DATE DUE

AP 26 00			

DEMCO 38-296

THE BLACK ROBE AND THE BALD EAGLE

THE SUPREME COURT AND THE FOREIGN POLICY OF THE UNITED STATES

1789 - 1953

DR. RANDALL WALTON BLAND

THE BLACK ROBE AND THE BALD EAGLE

THE SUPREME COURT AND THE FOREIGN POLICY OF THE UNITED STATES

1789 - 1953

DR. RANDALL WALTON BLAND

Austin & Winfield
San Francisco - London - Bethesda
1996

Library of Congress Cataloging-in-Publication Data

Bland, Randall Walton
        The black robe and the bald eagle: the Supreme Court and the
        foreign policy of the United States, 1789-present / Randall W.
        Bland.
            p. cm.
        Includes bibliographical references and indexes.
        ISBN 1-880921-40-5 (cloth : alk. paper). -- ISBN 1-880921-06-5
    (paper : alk. paper)
        1. War and emergency powers--United States--History. 2. Judicial
    review--United States--History. 3. Executive power--United States-
    -History. 4. United States--Foreign relations--Law and legislation.
    5. United States--Constitutional history. I. Title.
    KF5060.B55   1993
    342.73'0412--dc20
    [347.302412]   93-31327
                                                                  CIP

Editorial Inquiries:
Austin & Winfield, Publishers
7831 Woodmont Avenue, #345
Bethesda, MD 20814
(301) 654-7335

To Order: (800) 99-AUSTIN

Dedicated to two great associate justices, George Suther-land and Hugo Black, who had a greater impact on the formal mechanisms of foreign policy—whether for good or for ill—than *most* twentieth century presidents of the United States.

Acknowledgements

As a student of constitutional law, I have always found the area of American foreign policy to be extremely interesting. I was inspired by the words of such scholars as George Kennan, Arthur Schlesinger, Jr., John Spanier, Hans Morgenthau, and Louis Henkin, Cecil Crabb, among numerous others. I also agreed with Edward S. Corwin who wrote, with great concern, about the "high-flying men" surrounding a president who advised him to give more attention to "executive powers and prerogatives," than to the legal *restraints* of the Constitution on the presidential office. It is the matter of the latter concern that provides the focal point of this study.

As in the case of any written research effort, there are plenty of people to thank for their kind cooperation, unyielding support and freely-given advice. First among them are my friends, colleagues and fellow professors of political science: Henry Abraham, University of Virginia; David Adler, University of South Dakota; William Gangi, St. John's University, New York; David O'Brien, University of Virginia; Arnold Leder, Kenneth Grasso, Robert Gorman, Edward Mihaulhonin, and especially, Alfred B. Sullivan and my other associates at Southwest Texas State University.

I am also am quite appreciative of the assistance given by all of the secretaries in the Department of Political Science at Southwest Texas who typed several revisions of some chapters without complaint.

My senior research assistants were of tremendous succor, and three of them standout from the rest. Jeff McDermott who slaved tirelessly drawing up background briefs of the cases; Russell Zunker, who assisted in trimming down the full opinions of the Court's majority and separately-written ones; and Robert Drozd, whose skill at the computer keyboard is unmatched. Robert prepared the entire original text of the manuscript.

Of course, I wish to acknowledge the encouragement and unlimited patience of my publisher, Dr. Robert West, at Austin-Winfield Publishers. Nor can I downplay the contribution of Ms. Susan Peabody from the School of Law (Boalt Hall) at the University of California at Berkeley, who managed—in rather miraculous fashion—to mesh together hundreds of pages of material into a final, clean, beautiful draft.

Finally, I owe a word of thanks to my loving wife, Barbara, without whose support I would be a total wreck.

If there is anyone whom I have forgotten please accept my humble apologies and thanks.

Randall Walton Bland
Southwest Texas State University

Contents

Preface

The *Black Robe and the Bald Eagle* is a *major* text for college-level courses in constitutional law and interpretation, American foreign policy, and international law. It will also serve as a *supplementary* text for introductory courses in American government. It is designed to compare well to existing studies which presently fall into two categories: (1) those which focus on the *relationships* between the president and Congress with respect to all power and responsibilities under the United States Constitution, of which those on foreign policy are only a part;[1] and (2) those concentrating on operational activities: the formulation and execution of American foreign policy.[2] Most of the remaining studies are casebooks which, at best, give only partial treatment to foreign policy.[3]

The three main features of this study are its blending of theory, social and political factors, as well as examples and case studies. It also has an *evolutionary* theme running through the major historical periods, and a critical-thinking method of challenging the students in undergraduate courses to apply various arguments to the "reality" provided by the Court's opinions. Absent such features the existing texts are extremely limited.

This study also attempts to break out of the traditional casebook format by providing a narrative focus on Constitutional change, interpretive analysis of political, economic and social influences, and the evolutionary nature of the judicial process. It demonstrates *how* the Supreme Court has viewed its *functions* with respect to the interpretation and application of foreign affairs and in so doing has determined the extent to which it has employed judicial review.

Each period discussed reflects the economic and social dynamics of that particular historical epoch. The justices who served on the High Court were human beings *not* "political eunuchs"; nor did they operate in a "political vacuum." Various crises and popular movements—foreign and domestic—have, throughout history, had a *viable* impact on the Court's decision-making. All of these factors will be analyzed and evaluated. The struggles for individual minds continues to take place not only in the oval office, Congress, and the ballot box, but *also* in American courtrooms, as well.

The sequence of the material in this book is as follows: Chapter One combines an Introduction, which identifies the intrinsic value of this study, with an examination of the Constitutional Convention of 1787: the debates over the foreign policy apparatus; the public controversy between Alexander Hamilton and James Madison over which political branch will dominate; the drafting of the war powers and the role of the Supreme Court. Chapters Two through Five analyze the historical periods through which Court policy-making evolved including the Traditional Era: 1789-1945, during which the Supreme Court so expanded executive authority that Schlesinger, Jr. later called the Office the "imperial presidency." Chapter Six concentrates on the apex of presidential supremacy during the Truman years (1945-1954), and Chapter Seven (Conclusion) is a discussion of the future role of the Supreme Court in foreign policy questions as well as its position in a government of separated powers. Following the Conclusion, there is an Appendix which includes the Constitution of the United States, a Methodology (Research Note and Bibliography), and a Case Index.

Each chapter contains an opening narrative followed by excerpts from relevant cases. I do not claim to have cited all of the litigation or trivial cases somehow relating to foreign affairs reviewed by the Supreme Court of the United States. However, I have made every attempt to discuss, or at least mention, *most* of the significant decisions in our history. In many of the Court's opinions, I have taken the liberty of emphasizing by the use of italics the transcending or significant portions.

Notes

1. Those within this category are strictly interpretive and include: Joseph Bessette and Jeffrey Tulis, eds., *The Presidency in the Constitutional Order* (Baton Rouge: Louisiana State University Press, 1981); Louis Fisher, *Constitutional Conflicts Between Congress and the President*, 3rd edition (Lawrence: University Press of Kansas, 1991); Donald Robinson, *"To the Best of My Ability": The President and the Constitution*, (New York: Norton, 1987); and Arthur Schlesenger, Jr., *The Imperial Presidency*, Revised Edition (Boston: Houghton Mifflin, 1989).

2. These works include the following titles: Philip Brigs, *Making American Foreign Policy and the Constitution*, (New York: University Press of America, 1990); R.A. Falk, ed, *The Vietnam War and International Law*, (Princeton University Press, 1969); Louis Henkin, *Foreign Affairs and the Constitution*, (Mineola, N.Y.: Foundation Press, 1972); Edward Keyes, *Undeclared War: Twilight Zone of Constitutional Power*, (College Park:

Penn State University Press, 1991); Christopher May, *In the Name of War*, (Cambridge, Mass.: Harvard University Press, 1989); and Francis Wormouth and Edwin Firmage, *To Chain the Dog of War: The War Power of Congress in History and Law,* (Dallas: Southern Methodist University, 1986); and Cecil V. Crabb, Jr. and Pat M. Holt, *Invitation to Struggle* (Washington: CQ Press, 1992).

3.   The best of these texts include: David O'Brien, *Constitutional Law and Politics*, 2 volumes (New York: W.W. Norton & Company, 1996); Robert F. Cushman, *Cases in Constitutional Law*, 7th Edition (New York: Prentice-Hall, Inc., 1989); Gerald Gunther, *Constitutional Law*, 12th Edition (New York: Foundation Press, 1991); and Lawrence Tribe, *American Constitutional Law*, 2nd Edition (Cambridge: Harvard University Press, 1988).

Chapter One: Introduction & Constitutional Setting (1787-1789)

On August 2, 1990, Iraqi forces under orders from President Saddam Hussein invaded and ravaged its small neighbor Kuwait. Within days, President George Bush responded by committing roughly 200,000 American troops to Saudi Arabia to protect it against invasion. He then brought the matter before the United Nations Security Council. The President said he was responding to Iraq's act of "naked aggression."

Within weeks, twenty-seven other countries joined the United States's effort, either in a combatant or other role, and the Security Council issued twelve resolutions demanding, *inter alia*, unconditional withdrawal of Iraqi troops from Kuwait.

Congress was in recess when the first troops were sent to Saudi Arabia, its members recuperating from the congressional elections which had taken place in September and October. Accordingly, *few* congressional voices were raised in opposition to the President's actions, and the War Powers Resolution of 1973 was not invoked. However, after the November 8 elections, President Bush doubled the number of U.S. forces and successfully pressured the Security Council to adopt a January 15 deadline for Iraq's withdrawal from Kuwait. His position was *clear*: the decision to go to war was not a congressional one, but his alone: "I have the full authority to enforce the United Nations resolutions *without* a congressional resolution or declaration."

Soon after, what had seemed like a *defensive* posture for the United States (Desert Shield) began to develop into an *offensive* one (Desert Storm). At least that was the view of a number of Senators and Representatives who began to speak out in dissenting voices. Then, during the first week of January, when the 102nd Congress convened, Iowa Democratic Senator Tom Harkin called for a debate, despite the restraining efforts of the leaders of his own party, over the constitutionality of the President's use of American forces *without* congressional participation or approval.

A constitutional battle of the highest order seemed inevitable. But before this could happen, President Bush, under pressure from his advisors, reluctantly submitted a resolution to Congress on January 9, 1991, which supported the UN resolutions and thus his own actions. After three days of heated debate, the joint resolution passed in Senate by an extremely narrow vote of 52-47, and in the House by a vote of 250-183. On January 14, the President signed the resolution which he called "a clear expression of support" for the international community's demand of withdrawal.

Despite the resolution, debate over the need for congressional approval did not end here, since Presidsent Bush warned Saddam Hussein that if his government did *not* comply with the UN resolution to send investigative teams to inspect nuclear equipment, etc., the United States would once again *intervene* militarily. He felt free to make this threat because he believed that the President has certain war-making powers and does not need congressional approval before committing American troops to military action. His supporters in the executive branch and Congress cited 211 instances in American history in which a President had used military force *without* a declaration of war from Congress. Other arguments were also made in defense of his authority to so act: (1) his constitutional powers as Chief Executive and Commander in Chief; (2) the inherent or prerogative powers of the presidency stemming from extra-constitutional sources; and (3) the historical precedent of such presidential wars in the face of congressional inaction.

Since the Gulf War, President Clinton has also hinted at such executive prerogatives with respect to Somalia, the Dominican Republic, North Korea and even Bosnia. In 1996, using almost the same United

Nations assistance argument that his predecessor had employed, he sent a large contingent of U.S. troops to Bosnia.

Serious constitutional questions have arisen because of this continuing presidential assertion of authority: Does the United States Constitution make the President the single agent (sole organ) for the conduct of foreign policy *including* the decision to go to war? What judicial interpretation has the Supreme Court of the United States rendered on executive prerogatives particularly in view of the more than two-hundred "limited" or "presidential wars"?[1] What, if any, are the responsibilities of Congress in formulating American foreign policy and the decision to "go to war"? These are the questions that will be examined and answered by this study. No other book now available on the market makes such a detailed attempt to do so.

The theoretical framework of this study centers on the role of the Supreme Court of the United States in our country's foreign policy-making process, primarily through its manipulation of its most important prerogative—the power of judicial review. Moreover, it is an admittedly *controversial* analysis of judicial decision-making through various periods of our history with an evolving American foreign policy that was and is continually shaped by economic, political, cultural and social factors at home and, too often, abroad. Unfortunately, most citizens have little or no idea of the historical and political role of the Supreme Court in this external policy area. The overriding reason for this ignorance is quite disturbing: *most* constitutional scholars have made *false* assumptions concerning the "checks and balance" system relating to the Court's activity, and these assumptions have been passed on to generations of young Americans who are not equipped to challenge them.

As this study will attempt to prove, the Supreme Court since its inception in 1790 has taken an active and significant path as a constitutional referee or umpire in the on-going struggle between the political branches (the President and Congress), and has gone so far as to enforce a policy of *dual responsibility* for the formulation of external policy. Moreover, this judicial policy was based on the division of foreign policy power in the Constitution, and it resulted in a relatively stable, if often uneasy, period of mutual cooperation—as well as an equally-uniform course of constitutional interpretation until the watershed *Curtiss-Wright* case in 1936. Consequently, far from standing on the constitutional sidelines, the nation's High Court has, for most of its history, participated in the jurisdictional and even substantive debates within the foreign policy process. Only *after* the conclusion of the Korean War, has the Court taken a neutralist, non-active stance by avoiding these kinds of questions and by invoking the talisman of the "political question" doctrine. This was particularly the case during the 60s and 70s when United States involvement in Vietnam and Southeast Asia brought forth "bitter waters," *vox populii*; however, both historians and political scientists have failed to take note of these salient developments.

Most authors of political science texts specializing in American government and constitutional law would probably agree with Professor David O'Brien of the University of Virginia who has written that the Supreme Court has traditionally stood *aloof* from foreign policy questions since "the Court lacks both adequate standards for resolving disputes and the means to enforce its decisions."[2] Yet, O'Brien's assumptions, while universally accepted, are at best *questionable*. On his former point, if one accepted as prerequisites for the proper control of foreign policy the possession of "adequate standards," how could any reasonable scholar defend the authority of either the presidential establishment or the members of Congress based on the failures of American diplomacy throughout most of this century. More importantly, with regard to the Professor's latter contention, if one were to accept as the primary standard for the Supreme Court's active use of judicial review the appropriate or sufficient "means to enforce its decisions," then the judicial branch of the national government would *indeed* be "the least dangerous branch." With few exceptions in every area of litigation, the High Court ultimately relies on the good faith compliance of not only the other branches and the states, but the American *people* as well. For example, if the Court's pronouncements on prayers in the public schools or on Congress's legislative veto are at all noteworthy, it is because apparently all concerned have *ignored* the rulings altogether; yet, such negative reactions have *not* slowed down the Court's activism in even more controversial areas of law. But O'Brien and other young writers should not be singled out for criticism on these points since they learned from senior professors who had also accepted, and subsequently taught, these misinterpretations.

For example, Professor Walter F. Murphy, James E. Fleming and William F. Harris, make the above assumptions in their *American Constitutional Interpretation*. In examining "Structural Analysis: Sharing Power at the National Level" (Chapter 9), the authors argue that "the most difficult and consequential example of shared powers are those [shared by the President and Congress] over war and foreign policy."[3] Quite appropriately, they then discuss the division of authority between the two political branches contained in Articles I, II and VI of the United States Constitution. Thereafter, Murphy et al. make the predictable error of *eliminating* the non-political branch of government from the policy-making equation. These clauses, as Edward S. Corwin once remarked, are "an invitation to struggle" for the privilege of directing American foreign policy:

> And, of course, practical necessity seldom displays respect for constitutional texts. Presidents since George Washington have asserted Constitutional authority to take military action to defend the United States without a declaration of war or other congressional approval [the *Curtiss-Wright* Rule]. Individual legislators and occasionally Congress itself have contested this claim.... Although *sometimes* judges have become involved, citing *Little v. Barreme* (1804) and the *Prize Cases* (1836) as examples, the Supreme Court has *usually* been sufficiently fortunate or wise to *keep out* of this dangerous field.[4] (emphasis added)

If the authors are limiting the scope of their remarks to the Supreme Court being "sufficiently fortunate or wise to keep out of the actual making of decisions on the use of American troops or contrasting the provisions of treaties or the amount of millions of dollars to be appropriated for specific countries," then they are absolutely *correct*; however, if Murphy, Fleming and Harris are referring to questions of jurisdiction, the Court's assertion of its authority to review challenged actions by the other branches and, most significant, the Supreme Court's role as the "balance" in the tripartite constitutional system, then the authors are equally *wrong*! This study will attempt to fully expose and rectify the previously-mentioned declarations of erroneous scholarship.

A final example of the traditional theory on the lack of judicial participation may be seen in Kermit L. Hall's *The Oxford Companion to the Supreme Court of the United States*, a classic anthology on the political and legal salience of the High Court since 1789.[5] In it, one of the authors writes as follows:

> Of the three branches of the federal government, the judiciary has *least* to say on the subjects of foreign affairs and foreign policy...the Supreme Court has made *no* important foreign policies and *usually* defers to Congress and Presidents regarding foreign relations.[6] (emphasis added)

Of course, with full recognition of the constitutional responsibility of the Supreme Court to try cases involving foreign ambassadors (original jurisdiction) and to uphold the enforcement of treaties as "the Supreme law of the Land," Article VI, no serious scholar would disagree with the statement, above, that the Court does not itself formulate specific policies and that it also recognizes the primacy of the political branches in the relevant clauses of Articles I, II, and VI. On the other hand, since the Constitution does not *create* the power of judicial review, so it does not specifically *limit* it! There is *no* constitutional barrier to prevent the Court from extending its review powers to foreign policy matters *if* it chooses to do so. And it has chosen to do so on numerous and extremely significant occasions.

Indeed, as the nation rose as a super power, the federal courts *legitimated* the concentration of national and executive authority far more often than they *limited* it. The Constitution does govern foreign-policy makers, but their sources of authority are broader and their limits are less restrictive in foreign than in domestic affairs. The landmark decision, *United States v. Curtiss-Wright Export Corporation* (1935), "...*undergirds* claims of *hegemony* over foreign policy. It implies that the 'sovereign' states have no foreign power to surrender and that in the realm of relations with foreign countries, the president may do *anything* that the Constitution or statues do not expressly forbid."[7]

Amazing! How could the author of this statement (or other scholars for that matter) possibly attempt to *justify* or even to suggest the above conclusion. Either the Supreme Court embraced the "political question" doctrine and "stood aloof" from foreign policy questions *or* its decisions have had a *tremendous* impact, at certain times, on the entire formulation process. And if the power of review means only the *negation* of inter-branch policies rather than their ratification, legislation, or even expansion (in other words, if the Court plays no role) how can it possibly "legitimate" much less "undergird" claims—not claims of simple authority, but rather claims of "*hegemony* over foreign policy."

The *Curtiss-Wright* case stands as not only one of the most important foreign policy decisions by the Court, but as one of the most important decisions *ever* handed down by the Supreme Court in its history. Therefore, judicial power is much like pregnancy; just as a woman cannot be "kind a" pregnant, the Supreme Court cannot be "kind a" sterile. Consequently, if the President is "the sole organ of the federal government in the field of international relations," which continues to be a matter of controversy between the executive and legislative branches, it is simply because our constitutional scholars, and most politicians, have unquestionably supported the *Supreme Court's declaration*. Justice Sutherland's opinion may well be "flawed as history" but his *orbiter dicta* has been treated as "the supreme law of the land."

Finally, Professor Hall restates his original premise by taking note of the following:

> Separation of powers mostly *limits* the Court itself. Broadly speaking, most foreign policy decisions are *beyond* judicial review. The prime rationale is the fuzzy political question doctrine: that courts cannot subjects belonging by law function, or consider prudence to political branches.[8]

Since neither the Constitution nor statute limit the Court's authority to solely *domestic* policies, only the Supreme Court *itself* can impose its own limits, as it has since the 1960's. On the other hand, it may vigorously expand its scope of authority as it has done on even more numerous occasions throughout the history of our republic, subject only to the limits placed on its appellate jurisdiction by statute or organic law.

Consequently, those scholars who have argued that the Supreme Court has "had little or no impact on the formulation of foreign policy," as this text will clearly demonstrate, are placing their bets more on the *exception* (most notably in recent years) than the long-existing *rule*!

Of course, there are always exceptions even in the academic world of political science and government. Some relatively few scholars have been shouting over the roof tops that there was a great deal *more* to the operations of separated national responsibility in foreign affairs. Dr. Louis Henkin, along with a few others, has contributed several note-worthy works, most notably his book, *Constitutionalism Democracy and Foreign Affairs,* in which he addresses the "highly controversial yet neglected aspect of United States constitutional jurisprudence and the governance of foreign affairs."[9] Even so, Henkin makes the same flawed assumptions that most text writers have made through the years with respect to the jurisprudential issues conceded in the foreign policy area. First, he embraces the argument that the Constitution is, at best, vague and ambiguous in dividing these shared powers:

> For the deep issues of foreign affairs, notably those of the "twilight zone," there is little or no text to construe, and what is available of these is hopelessly opaque and nondeterminative. Looking at the text or elsewhere for the intent of the fram-ers—however one defines and identifies them—is no more helpful, for their intent is unknown or hopelessly ambigu-ous.[10]

Second, Henkin implies from this premise that judicial review in foreign affairs is not possible,

> [because of] ...the Supreme Court's jurisprudence of not hearing cases, from the constitutional requirement of case or controversy to prudential avoidance of "political questions," the courts have resolved few of these perennial foreign affairs issues. Indeed, judicial abstention may have perpetuated and even extended and aggravated uncertainties and has created a judicial "twilight zone" of uncertainty as well.[11]

As we shall see, *both* of these assumptions, with minor exceptions, are seriously defective.

This study will not only show that the Supreme Court has had an active role in foreign policy-making (making it clear that it has the right to do so), in the Conclusion I will advance the theory that if the political branches (the President and Congress) are gripped by deadlock ("gridlock") and are unable to confront a justiciable foreign policy issue of national importance, then the Supreme Court *must* serve as the "balancing agency" in our triparte system, i.e. the Court's intervention during the Korean War when President Harry Truman seized the nation's steel industry during a threatened strike over the heads of Congress (*Youngstown Sheet & Tube Co., v. Sawyer*). In other words, the Supreme Court, as it did in 1952 (in calmness and solitude) should meet the question head-on and resolve it. But, such a decision must reject the extremes on either side of the question and produce that which the Framers of the Constitution intended—judicial *weight* on the side of the *ordained* authority! In our constitutional scheme, as the Framers recognized, the people's will is *most likely* to reside in the popularly-elected legislature, *not* the executive.

In such instances, a straight-out decision by the nation's Highest Court is *absolutely* necessary. If American foreign policy is to operate successfully on a global basis, political stalemate cannot be allowed to shove such critical issues on to the "back burner" with no timely resolution in sight. This is a theory that advocates of judicial "interpretavism" may not accept; however, it does provide the only workable yet available solution to political inertia, save, of course, for presidential *fiat!* And President Lyndon Johnson's near "resignation" in 1968 over the Vietnam War clearly showed the failure of such executive action in the face of overwhelming public opposition.

Constitutional Setting
1787-1789

Arthur M. Schlesinger, Jr. has written that from within the area of foreign policy "above all, [it is] from the capture by the presidency of the most vital of national decisions, the decision to go to war...that the imperial presidency received its *decisive* impetus."[12] He further observed:

The result of calculated ambiguities of the founding fathers was
to design not a machine but a battle field—to create the
conditions for permanent guerrilla warfare between the two
branches of the national government [the President and
Congress] with powers for initiative.

Now you might ask: What legal philosophy or conceptual framework of
the Framers led to these sets of circumstances?

Very clearly, as the results of the Philadelphia Convention of 1787
verify, the Framers intended that the conduct of foreign policy should be
carried on *jointly* by the political departments of the national government
at the exclusion of the individual states.[13] Even Alexander Hamilton,
who argued for a high visibility of the President in foreign affairs,
maintained that a number of powers, like the treaty-making power, for
example, should not be vested in the President alone but should be
shared with the Senate:

The history of human conduct does not warrant the exalted
opinion of human virtue which would make it wise in a nation,
to commit interests of so delicate a momentous a kind, as those
which concern is intercourse with the rest of the world, to the
sole disposal of a magistrate created and circumstanced as
would be a President of the United States.[14]

At the Philadelphia Convention, Edmond Randolph of Virginia,
arguing for *mutual* participation of the political branches, was prompted
to explain that since "the Executive will have more influence over the
Senate" the power to declare war should be placed in the House.[15] John
Rutledge of South Carolina rejected this view contending that the power
should be vested in the Senate since it is "more conversant in business"
and has "more leisure" than the House.[16] However, most of the
Framers believed that the "war powers"—Article I, section 7, paragraph
11 along with paragraphs 12,13,14,15,16, and 18—must be vested in the
whole Congress; while, the powers of the Commander in Chief in Article
II, section 2, paragraph 1 should be given to the President. As Hamilton
had reasoned, the war-making authority consists of "an aggregate of
powers"; the national government "ought to be clothed with all the
powers requisite to complete execution for its trust."[17] But no one at the
Convention seriously argued that the war powers should be vested in the

President *alone* except for Pierce Butler of South Carolina. James Madison and Elbridge Gerry specifically amended the original draft of the Committee of Detail's, to read that Congress shall "declare war" instead of "*make* war," so that the military responsibility for conducting a war was vested in the President who, for example, must respond to foreign attack. The Constitution absorbed the revision as amended, any possible change in this allocation of power could only be made in the future by a constitutional amendment or by interpretation of a newly-created membership on the Supreme Court of the United States.

Notes

1. The term originated in Francis D. Warmuth, "Presidential Wars: The Convenience of 'Precedent', " *The Nation* (October 9, 1972) p. 301.
2. David M. O'Brien. *Constitutional Law and Politics: Struggles for Power and Governmental Accountability* (New York: W.W. Norton & Company, 1991), p. 111.
3. *American Constitutional Interpretation* (Mineola, NY: The Foundation Press, 1986), p. 323.
4. Ibid.
5. Hall is listed as editor in chief, while James W. Ely, Jr., Joel B. Grossman, and William M. Wiecek are designated as editors of The Oxford Companion to the Supreme Court of the United States (New York: Oxford University Press, 1992).
6. Ibid., p. 307.
7. Ibid.
8. Ibid.
9. Professor Henkin's earlier text, *Foreign Affairs and the Constitution* (New York: W.W. Norton, 1975) was the first work in the field of the jurisprudence of foreign policy. Also, other writers deserve credit for following his lead. At the top of this list I would cite the excellent works of Professor David Adler, but I would also include Cecil Crabb, Jr., Pat Holt, Edward Keyes and Thomas E. Mann, among others. Full citations of their works are provided later in this study.
10. *Constitutionalism, Democracy, and Foreign Affairs* (New York: Columbia University Press, 1990), p. 73.
11. Ibid., p. 2.
12. *The Imperial Presidency*. (Boston: Houghton Mifflin, 1973), ix.
13. Max Farrand. *The Framing of the Constitution* (New Haven: Yale University Press, 1913) pp. 153-154.

14. Paper #75 in Clinton Rossiter, editor, *The Federalist Papers* (New York: A Mentor Book, 1961) p. 451.
15. Madison's Notes on Monday, August 13 in Willbourne Benton, 1787: *Drafting the US. Constitution*, Volume I (College Station: Texas A&M University Press. 1986) p. 784.
16. Ibid.
17. Paper #23 in Rossiter, *The Federalist Papers*, pp. 153-154

Chapter Two:
The Early Court and Judicial Precedent (1790-1845)

The Supreme Court of the United States began as an organ of government within the Constitution's tripartite national system in 1790, under Chief Justice John Jay. Even during the so-called "dark ages" of the pre-Marshall Court, the Tribunal initiated the legal precedent, stemming directly from Article I, that the *responsibility* for the making of foreign policy was a matter of *mutual cooperation* between the President and Congress. For the most part, until 1936, it did *not* hesitate, when properly called upon, to serve as umpire or referee on those occasions when "mutual cooperation" turned unwittingly to "bipolar hostilities" between the two political branches.

In the afterglow of constitutional ratification in 1789, the Republic encountered hemispheric, if not global, crises with Great Britain, Spain, and even our one-time ally, France. The heavily disputed Jay Treaty of 1795 resulted from our serious objections over England's conduct of its European war, particularly its claimed authority to "impress" or kidnap sailors to serve in its wartime shipping. In addition, the British refusal to evacuate certain commercial posts on American territory in defiance of the Peace Treaty of 1783, led to an outgrowth of popular resentment in the United States. This ill-will eventually boiled over under President James Madison in the War of 1812. Twenty-five years later, however, it would be Great Britain that would substitute for a weak United States as the *one* European power willing to protect the integrity of the Western Hemisphere under the Monroe Doctrine.

Also during this period, His Most Catholic Majesty, Philip of Spain, cast his greedy eyes on the territories of America. His government refused to recognize American claims that the Republic's southern boundary lay along the thirty-first parallel since Spain controlled *both* sides of the Mississippi River. Open warfare was avoided only by the conclusion of the Pinkney Treaty of 1795—obviously a critical year for the new Republic—under which the United States was grudgingly ceded navigation rights on the Mississippi.

Finally, in 1793, France, our primary ally during the American Revolution, made the tragic error of sending the proud and boastful Edmund Genêt as Minister to the United States. Once here, Genêt repeatedly insisted, *inter alia*, that American ports be used for France's privateering raids against the British fleet, that this Country owed its existence to France, and, finally, that the use of our ports was the very least the United States could do to repay its debts. Needless to say, the already Francophobic Federalist Administration was incensed by Genêt's activities. President Washington not only issued a Proclamation of Neutrality, he asserted that France was the aggressor in the war and thus denied its request to assist her in the defense of the West Indies. Consequently, Genêt's public pleas for support were rebuffed and he was recalled to France.

The turn of events during the Revolution led to the creation of the Republican French government and the slaughter of the nobility. In reaction to American hostility, the new French government refused to receive Charles C. Pinkney as American Minister, a post previously held by James Monroe. In 1797, the new Federalist President, John Adams, dispatched Elbridge Gerry and John Marshall to work with Pinkney as a three-membered "commission" for the re-establishment of diplomatic relations. The French Foreign Minister Talleyrand, usually skillful in the diplomatic arts, overplayed his hand by using three of his agents to intervene with the "commission." Later referred to as the "X, Y and Z" Affair, the agents promised the Americans its cooperation if certain conditions, including the payment of large sums of money, were met by the United States government. Once informed, the Adams administration angrily prepared for war as a matter of national honor; however, the

American people, while upset by the "X, Y, Z" Affair wanted to maintain peace with France. Consequently, in 1800, the President sent another mission to Paris and concluded a treaty which nullified the earlier attempt of 1778, thus ending hostile relations with France.

The earliest cases arising under the Supreme Court concerning foreign relations were related to the diplomatic entanglements described above. One noted student of the Court, Leonard W. Levy, has written that the first two decisions were handed down in 1793-94: Henfield's case in which the Court decided that, even though Congress had *not* enacted a specific criminal statute, an American seaman serving on a French privateer which was attacking British ships was guilty of an indictable offense violating our Proclamation of Neutrality; the other decision, *Glass v. Sloop Betsy (1794)* was far more significant.[1] In it, the Court upheld the government's policy of neutrality by forbidding France, after capturing a neutral vessel, from holding her as a "prize" in an American port. The message was clear: only the courts of the United States were empowered to determine the validity of such awards or American inherent rights of sovereignty would be jeopardized. One year later, the first Supreme Court decision directly involving the distribution of responsibility over foreign policy was to firmly establish legal precedent for nearly a century and a half.

In *Penhallow v. Doane*, 3 Dallas 54 (1795), Justice James Iredell, speaking for the Court, stated that during the transitional period from 1776 through 1789, complete and unfettered sovereignty in international affairs passed from the several States to the *national* government. Moreover, while foreign policy-making was a shared power between Congress and the President, the war powers were consolidated within the power of Congress, *alone!*[2] Five years later, the question of "limited wars" was brought before the Court in *Bas v. Tingy,* 4 Dall. 36 (1800). The case centered on the question of salvage during the undeclared American-French Naval War (1799-1800), and the Court agreed that even in the case of a small or "imperfect" war *Congress* had the power to *determine* policy. Justice Bushrod Washington pointed out that in an Act of March 2nd, 1799:

> Congress had raised an army; stopped all intercourse with France; dissolved our treaty; built and equipped ships of war; and commissioned private armed ships: enjoining the former

and authorizing the latter, to defend themselves against the armed ships of France, to attack them on the high seas, to subdue and take them as prize...the contention was external and authorized by the legitimate authority of the two governments. If they were not our enemies, I know not what constitutes an enemy.[3]

In 1801, the Supreme Court reaffirmed *Bas* in a related case, *Talbot v. Seeman*, in which the newly appointed Chief Justice John Marshall was even more explicit:

The whole powers of war being, by the Constitution of the United States, vested in Congress, the acts of that body can alone be resorted to as our guides in this inquiry...Congress may authorize general hostilities...or partial hostilities in which case the laws of war, so far as they actually apply to our situation, must be noticed.[4]

But had not Marshall, *himself*, just two years earlier, argued that "the President is the sole organ of the nation in its external relations and its sole representative with foreign nations." He had spoken these words as a member of the House of Representatives to defend the extradition powers of President John Adams under the Jay Treaty. As Edward S. Corwin has amply pointed out: "Clearly, what Marshall had foremost in mind was simply the President's role as an instrument of *communication* with other governments."[5] He certainly did not mean that all foreign power should be vested *solely* in the presidential office! On this point, Corwin agreed:

In short, the President has all powers that the facts of international intercourse may at any time make conveniently applicable if the Constitution does not vest them elsewhere in clear terms...this means that the initiative in the foreign field rests with him.[6]

Yet, by no stretch of the imagination does this "initiative" of the President include the authority to *initiate* war except in response to our being attacked *by* foreign forces. As James Madison wrote in 1793:

The power to declare war, including the power of judging the causes of war is *fully* and *exclusively* vested in the legislature; that the executive has no right, in any case, to decide the question, whether there is or is not a cause for declaring war....

He also stated that,

Those who are to conduct a war cannot in the nature of things, be proper or safe judges, whether a war ought to be commenced, continued or concluded. They are banned from the latter functions by a great principle in free government, analogous to that which separates the sword from the purse, or the power of executing the power of enacting laws.[7]

Nor, did the early Court *hesitate*, during this traditional period, to call the President into account if he exceeded his authority in foreign affairs. In one extremely significant decision, that is usually referred to by most writers without much discussion, the Supreme Court of the United States constitutionally nullified a presidential attempt to exercise foreign policy.

During the undeclared Naval War between France and the United States, President John Adams issued instructions to seize certain ships. In 1804, in *Little v. Barreme,* the Court held that the President's orders *conflicted* with an Act of Congress dated February 9, 1799. Otherwise, Chief Justice Marshall noted:

It is by *no means clear* that the President of the United States whose high duty it is to take care that the laws be faithfully executed, and who is Commander in Chief of the armies and navies of the United States, might not, *without* any special authority for that purpose, in the then existing state of things, have empowered the officers commanding the armed vessels of the United States, to seize and send into port for adjudication, American vessels which were forfeited by being engaged in this illicit commerce.[8] (emphases added)

It would not be for *another* 130 years, that the Court would hold *invalid* another presidential order.[9] In 1829, however, the Court did make clear its position on the disposition of treaties and, for the *first* time in its history, declared that the concept of separated powers in the Constitution requires that the "political question" doctrine be extended to the formulation of American foreign policy. It should be noted that this decision was one of a few rare cases *prior* to the Vietnam fiasco in which the Court demurred to either congressional or, much less, to presidential claims of hegemony.

The question centered on whether certain land lying east of the Mississippi River up to the Perdido River belonged to the United States or Spain under a Treaty of 1803. Speaking for the Court, Chief Justice John Marshall proclaimed:

> The judiciary is *not* that department of the government, to which the assertion of [American] interests against foreign powers is confided: and its duty commonly is to decide upon individual rights according to those principles which the *political departments* of the nation have established. If the course of a nation has been a plain one, its Courts would *hesitate* to pronounce it erroneous. [emphases added.][10]

Once again, as to the *specific* language of the Treaty, Marshall demurred:

> Our Constitution declares a treaty to be the law of the land. It is, consequently, to be regarded in courts of justice as equivalent to an Act of the legislature, whenever it operates of itself without the aid of any legislature provision. But when the terms of the stipulation import a contract, when either of the parties engages to perform a particular act, the treaty addresses itself to the *political*, not the *judicial* department; and the legislature must execute the contract before it can become a rule for the Court. [emphases added.][11]

Even though unrefined and seemingly tentative, this was the *first* case in which the Court applied the "political question" doctrine. It would not be applied by the Court again—in a regular and serious manner—until the Vietnam War years.

During the second Republican administration of President James Madison, an open naval war broke out between Great Britain and the United States. As an outgrowth of the War of 1812, two cases of legal significance were brought before the nation's Highest Court. The first case *Armitz Brown v. United States* (1814) centered on the gravamen of American ownership of seized goods and the second, *Martin v. Mott* (1827) questioned the supremacy of a presidential proclamation during an enemy invasion of the United States. Significantly, on the power of the President to repel invasions, Edward S. Corwin left no doubt when he wrote:

> By the Acts of 1795 and 1807 [the President] is authorized to call upon the militia and to employ the armed forces of the United States not only in cases of actual invasion, but also whenever there is [under *Mott*] "eminent danger of invasion," a question to be determined exclusively by *himself*.[12]

Later, as we shall observe, Presidents Woodrow Wilson, in the case of Mexico in 1916, and Franklin D. Roosevelt, in the Relocation Orders of 1942, were to rely on the rule of *Mott* and its usage of "*eminent danger*." These citations of legal precedent clearly demonstrated that *Mott* was, in fact, the exception and *not* the rule during the first 150 years of our constitutional history.

PENHALLOW v. DOANE
3 Dall. 54 (1795)

Prior to and after the Articles of Confederation, Congress was the "final court for appeals" stemming from the Admiralty courts of the states. During the American Revolution, Congress had supreme "sovereign power of war and peace." On 25 November 1775, Congress passed a series of resolutions concerning the unwarranted capture of "colonial vessels" by the British Navy; these resolutions gave the "United Colonies" under Congress the power to seize British ships of war and confiscate their goods. In October of 1777, the armed brigantine M'Clary, acting under authority of Congress, captured the brigantine, Susanna. Penhallow and other owners of the M'Clary filed a libel suit in the maritime court of New Hampshire; subsequently, the Susanna and her cargo were declared to be their "lawful prize." Doane, an owner of the Susanna appealed to the superior court of New Hampshire which upheld the lower court's ruling. Another appeal was made to Congress, which issued a decree which reversed the prior ruling. The case reached the Supreme Court by writ of error.

[excerpts]

MR. JUSTICE WILLIAM PATTERSON delivered the opinion of the Court:

The pleadings consist of a heap of materials, thrown together in an irregular manner, and, if examined by the strict rules of common law, cannot stand the test of legal criticism. We are, however, to view the proceedings as before a court of admiralty, which is not governed by the rigid principles of common law....

...The jurisdiction of the commissioners of appeals has been questioned. The jurisdiction of the court of appeals has been questioned.

These jurisdictions turning on the competency of Congress, it has been questioned, whether that body had authority to institute such tribunals.

And, lastly, the jurisdiction of the district court of New Hampshire has been questioned.

The pleadings consist of a heap of materials, thrown together in an irregular manner, and, if examined by the strict rules of common law, cannot stand the test of legal criticism. We are, however, to view the proceedings as before a *court of admiralty, which is not governed by the rigid principles of common law.*

The jurisdiction of the commissioners of appeals has been questioned. The jurisdiction of the court of appeals has been questioned.

These jurisdictions turning on the competency of Congress, it has been questioned, whether that body had authority to institute such tribunals.

And lastly, the jurisdiction of the district court of New Hampshire has been questioned. In every step we take, the point of jurisdiction meets us.

1. The question first in order is, whether the commissioners of appeals had jurisdiction, or, in other words, whether Congress, before the ratification of the Articles of Confederation, had authority to institute such a tribunal, with appellate jurisdiction in cases of prize?

Much has been said respecting the powers of Congress. On this part of the subject the counsel on both sides displayed great ingenuity and erudition, and that too in a style of eloquence equal to the magnitude of the question. *The powers of Congress were revolutionary in their nature, arising out of events, adequate to every national emergency, and co-extensive with the object to be attained. Congress* was the general, *supreme*, and *controlling* council of the nation, the center of union, the *center* of force, and the *sun* of the political system. To determine what their powers were we must inquire what powers they exercised. Congress raised armies, fitted out a navy, and prescribed rules for their government: Congress conducted all military operations both by land and sea. Congress emitted bills of credit, received and sent ambassadors, and made treaties. Congress commissioned privateers to cruise against the enemy, directed what vessels should be liable to capture, and prescribed rules for the distribution of prizes. These high acts of sovereignty were submitted to, acquiesced in, and approved of, by the people of America. In Congress were vested, because by Congress were exercised with the approbation of the people, the rights and powers of war and peace....

That Congress, or such person or persons as they appoint, to hear and determine appeals from the courts of admiralty, have necessarily the power to examine as well into decisions on facts as decisions on the law, and to decree finally thereon, and that no finding of a jury in any court of admiralty, or court for determining the legality of captures on the high seas, can or ought to destroy the right of appeal, and the re-examination of the facts reserved to Congress....

"That the power of executing the law of nations is essential to the sovereign supreme power of war and peace:

"That the legality of all captures on the high seas must be determined by the law of nations:

"That the authority ultimately and finally to decide on all matters and questions touching the law of nations, does reside and is vested in the sovereign supreme power of war and peace:

"That a control by appeal is necessary, in order to compel a just and uniform execution of the law of nations...."

...the first question is, whether by the death of Elisha Doane, before the judgment rendered in the court of appeals, that judgment is not avoided? The death of Doane does not appear on the record of the proceedings before the court of appeals; it is in evidence from the certificate of the judge of probates, which is annexed to the record transmitted from the circuit court of New Hampshire. Many answers have been given to this question; some of which are cogent as well as plausible. On this subject, it will be sufficient to observe, that admitting the death of Doane, and that it can be taken notice of in this court, it is unavailing, because the proceedings in a court of admiralty are *in rem.* The sentence of a court of admiralty, or of appeal in questions of prize, binds all the world, as to everything contained in it, because all the world are parties to it. The sentence, so far as it goes, is conclusive to all persons

...The powers of Congress at first were indeed little more than advisory: but, in proportion as the danger increased, their powers were gradually enlarged, either by express grant, or by implication arising from a kind of indefinite authority, suited to the unknown exigencies that might arise. That an undefined authority is dangerous, and ought to be entrusted as cautiously as possible, every man must admit, and none could take more pains, than Congress for a long time did, to get their authority regularly defined by a ratification of the Articles of Confederation. But that previously thereto they did exercise, with the acquiescence of the states, high powers, of what I may, perhaps, with propriety for distinction, call external sovereignty, is unquestionable. Among numerous instances that might be given of this, (and which were recited very minutely at the bar) were the treaties of France in 1778, which no friend to his country at the time questioned in point of authority, nor has been capable of reflecting upon since without gratitude and satisfaction. Whether among these powers comprehended within their general authority, was that of instituting courts for the trial of all prize causes, was a great and awful question; a question that demanded deep consideration, and not perhaps susceptible of an easy decision. That in point of prudence and propriety it was a power most fit for Congress to exercise, I have no doubt. I think all prize causes whatsoever ought to belong to the national sovereignty....

...1. It is taking for granted the very point in dispute, that this decision was retrospective. If Congress possessed this authority before, and the Articles of Confederation amounted only to a solemn confirmation of it, it was in no manner retrospective. It was in effect a continuance of the same court acting under an express, instead (as before) of acting under an implied authority, and allowing the full benefit of an appeal regularly prayed, and rightfully enforced by the superior tribunal, after an unwarranted disallowance by the inferior.

2. Whether the article in the confederation giving authority to this court as a superior tribunal in all cases of capture, did authorize them to receive appeals in cases circumstances like this, was a point for them to decide; since it was a question arising in a case of capture, of all which cases (without any exception) they were constituted judges in the last resort. The merits of their decision we surely cannot now inquire into, but their authority to decide not being limited, there was no method, by applying to any other court, of correcting any error they might commit, if in reality they should have committed any.

3. Whether their decision was right or wrong, yet nobody can deny that the jurisdiction of the commissioners was at least doubtful; of course the court of appeals found a case then depending in the former court of the commissioners, after a preliminary, but not a final, determination, for such I consider it to have been. It was therefore a cause then *sub judice,* and it being a case of capture and a question of appeal, no other court on earth, but that, in my opinion, could decide it. And no objection can be urged in this case against the authority of such a decision, or the propriety of its being final, but such as may be urged against all courts in the last resort, with respect to the merits of whose decisions there may be eternal disputes, but such disputes would be productive of eternal war, if some court had not authority to settle such questions forever.

I, therefore, have not the smallest doubt, that the decision of the court in 1783, was *final* and *conclusive* as to the parties to the decree. And this point appears to me so plain, that I think it useless to take notice of any authorities quoted on either side, in relation to it, none of them, I conceive, in any manner contravening the conclusive quality of such decrees upon the principles I have stated, and some of them clearly, and beyond all question, supporting it.

The decree of September, 1783, being by me thus deemed final and conclusive.

I have already, however, stated my opinion, that from the nature of our political situation, it was highly reasonable and proper that Congress should be possessed of such an authority, and this is a consideration of no small weight to induce an inference, that they actually possessed it when their powers were so indefinite, and when it seems to have been the sense of all states, that Congress should possess all the incidents to external sovereignty, or, in other words, the power of war and peace, so far as other nations were concerned, though the states in some particulars differed, as to the construction of the general powers given for that purpose. Two principles appear to me to be clear. 1. The authority was not possessed by Congress, unless given by all the states. 2. If once given, no state could, by any act of its own, disavow and recall the authority previously given without withdrawing from the confederation....

I should indeed have had some doubts as to the subsequent interest, had it appeared that the defendants had been unable to comply substantively with the decree, owing to the death of Doane, and the want, (had that been the case) of a subsequent demand by the administrators. But as that is not alleged, and they set up their whole defense upon the point of right, merely, we are not to presume, that those circumstances (if the administrators did not make a demand, with respect to which nothing appears) had any weight in inducing their non-compliance with the decree....

...Damages against all the defendants jointly, ought not to have been given. We are to look at substance, not form. There were, in effect, two decrees originally, one half of the value of the property to one party the other half to another. The reversal of the decree ought to affect the decree itself, in the manner in which it was given. Consequently, each party ought only to be required to restore what he was adjudged to receive....

As owners are, in all instances, made jointly liable ex *contract,* and their respective shares are matters of private cognizance, so that they, in all instances, appear jointly before the court, and a payment to one owner is, in law, a payment to all; I can discover no principle, upon which any discrimination could be properly made in this case, in regard to the different interests and actual receipts of the owners. I think, therefore, the decree in regard to one moiety, ought to be jointly against all the owners.

The third error in the decree, in my opinion, is, making George Wentworth, the agent, liable for any part. I have had considerable doubts on this subject, but upon the fullest consideration I have been able to bestow on it, I think he is not liable. Had he held any of the property, at the time of the decree of the court of appeals, he would have been undoubtedly liable.

The 4th question is, whether this court can now rectify the decree in respect to the parts of it considered to be erroneous, or must affirm or reverse in the whole.

The latter is certainly the general method at common law, and it has been contended, that as this proceeding is on a writ of error it must have all the incidents of a writ of error at common law. The argument would be conclusive, if this was a common law proceeding, but as it is not, I do not conceive, that it necessarily applies. An incident to one subject cannot be presumed, by the very name of such an incident, to be intended to apply to a subject totally different. I presume the term, "writ of error," was made use of, because we are prohibited from reviewing facts, and therefore must be confined to the errors on the record. But as this is a civil law proceeding, I conceive the word "error" must be applied to such errors as are deemed such, by the principles of the civil law, and that in rectifying the error we must proceed according to those principles.

Upon the whole, my opinion is, that the decree be affirmed in respect to the recovery of the libellants, in the original action against all the defendants but George Wentworth; that the libel against him, be adjudged to be dismissed, but that there be recovered against the other defendants in the original action, the value of the property they received, as ascertained in the circuit court, with interest from the 17th of September, 1783.

I am also of opinion, that the respective parties should pay their own costs.

But it is objected, that at most, no greater power was given to Congress than to enter into a definite war with Great Britain, not the right of war and peace generally; and even that war, till the declaration of independence, would be only a civil war. But why is not a definite war against Great Britain (call it if you will, a civil war) to be conducted on the same principles as any other: If it was a civil war, still we do not allow it to have been a rebellion America resisted and became thereby engaged in what she deemed a just war. It was not the war of a lawless banditti, but of freemen fighting for their dearest rights, and of men, lovers of order and good government. Was it not as necessary in such a war, as in any between contending nations, that the law of nations should be observed, and that those who had the conducting of it, should be armed with every authority for preventing injuries to neutral powers, and their subjects, and even cruelty to the enemy? The *power* supposed to have been *given* to *Congress* being confined to a definitive war against Great Britain, and not extending to the rights of peace and war generally, appears to me to make no material difference; still the same necessity recurs, of confining the evil of the war to the enemy against whom it is waged....

...As the supposition that Congress was invested with all the rights of war, in respect to Great Britain, is of great moment in the present cause, and as the power may not be so satisfactorily conveyed by the instructions to the several delegates as might be wished, partly because some of them did not exhibit farther instructions than to attend Congress, and partly because the instructions given to the rest, may be satisfied by a different construction, it may be proper to consider the manner in which Congress, by their proceedings, appear to have considered their powers; not that by anything of this sort, they had a right to extend their authority to the desired point, if it was not given, but because in showing by such means, their sense of the extent of their power, they gave an opportunity to their constituents to express their disapprobation, if they conceived Congress to have usurped power, or by their co-operation to confirm the construction of Congress; which would be as legitimate a source of authority, as if it had been given at first....

But if Congress possessed the right of war, they had also authority to equip a naval force; they did so, and exercised the same authority over it, as they had done over the army; they passed a resolution for permitting the inhabitants of the colonies to fit out armed vessels to cruise against the enemies of America; directed what vessels should be subject to capture, and prescribed a rule of distribution of prizes, together with a form of commission, and instructions to the commanders of private ships of war; they directed that the general assemblies, conventions and councils or committees of safety of the united colonies, should be supplied with blank commissions, signed by the president of Congress, to be by them filled up, and delivered to any person intending to fit out private ships of war, on his executing a bond, forms of which were to be sent with the commissions, and the bonds to be returned to Congress.

BY THE COURT. Ordered, That against all the plaintiffs in error, sixteen thousand three hundred and sixty dollars and sixty-eight cents, be recovered by the defendants in error and the same sum against George Wentworth; and that against the plaintiffs in error the costs of the circuit court be recovered.

BAS v. TINGY
4 Dall. 36 (1800)

This case involved the capture of an American vessel on the high seas by a French privateer and the subsequent recapture of the same by an armed American ship. The controversy centered on two separate acts of 1798 and 1799 by Congress which set out guidelines for returning re-captured ships to their original owner(s) based on the payment of a salvage fee. Bas, one of the owners, sought enforcement of the first, the 1798 act, which allowed for payment of a smaller salvage fee than did the Act of 1799. On the basis that the former Act targeted France only, it was considered merely temporary in nature. He claimed that the latter enactment of 1799 had a more general designation of "the enemy," and therefore, it should apply only to future hostilities resulting from a declared war. Since the term "enemy" was present in the second Act and not in the first, Mr. Bas argued that only the first Act should apply to France which was, as he viewed it, not an enemy as defined by a formal declaration of war. Consequently, the focal point of the decision rested on the definition of the term "enemy."

[excerpts]

MR. ASSOCIATE JUSTICE BUSHROD WASHINGTON gave the unanimous opinion of the Court:

The decision of this question must depend upon another; which is, whether, at the time of passing the Act of Congress of the 2d of March, 1799, there subsisted a state of war between the two nations? It may, I believe, be safely laid down, that every contention by force between two nations, in external matters, under the authority of their respective governments, is not only war, but public war. If it be declared in form, it is called solemn, and is of the perfect kind; because one whole nation is at war with another whole nation; and all the members of the nation declaring war, are authorized to commit hostilities against all the members of the other, in every place, and under every circumstance. In such a war all the members act under a general authority, and all the rights and consequences of war attach to their condition.

But hostilities may subsist between two nations, more confined in its nature and extent; being limited as to places, persons, and things; and this is more properly termed *imperfect war;* because not solemn, and because those who are authorized to commit hostilities, act under special authority, and can go farther than to the extent of their commission. Still, however, it is a public war, because it is an external contention by force between some of the members of the two nations, authorized by the legitimate powers. It is a war between the two nations, *though all the members are not authorized to commit hostilities such as in a solemn war, where the government restrains the general power....*

...Congress had raised an army, stopped all intercourse with France; dissolved our treaty, built and equipped ships of war; and commissioned private armed ships; enjoining the former, and authorizing the latter, to defend themselves against the armed ships of France, to attack them on the high seas, to subdue and take them as prize, and to re-capture armed vessels found in their possession....

The contention was external, and authorized by the legitimate authority of the two governments. If they were not our enemies, I know not what constitutes an enemy....

The opinion which I delivered at New York, in *Talbot v. Seeman,* was, that although an American vessel could not justify the re-taking of a neutral vessel from the French, because neither the sort of war that subsisted, nor the special commission under which the American acted, authorized the proceeding; yet, that the 7th section of the Act of 1799, applied to re-captures from France as an enemy, in all cases authorized by Congress. And on both points, my opinion remains unshaken; or rather has been confirmed by the very able discussion which the subject has lately undergone in this court, on the appeal from my decree. Another reason has been assigned by the defendant's counsel, why the former law [1798] is not to be regarded as repealed by the latter, to wit: that a subsequent affirmative general law cannot repeal a former affirmative special law, if both may stand together....

What then is the evidence of legislative will? In fact and in law we are at war: an American vessel fighting with a French vessel, to subdue and make her prize, is fighting with an enemy, accurately and technically speaking: and if this be not sufficient evidence of the legislative mind, it is explained in the same law. The sixth and the ninth sections of the Act speak of prizes, which can only be of property taken at sea from an enemy, *jure belli;* and the 9th section speaks of prizes as taken from an enemy, in so many words, alluding to prizes which had been previously taken....

The two laws, upon the whole, cannot be rendered consistent, unless the court could wink so hard as not to see and know the possession by a French armed vessel of an American vessel, was the possession of an enemy; and, therefore, in my opinion, the decree of the circuit court ought to be *affirmed*....

As there may be a public general war, and a public qualified war; so there may, upon correspondent principles, be a general enemy, and a partial enemy. The designation of *"enemy"* extends to a case of perfect war; but as a general designation, it surely includes the *less, as well as the greater, species of warfare.* If Congress had chosen to declare a general war, France would have been a general enemy; having chosen to wage a partial war, France was, at the time of the capture, only a partial enemy; but still she was an enemy....

TALBOT v. HANS FREDERICK SEEMAN
1 Cr. 15 (1801)

In an effort to protect American interests in commercial shipping in the late 1790's, Congress enacted a series of statutes which put it in a state of open hostilities with France. This "quasi-war" brought havoc on the trading vessels of both nations and quite often, it also adversely affected neutral vessels of non-participating countries. The latter factor gave rise to the present case.

*In September of 1799, the **Amelia**, a trading vessel owned by a citizen and merchant of Hamburg, Germany, was captured (and her cargo seized) in the Bay of Bengal by a French warship. The captain ordered that the **Amelia** be taken to St. Domingo and be judged as a lawful prize of war. Less than two weeks later—before reaching port—the same ship was captured without any resistance by the **Constitution,** an American ship of war. Talbot was the commander of the **Constitution** who brought the **Amelia** into the port of New York to seek a salvage fee from the original owners were represented by Hans Frederick Seeman. The district court of New York ruled that one-half of the gross value of the ship and cargo were to be paid to the plaintiff as salvage, but on appeal the circuit court reversed this decision. A writ of error was granted on behalf of the plaintiff, bringing the case before the United States Supreme Court.*

[excerpts]

MR. CHIEF JUSTICE JOHN MARSHALL delivered the opinion of the Court:

...Is Captain Talbot, the plaintiff in error, entitled to any, and if to any, to what salvage in the case which has been stated?

Salvage is a compensation for actual service rendered to the property charged with it.

It is demandable of right for vessels saved from pirates, or from the enemy.

In order, however, to support the demand, two circumstances must concur..

1. The taking must be lawful.
2. There must be a meritorious service rendered to the recaptured.

1. The taking must be lawful; for no claim can be maintained in a court of justice founded on an act in itself tortious. On a recapture, for salvage can arise, because that act of retaking is a hostile act, not justified by the situation of the nation to which the vessel making the recapture belongs, in relation to that from the possession of which such recaptured vessel was taken. The degree of service rendered the rescued vessel is precisely the same as if it had been rendered by a belligerent; yet the rights accruing to the recaptor are not the same, because no right can accrue from an act in itself unlawful....

The whole powers of war being, by the Constitution of the United States, vested in Congress, the acts of that body can alone be resorted to as our guides in this inquiry [sic]. It is not denied, nor in the course of the argument has it been denied, that Congress may authorize general hostilities, in which case the general laws of war apply to our situation; or partial hostilities, in which case the laws of war, so far as they actually apply to our situation, must be noticed....

The first Act on this subject passed on the 28th of May, 1798, an is entitled "An Act More Effectually To Protect the Commerce and Coasts of the United States."

This Act authorized any armed vessel of the United States to capture any armed vessel sailing under the authority, or pretense of authority, of the republic of France, which shall have committed depredations on vessels belonging to the citizens of the United States, or which shall be found hovering on the coasts for this purpose of committing such depredations. It also authorizes the recapture of vessels belonging to the citizens of the United States.

On the 25th of June, 1798, an Act was passed "to authorize the defense of the merchant vessels of the United States against French depredations."

This Act empowers merchant vessels, owned wholly by citizens of the United States, to defend themselves against any attack which may be made on them by the commander or crew of any armed vessel sailing under French colours, or acting, or pretending to act, by or under the authority of the French republic; and to capture any such vessel. This Act also authorizes the recapture of merchant vessels belonging to the citizens of the United States. By the 2d section, such armed vessel is to be brought in and condemned for the use of the owners and captors.

By the same section, recaptured vessels belonging to the citizens of the United States, are to be restored, they paying for salvage not less than one-eighth, nor more than one-half the true value of such vessel and cargo.

On the 28th of June, an Act passed "in addition to the act more effectually to protect the commerce and coasts of the United States."

This authorized the condemnation of vessels brought in under the first act, with their cargoes, excepting only from such condemnation the goods of any citizen or person resident within the United States, which shall have been before taken by the crew of such captured vessel....

On the 9th of July another law was enacted, "further to protect the commerce of the United States."

This Act authorizes the public armed vessels of the United States to take any armed French vessel found on the high seas. It also directs such armed vessel, with her apparel, guns, &c., and the goods and effects found on board, being French property to be condemned as forfeited.

The same power of capture is extended to private armed vessels....

On the 3d of March, 1800, Congress passed "An Act Providing for Salvage in Cases of Recapture."

This law regulates the salvage to be paid "when any vessels or goods, which shall be taken as a prize as aforesaid, shall appear to have before belonged to any person or persons permanently resident within the territory, and under the protection, of any foreign prince, government or state, in amity with the United States, and to have been taken by an enemy of the United States, or by authority, or pretense of authority, from any prince, government, or state, against which the United States have authorized, or shall authorize, defense or reprisals."

These are the laws of the United States, which define their situation in regard to France, and which regulate salvage to accrue on recaptures made in consequence of that situation.

A neutral armed vessel which has been captured, and which is commanded and manned by Frenchmen, whether found cruising on the high seas, or sailing directly for a French port, does not come within the description of those which the laws authorize an American ship of war to capture, unless she be considered *quoad hoc* as a French vessel.

Very little doubt can be entertained but that a vessel thus circumstanced, encountering an American unarmed merchantman, or one which should be armed, but of inferior force, would as readily capture such merchantman as if she had sailed immediately from the ports of France. One direct and declared object of the war, then, which was the protection of the American commerce, would as certainly require the capture of such a vessel as of others more determinately specified. But the rights of a neutral vessel, which the government of the United States cannot be considered as having disregarded, here Intervene, and the vessel certainly is not, correctly speaking, a French vessel.

If the Amelia was not, on the 15th of September, 1799, a French vessel within the description of the Act of Congress, could her capture be lawful?

It is, I believe, a universal principle, which applies to those engaged in a partial, as well as those engaged in a general war, that where there is probable cause to believe the vessel met with at sea is in the condition of one liable to capture, it is *lawful* to take her and subject her to the examination and adjudication of the courts.

The Amelia was an armed vessel commanded and manned by Frenchmen. It does not appear that there was evidence on board to ascertain her character. It is not then to he questioned, but that there was probable cause to bring her in for adjudication. The recapture, then, was lawful.

The opinion of the court is, that had the character of the Amelia been completely ascertained by Captain Talbot, yet as she was an armed vessel under French authority, and in a condition to annoy the American commerce, it was his duty to render her incapable of mischief. To have taken out the arms, or the crew, was as little authorized by the construction of the Act of Congress contended for by the claimants, as to have taken possession of the vessel herself.

There must, then, be incidents growing out of those acts of hostility specifically authorized, which a fair construction of the acts will authorize likewise. This was obviously the sense of Congress.

If by the laws of Congress on this subject that body shall appear to have legislated upon a perfect conviction that the state of war in which this country was placed, was such as to authorize recaptures generally from the enemy; if one part of the system shall be manifestly founded on this construction of the other part it would have considerable weight in rendering certain what might before have been doubtful.

Upon a critical investigation of the acts of Congress it will appear, that the right of recapture is expressly given in no single instance, but that of a vessel or goods belonging to a citizen of the United States.

It will also appear that the quantum of salvage is regulated, as if the right to it existed previous to the regulation.

Although no right of recapture is given in terms for the vessels and goods belonging to persons residing within the United States not being citizens, yet an act, passed so early as the 28th of June, 1798, declares, that vessels and goods of this description, when recaptured, shall be restored on paying salvage; thereby plainly indicating that such recapture was sufficiently warranted by law to be the foundation
of a claim for salvage.

If the recapture of vessels of one description, not expressly authorized by the very terms of the Act of Congress...be yet a rightful act recognized by Congress, as the foundation for a claim to salvage, which claim *Congress proceeds to regulate*, then it would seem that other recaptures from the same enemy are equally rightful; and where the claim they afford for salvage has not been *regulated by Congress* such claim must be determined by the principles of general law....

It is not unworthy of notice that the first regulation of the right of salvage in the case of a recapture, not expressly enumerated among the specified acts of hostility warranted by the law Is to be found in one of those acts which constitute a part of the very system of defense determined on by *Congress*, and is the first which subjects to condemnation the prizes made by our public ships of war.

It has not escaped the consideration of the court that a legislative act founded on a mistaken opinion of what was law, does *not* change the actual state of the law as to pre-existing cases.

This principle is not shaken by the opinion now given. The court goes no further than to use the provisions in one of several acts forming a general system, as explanatory of other parts of the same system; and this appears to be in obedience to the best established rules of exposition, and to be necessary to a sound construction of the law....

It is, then, the opinion of the court, on a consideration of the acts of Congress, and of the circumstances of the case, that the recapture of the Amelia was lawful, and that, if the claim to salvage be in other respects well founded there is nothing to defeat it in the character of the original taking....

Whether there has been such a meritorious service rendered to the recaptured as entitles the recaptor to salvage....

It is stated to be the settled doctrine of the law of nations, that a neutral vessel captured by a belligerent is to be discharged without paying salvage: and for this several authorities have been quoted, and many more might certainly be cited. That such has been a general rule is not to be questioned. As little is it to be questioned that this rule is founded exclusively on the supposed safety of the neutral. It is expressly stated in the case of the *War Onskan* cited from Robinson's Reports, to be founded on this plain principle, "that the liberation of a clear neutral from the hand of the enemy, is no essential service rendered to him, inasmuch as that the same enemy would be compelled, by the tribunals of his own country, after he had carried the neutral into port, to release him with costs and damages for the injurious seizure and detention." It is not infrequent to consider and speak of a regular practice under a rule, as itself forming a rule. A regular course of decisions on the text of the law constitutes a rule of construction by which that text is to be applied to all similar cases: but alter the text, and the rule no longer governs. So [it is] in the case of salvage. [If] [t]he general principle [that] the Act of Congress be yet a rightful Act recognized by Congress, as the foundation for a claim to salvage, which claim Congress proceeds to regulate, then it would seem that other recaptures from the same enemy are equally rightful; and where the claim they afford for salvage has not been regulated by Congress such claim must be determined by the principles of general law.

It is not unworthy of notice that the first regulation of the right of salvage in the case of a recapture, not expressly enumerated among the specified acts of hostility warranted by the law Is to be found in one of those acts which constitute a part of the very system of defense determined on by *Congress*, and is the first which subjects to condemnation the prizes made by our public ships of war.

It has not escaped the consideration of the court that a legislative act founded on a mistaken opinion of what was law, does *not* change the actual state of the law as to pre-existing cases.

This principle is not shaken by the opinion now given. The court goes no further than to use the provisions in one of several acts forming a general system, as explanatory of other parts of the same system; and this appears to be in obedience to the best established rules of exposition, and to be necessary to a sound construction of the law....

It is, then, the opinion of the court, on a consideration of the acts of Congress, and of the circumstances of the case, that the recapture of the Amelia was lawful, and that, if the claim to salvage be in other respects well founded there is nothing to defeat it in the character of the original taking....

Whether there has been such a meritorious service rendered to the recaptured as entitles the recaptor to salvage....

It is stated to be the settled doctrine of the law of nations, that a neutral vessel captured by a belligerent is to be discharged without paying salvage: and for this several authorities have been quoted, and many more might certainly be cited. That such has been a general rule is not to be questioned. As little is it to be questioned that this rule is founded exclusively on the supposed safety of the neutral. It is expressly stated in the case of the *War Onskan* cited from Robinson's Reports, to be founded on this plain principle, "that the liberation of a clear neutral from the hand of the enemy, is no essential service rendered to him, inasmuch as that the same enemy would be compelled, by the tribunals of his own country, after he had carried the neutral into port, to release him with costs and damages for the injurious seizure and detention." It is not infrequent to consider and speak of a regular practice under a rule, as itself forming a rule. A regular course of decisions on the text of the law constitutes a rule of construction by which that text is to be applied to all similar cases: but alter the text, and the rule no longer governs. So in the case of salvage. The general principle is, that salvage is only payable where a meritorious service has been rendered. In the application of this principle, it has been decided that neutrals carried in by a belligerent for examination, being in no danger, receive no benefit from recapture; and ought not, therefore, to pay salvage.

The principle is that without benefit, salvage is not payable: and it is merely a consequence from this principle which exempts recaptured neutrals from its payment. But let a nation change its laws and its practice on this subject; let its legislation be such as to subject to condemnation all neutrals captured by its cruisers and who will say that no benefit is conferred by a recapture? In such a course of things the state of a neutral is completely changed. So far from being safe, he is in as much danger of condemnation as if captured by his own declared enemy. A series of decisions, then, and of rules founded on his supposed safety, no longer apply. Only those rules are applicable, which regulate a situation of actual danger. This is not, as it has been termed, a change of principle; but a preservation of principle by a practical application of it according to the original substantial good sense of the rule.

It becomes, then, necessary to inquire whether the laws of France were such as to have rendered the condemnation of the Amelia so extremely probable, as to create a case of such real danger, that her recapture by Captain Talbot must be considered as a meritorious service entitling him to salvage....

To prove this the counsel for the plaintiff in error has offered several decrees of the French government, and especially one of the 18th of January, 1798.

That the laws of a foreign nation, designed only for the direction of its own affairs, are not to be noticed by the courts of other countries unless proved as facts. and that this court, with respect to facts is limited to the statement made in the court below, cannot be questioned. The real and only question is, whether the public laws of a foreign nation, on a subject of common concern to all nations, promulgated by the governing powers of a country, can be noticed as law by a court of admiralty of that country, or must be still further proved as a fact.

It is therefore the opinion of the court that the decree should be read as an authenticated copy of a public law of France interesting to all nations.

The decree ordains, that "the character of vessels, relative to their quality of neuter or enemy, shall be determined by their cargo; in consequence, every vessel found at sea loaded in whole or in part with merchandise, the production of England or her possessions, shall be declared good prize, whoever the owner of these goods or merchandise may be."...

This decree subjects to condemnation in the courts of France a neutral vessel laden, in whole or in part, with articles the growth of England or any of its possessions. A neutral thus circumstanced cannot be considered as in a state of safety. His recaptor cannot be said to have rendered him no service. It cannot reasonably be contended that he would have been discharged in the ports of the belligerent, with costs and damages.

Let us, then, inquire, whether this was the situation of the Amelia. The first fact states her to have sailed from Calcutta in Bengal, in April, 1799, laden with a cargo of the product and manufacture of that country. Here it is contended that the whole of Bengal may possibly not be in possession of the English, and therefore it does not appear that the cargo was within the description of the decree. But to this it has been answered, that in inquiring whether the Amelia was in danger or not, this court must put itself in the place of a French court of admiralty, and determine as such court would have determined. Doing this, there seems to be no reason to doubt that the cargo without inquiring into the precise situation of the British power in every part of Bengal, being prima facie of the product and manufacture of a possession of England, would have been so considered, unless the contrary could have been plainly shown.

The next fact relied on by the defendant in error is, that the Amelia was sent to be adjudged according to the laws of war, and from thence it is inferred that she could not have been judged according to the decree of the 18th of January.

It is to be remembered that these are the orders of the captor, and without a question in the language of a French cruiser, a law of his own country furnishing a rule of conduct in time of war, will be spoken of as one of the laws of war.

But the third and fourth facts in the statement admit the Amelia, with her cargo, to have belonged to a citizen of Hamburgh, which city was not in a state of hostility with the Republic of France, but was to be considered as neutral between the then belligerent powers.

It has been contended that these facts not only do not show the recaptured vessel to have been one on which the decree could operate, but positively show that the decree could not have affected her.

The whole statement taken together amounts to nothing more than that Hamburgh was a neutral city; and it is precisely against neutrals that the decree is in terms directed. To prove, therefore, that the Amelia was a neutral vessel is to prove her within the very words of the decree, and, consequently, to establish the reality of her danger....

It has been contended that this decree might have been merely *in terrorem;* that it might never have been executed; and that, being in opposition to the law of nations, the court ought to presume it never would have been executed.

But the court cannot presume the laws of any country to have been enacted *in terrorem*; nor that they will be disregarded by its judicial authority. Their obligation on their own courts must be considered as complete, and without resorting either to public notoriety, or the declarations of our own laws on the subject, the decisions of the French courts must be admitted to have conformed to the rules prescribed by their government....

It is true that a violation of the law of nations by one power does not justify its violation by another; but that remonstrance is the proper course to be pursued, and this is the course which has been pursued. America did remonstrate, most earnestly remonstrate, to France against the injuries committed on her; but remonstrance having failed, she appealed to a higher tribunal, and authorized limited hostilities. This was not violating the law of nations, but conforming to it. In the course of these limited hostilities the Amelia has been recaptured, and the inquiry now is not whether the conduct of France would justify a departure from the law of nations, but that is the real law in the case. This depends on the danger from which she has been saved....

It has been contended that an illegal commission to take, given by France, cannot authorize our vessels to retake; that we have no right by legislation to grant salvage out of the property of a citizen of Hamburgh, who might have objected to the condition of the service.

But it is not the authority given by the French government to capture neutrals, which is legalizing the recapture made by Captain Talbot; it is the state of hostility between the two nations which is considered as having authorized that act. The recapture having been made lawfully, then the right to salvage, on general principles, depends on the service. We cannot presume this service to have been unacceptable to the Hamburgher, because it has bettered his condition; but a recapture must always be made without consulting the recaptured. The Act is one of the incidents of war, and is in itself only offensive as against the enemy. The subsequent fate of the recaptured depends on the service he has received, and on other circumstances.

To give a right to salvage, it is said there must be a contract either express or implied.

It is also urged that to maintain this right, the danger ought not to be merely speculative, but must be imminent and the loss certain.

That a mere speculative danger will not be sufficient to entitle a person to salvage is unquestionably true. But that the danger must be such, that escape from it by other means was inevitable, cannot be admitted.

In all the cases stated by the counsel for the defendant in error, safety by other means was possible, though not probable. The flames of a ship on fire might be extinguished by the crew, or by a sudden tempest. A ship on the rocks might possibly be got off by the aid of wind and tides without assistance from others. A vessel captured by an enemy might be separated from her captor, and if sailors had been placed on board the prize, a thousand accidents might possibly destroy them; or they might even be blown by a storm into a port of the country to which the prize vessel originally belonged.

It has been contended that the case before the court is in the very words of the act. That the owner of the Amelia. is a citizen of a state in amity with the United States, retaken from the enemy. That the description would have been more limited had the intention of the Act been to restrain its application to a recaptured vessel belonging to a nation engaged with the United States against the same enemy.

The words of the Act would certainly admit of this construction.

Against it has been urged, and we think with great force, that the laws of the United States ought not, if it be avoidable, so to be construed as to infract the common principles and usages of nations, or the general doctrines of national law. If the construction contended for be given to the act, it subjects to the same rate of salvage a recaptured neutral, and a re captured belligerent vessel. Yet, according to the law of nations, a neutral is generally to be restored without salvage.

This act, then, if the words admit it, since it provides a permanent rule for the payment of salvage, ought to be construed to apply only to cases in which salvage is permanently payable.

On inspecting the clause in question, the court is struck with the description of those from whom the vessel is to he retaken in order to come within the provisions of the act. The expression used is the enemy. A vessel retaken from the enemy. The enemy of whom? The court thinks it not unreasonable to answer of both parties. *By this construction the Act of Congress will never violate those principles which we believe, and which it is our duty to believe, the legislature of the United States will always hold sacred.*

It is therefore the opinion of the court, that the decree of the circuit court, held for the district of New York, was correct in reversing the decree of the district court, but not correct in decreeing the restoration of the Amelia without paying salvage. This court, therefore, is of opinion, that the decree, so far as the restoration of the Amelia without salvage is the Amelia and her cargo ought to be restored to the claimant, on paying for salvage one sixth part of the net value, after deducting therefrom the charges which have been incurred.

LITTLE v. BARREME
2 Cr. 170 (1804)

On 2 December 1799, Captain Little, the Commander of a U.S. warship, ordered and procured the capture of a Danish vessel for an alleged violation of an Act passed by Congress on February 9 of the same year. This "nonintercourse law" forbade American ships from sailing to any port within the territory of France. The district court of Massachusetts found that Captain Little did have probable cause to believe that the Danish ship was American-owned, and it upheld his action. The Circuit Court reversed and awarded damages to the owners and crew of the Danish vessel. The question before the Supreme Court was whether or not an American military officer, acting under authority of the President, is accountable for damages resulting from the execution of orders that are not warranted by a congressional statute. The Supreme Court's decision in this case was its most significant in the area of foreign policy and war-making until the notorious Curtiss-Wright (1936) decision which, in effect, overruled it.

[excerpts]

MR. CHIEF JUSTICE JOHN MARSHALL delivered the opinion of the Court:

> During the hostilities between the United Sates and France, an act for the suspension of all intercourse between the two nations was annually passed.

The 5th section of this Act authorizes the President of the United States to instruct the commanders of armed vessels "to stop and examine any ship or vessel of the United States on the high seas, which there may be reason to suspect to be engaged in any traffic or commerce contrary to the true tenor of the act, and if upon examination it should appear that such ship or vessel is bound, or sailing to, any port or place within the territory of the French republic or her dependencies, it is rendered lawful to seize such vessel, and send her into the United States for adjudication.

It is by *no means clear* that the President of the United States, whose high duty it is to "take care that the laws be faithfully executed," and who is Commander in Chief of the armies and navies of the United States, might not, *without any special authority* for that purpose, in the then existing state of things, have empowered the officers commanding the armed vessels of the United States, to seize and send into port for adjudication, American vessels which were forfeited by being engaged in this illicit commerce. But when it is observed that the general clause of the first section of the "act, which declares that such vessels may be seized, and may be prosecuted in any district or circuit court, which shall be holden within or for the district where the seizure shall be made," obviously contemplates a seizure within the United States; and that the 5th section gives a special authority to seize on the high seas, and limits that authority to the seizure of vessels bound, or sailing to, a French port, the legislature seems to have prescribed that the manner in which this law shall be carried into execution, was to exclude a seizure of any vessel not bound to a French port. Of consequence, however strong the circumstances might be, which induced Captain Little to suspect the Flying Fish to be an American vessel, they could not excuse the detention of her, since he would not have been authorized to detain her had she been really American.

It was so obvious, that if only vessels sailing to a French port could be seized on the high seas, that the law would be very often evaded, that this Act of Congress appears to have received a different construction from the executive of the United States; a construction much better calculated to give it effect.

A copy of this Act was transmitted by the Secretary of the Navy, to the captains of the armed vessels, who were ordered to consider the 5th section as part of their instructions. The same letter contained the following clause: "A proper discharge of the important duties enjoined on you, arising out of this act, will require the exercise of a sound and an impartial judgment. You are not only to do all that in you lies to prevent all intercourse, whether direct or circuitous, between the ports of the United Sates and those of France or her dependencies, where the vessels are apparently as well as really American, and protected by American papers only, but you are to be vigilant that vessels or cargoes really American, but covered by Danish or other foreign papers, and bound to or from French ports, do not escape you."

These orders given by the executive under the construction of the Act of Congress made by the department to which its execution was assigned, *enjoin* the seizure of American vessels sailing from a French port. Is the officer who obeys them liable for damages sustained by this misconstruction of the act, or will his orders excuse him? If his instructions afford him no protection, then the law must take its course, and he must pay such damages as are legally awarded against him; if they excuse an act not otherwise excusable, it would then be necessary to inquire whether this is a case in which the probable cause which existed to induce a suspicion that the vessel was American, would excuse the captor from damages when the vessel appeared in fact to be neutral....

...the instructions *cannot* change the nature of the transaction, or *legalize* an act which, without those instructions, would have been a plain trespass.

It becomes, therefore, unnecessary to inquire whether the probable cause afforded by the conduct of the Flying Fish to suspect her of being an American would excuse Captain Little from damages for having seized and sent her into port, since, had she *been* an American, the seizure would have been *unlawful*....

There appears, then, to be *no error in this judgment of the circuit court,* and it must be *affirmed* with costs.

ARMITZ BROWN v. UNITED STATES
8 Cranch 504 (1814)

*Prior to the outbreak of hostilities in Anglo-American relations during the War of 1812, an American ship, the **Emulous**, was chartered to a British company to transport goods from Savannah to Plymouth. After the United States's declaration of war, the British owners of the cargo sold it to Armitz Brown, an American merchant. The goods, which included—among another things—550 tons of pine timber that had been secured in a shallow creek in Massachusetts, were seized as enemy property under a libel filed by the U.S. District Attorney. The District Court dismissed this cause of action; however, the U.S. Circuit Court reversed this decision and condemned the goods as enemy property and thus subject to forfeiture. The case reached the Supreme Court on an appeal filed by the appellant.*

[excerpts]

MR. CHIEF JUSTICE JOHN MARSHALL delivered the opinion of the Court:

The material question made at bar is this: Can the pine timber, even admitting the property not to be changed by the sale in November, be condemned as prize of war?

The cargo of the Emulous having been legally acquired and put on board the vessel, having been detained by an embargo not intended to act on foreign property, the vessel having sailed before the war, from Savannah, under a stipulation to re-land the cargo in some port of the United States, the re-landing having been made with respect to the residue of the cargo, and the pine timber having been floated into shallow water, where it was secured and in the custody of the owner of the ship, an American citizen, the court cannot perceive any solid distinction, so far as respects confiscation between this property and other British property found on land at the commencement of hostilities. It will therefore be considered as a question relating to such property generally, and to be governed by the same rule.

Respecting the power of government no doubt is entertained. That war gives to the sovereign full right to take the persons and confiscate the property of the enemy wherever found, is conceded. The mitigations of this rigid rule, which the humane and wise policy of modern times has introduced into practice, will more or less affect the exercise of this right, but cannot impair the right itself. That remains undiminished, and when the sovereign authority shall choose to bring it into operation, the judicial department must give effect to its will. But until that will shall be expressed, no power of condemnation can exist in the court.

The questions to be decided by the court are:

1st. May enemy's property, found on land at the commencement of hostilities, be seized and condemned as a necessary consequence of the declaration of war?

2d. Is there any legislative Act which authorized such seizure and condemnation?

Since, in this country, from the structure of our government, proceedings to condemn the property of an enemy found within our territory at the declaration of war can be sustained only upon the principle that they are instituted in execution of some existing law, we are led to ask,

Is the declaration of war such a law? Does that declaration, by its own operation, so vest the property of the enemy in the government as to support proceedings for its seizure and confiscation, or does it vest only a right, the assertion of which depends on the will of the sovereign power?

The universal practice of forbearing to seize and confiscate debts and credits, the principle universally received, that the right to them revives on the restoration of peace, would seem to prove that war is not an absolute confiscation of this property, but simply confers the right of confiscation.

Between debts contracted under the faith of laws, and property acquired in the course of trade, on the faith of the same laws, reason draws no distinction; and, although, in practice vessels with their cargoes, found in port at the declaration of war, may have been seized, it is not believed that modern usage would sanction the seizure of the goods of an enemy on land which were acquired in peace in the course of trade. Such a proceeding is rare ad would be deemed a harsh exercise of the rights of war. But although the practice in this respect may not be uniform, that circumstance does not essentially affect the question. The inquiry is, whether such property vests in the sovereign by the mere declaration of war, or remains subject to a right of confiscation, the exercise of which depends on the national will; and the rule which applies to one case, so far as respects the operation of a declaration of war on the thing itself, must apply to all others over which war gives an equal right. The right of the sovereign to confiscate debts being precisely the same with the right to confiscate other property found in the country, the operation of a declaration of war on debts and on other property found within the country must be the same....

The modern rule, then, would seem to be, that tangible property belonging to an enemy and found in the country at the commencement of war, ought not to be immediately confiscated; and in almost every commercial treaty an article is inserted stipulating for the right to withdraw such property.

This rule appears to be totally incompatible with the idea that war does of itself vest the property in the belligerent government. It may be considered as the opinion of all who have written on the *jus belli*, that war gives the right to confiscate, but does not itself confiscate the property of the enemy; and their rules go to the exercise of this right. The constitution of the United States was framed at a time when this rule, introduced by commerce in favor of moderation and humanity, was received throughout the civilized world. In expounding that constitution, a construction ought not lightly to be admitted which would give to a declaration of war an effect in this country it does not possess elsewhere, and which would fetter that exercise of entire discretion respecting enemy property, which may enable the government to apply to the enemy the rule the he applies to us.

If we look to the constitution itself, we find this general reasoning much strengthened by the words of that instrument.

That the declaration of war has only the effect of placing the two nations in a state of hostility, of producing a state of war, of giving those rights which war confers; but not of operating, by its own force, any of those results, such as a transfer of property, which are usually produced by ulterior measures of government, is fairly deducible from the enumeration of powers which accompanies that of declaring war. *"Congress shall pave power" to declare war, grant letters of marquee and reprisal, and make rules concerning captures on land and water."*

It would be restraining this clause within narrower limits than the words themselves import to say that the power to make rules concerning captures on land and water is to be confined to captures which are extraterritorial. If it extends to rules respecting enemy property found within the territory, then we perceive an express grant to Congress of the power in question as an independent substantive power, not included in that of declaring war.

The acts of Congress furnish many instances of an opinion that the declaration of war does not, of itself, authorize proceedings against the persons or property of the enemy found, at the time, within the territory.

War gives an equal right over persons and property; and if its declaration is not considered as prescribing a law respecting the person of an enemy found in our country, neither does it prescribe a law for his property. The *Act* concerning alien enemies, which *confers* on the President very great discretionary powers respecting their persons, affords a strong implication that he did *not* possess those powers by virtue of the declaration of war.

The "act for the safe keeping and accommodation of prisoners of war" is of the same character.

The Act prohibiting trade with the enemy contains this clause:

"And be it further enacted, That the President of the United States be, and he is hereby authorized to give, at any time within six months after the passage of this act, passports for the safe transportation of any ship or other property belonging to British subjects, and which is now within the limits of the United States."

The phraseology of this law shows that the property of a British subject was not considered by the legislature as being vested in the United States by the declaration of war; and the authority which the Act confers on the President is manifestly considered as one which he did not previously possess.

The proposition that a declaration of war does not, in itself, enact a confiscation of the property of the enemy within the territory of the belligerent, is believed to be entirely free from doubt. Is there in the Act of Congress, by which war is declared against Great Britain, any expression which would indicate such an intention?

That *act*, after placing the two nations in a state of war, *authorizes* the *President of the United States* to use the whole land and naval force of the United States *to carry the war into effect*, and "to issue to private armed vessels of the United States commissions or letters of marquee and general reprisal against the vessels, goods and effects of the government of the united kingdom of Great Britain and Ireland, and the subjects thereof."

That reprisals may be made on enemy property found within the United States at the declaration of war, if such be the will of the nation, has been admitted; but it is not admitted that *in the declaration of war, the nation has expressed its will to that effect.*

It cannot be necessary to employ argument in showing that when the attorney for the United States institutes proceedings at law for the confiscation of enemy property found on land, or floating in one of our creeks, in the care and custody of one of our citizens, he is not acting under the authority of letters of marquee and reprisal, still less under the authority of such letters issued to a private armed vessel.

The "act concerning letter of marquee, prizes and prize goods," certainly contains nothing to authorize this seizure.

There being no other Act of Congress which bears upon the subject, it is considered as proved that the legislature has not confiscated enemy property which was within the United States at the declaration of war, and that this sentence of condemnation cannot be sustained....

The rule is, in its nature, flexible. It is subject to infinite modification. It is not an immutable rule of law, but depends on political considerations which may continually vary.

Commercial nations, in the situation of the United States, have always a considerable quantity of property in the possession of their neighbors. When war breaks out, the question, what shall be done with enemy property in our country is a question rather of policy than of law. The rule which we apply to the property of our enemy will be applied by him to the property of our citizens. Like all other questions of policy, it is proper for the consideration of a department which can modify it at will; not for the consideration of a department which can pursue only the law as it is written. It is proper for the consideration of the legislature, not of the executive or judiciary.

It appears to the court, that the power of confiscating enemy property is in the legislature, and that the legislature has not yet declared its will to confiscate property which was within our territory at the declaration of war.

The court is therefore of opinion that there is error in the sentence of condemnation pronounced in the Circuit Court in this case, and doth direct that the same be reversed and annulled, and that the sentence of the District Court be affirmed.

MARTIN v. MOTT
12 Wheaton 37 (1827)

The War of 1812 began with the Declaration of War by Congress on June 18, 1812. Until December 25, 1814, the exigencies of the armed conflict necessitated the calling forth of various state militia to aid the army of the United States. The congressional Act of 28 February 1795 empowered the President to call forth the state militia under Article IV "to execute the laws of the Union, suppress insurrections, and repel invasions. "

Subsequent orders of requisition by the President forced the governor of New York to issue a declaration placing the militia of his state into service for the United States government. Refusing to comply with the stipulations in the declaration Private Jacob E. Mott and other New Yorkers were charged and convicted in a court-martial presided over by U.S. Deputy-Magistrate Marshall Martin.

Mott filed a suit in the New York Supreme Court challenging the validity and applicability of the governor's declaration. That court, and subsequently, the court for the trial of impeachments, ruled in Mr. Mott's favor. Subsequently, Deputy-Magistrate Marshall Martin sought and received a writ of error which facilitated review by the Supreme Court of the United States.

[excerpts]

MR. JUSTICE STORY delivered the opinion of the Court:

The authority to decide whether the exigencies contemplated in the constitution of the United States, and the Act of Congress of 1795, ch. 101, in which the President has authority to call forth the militia, "to execute the laws of the Union, suppress insurrections, and repel invasions," have arisen, is exclusively vested in the President, and his decision is conclusive upon all other persons....

The constitution declared that Congress shall have power "to provide for calling forth the militia, to execute the laws of the Union, suppress insurrections, and repel invasions;" and also "to provide for organizing, arming and disciplining the militia, and for governing such part of them as may be employed in the service of the United States." In pursuance of this authority, the Act of 1795 has provided, "that whenever the United States shall be invaded, or be in imminent danger

of invasion from any foreign nation or Indian tribe, it shall be lawful for
the President of the United States to call forth such number of the militia
of the state or states most convenient to the place of danger, or scene of
action, as he may judge necessary to repel such invasion, and to issue his
order for that purpose to such officer or officers of the militia as he shall
think proper. " And like provisions are made for the other cases stated in
the Constitution. It has not been denied here that the Act of 1795 is
within the constitutional authority of Congress, or that Congress may not
lawfully provide for cases of imminent danger of invasion, as well as for
cases where an invasion has actually taken place. In our opinion there is
no ground for a doubt on this point, even if it had been relied on, for the
power to provide for repelling invasions includes the power to provide
against the attempt and danger of invasion, as the necessary and proper
means to effectuate the object. One of the best means to repel invasion
is to provide the requisite force for action before the invader himself has
reached the soil....

A free people are naturally jealous of the exercise of military power;
and the power to call the militia into actual service is certainly felt to be
one of no ordinary magnitude. But it is not a power which can be
executed without a correspondent responsibility. It is, in its terms, a
limited power, confined to cases of actual invasion, or if imminent
danger of invasion....

We are all of opinion that the authority to decide whether the
exigency has arise, belongs *exclusively* to the *President*, and that his
decision is *conclusive* upon all other persons. We think that this
construction necessarily *results* from the nature of the power itself, and
from the manifest object contemplated by the Act of *Congress*. The
power itself is to be exercised upon sudden emergencies, upon great
occasions of state, and under circumstances which may be vital to the
existence of the Union. A prompt and unhesitating obedience to orders
is indispensable to the complete attainment of the object....

If a superior officer has a right to contest the orders of the President
upon his own doubts as to the exigency having arisen, it must be equally
the right of ever inferior officer and soldier; and any act done by any
person in furtherance of such orders would subject him to responsibility
in a civil suit, in which his defense must finally rest upon his ability to
establish the facts by competent proofs. Such a course would be

subversive of all discipline, and expose the best disposed officers to the chances of ruinous litigation....

The power itself is confined to the Executive of the Union, to him who is, by the constitution, "the Commander in Chief of the militia, when called into the actual service of the United States," whose duty it is to "take care that the laws be faithfully executed," and whose responsibility for an honest discharge of his official obligations is secured by the highest sanctions. He is necessarily constituted the judge of the existence of the exigency in the first instance, and is bound to act according to his belief of the facts. *If he does so act, and decides to call for the militia, his orders for this purpose are in strict conformity with the provisions of the law;* and it would seem to follow as a necessary consequence, that every act done by a subordinate officer, in obedience to such orders, is equally justifiable....

When the President exercises an authority confided to him by law, the presumption is, that it is exercised in pursuance of law. Every public officer is presumed to act in obedience to his duty, until the contrary is shown; and *a fortiori*, this presumption ought to be favourably applied to the chief magistrate of the Union. It is not necessary to aver that the act which he may rightfully do was so done. If the fact of it would be traversable, and of course might be passed upon by a jury; and thus the legality of the orders of the President would depend, not on his own judgment of the facts, but upon the finding of those facts upon the proofs submitted to a jury....

Another objection is that the orders of the President are not set forth; nor is it averred that he issued any orders, but only that the Governor of New York called out the militia, upon the requisition of the President. The objection, so far as it proceeds upon a supposed difference between a requisition and an order, is untenable; for a requisition calling forth the militia is, in legal intendment, an order and must be so interpreted in this avowry. The majority of the court understood and acted upon this sense, which is one of the acknowledged sense of the work, in *Houston v. Moore*, 5 Wheat. Rep. 1. It was unnecessary to set forth the orders of the President at large; it was quite sufficient to state that the call was in obedience to them. No private citizen is presumed to be conversant the particulars of those orders; and if we were, he is not bound to set them forth in *haec verba*....

It is said that the original plaintiff was never employed in the service of the United States, but refused to enter that service, and that consequently, he was not liable to the rules and Articles of War, or to be tried for the offense by any court-martial organized under the authority of the United States. The case of *Houston v. Moore*, 5 Wheat. Rep. 1, affords a conclusive answer to this suggestion. It was decided in that case, that although a militiaman, who refused to obey the orders of the President calling him into the public service, was not, in the sense of the Act of 1795, "employed in the service of the United States" so as to be subject to the rules and Articles of War, yet that he was liable to be tried for the offense under the 5th section of the same act, by a court-martial called under the authority of the United States. The great doubt in that case was, whether the delinquent was liable to be tried for the offense by a court-martial organized under state authority.

In the next place, it is said the court-martial was not composed of the proper number of officers required by law. In order to understand the force of this objection, it is necessary to advert to the terms of the Act of 1795, and the rules and Articles of War. The Act of 1795, s. 5, provides, "that every officer, non-commissioned officer, or private of the militia, who shall fail to obey the orders of the President of the United States," etc., "shall forfeit a sum not exceeding on year's pay, and not less than one month's pay, to be determined and adjudged by a court-martial." And it further provides, s. 6, "that court-martial for the trial of militia shall be composed of militia officers only." These are the only provisions in the Act on this subject. It is not stated by whom the courts-martial shall be called, nor in what manner, nor of what number they shall be composed. But he court is referred to the 64th and 65th of the rules and Articles of War, enacted by the Act of the 10th of April, 1806, ch. 20, which provide, "that general courts-martial may consist of any number of commissioned officers from five to thirteen inclusively; but they shall not consist of less than thirteen, where that number can be convened without manifest injury to the service;" and that "any general officer commanding an army, or colonel commanding a separate department, may appoint general courts-martial when necessary." Supposing these clauses applicable to the court-martial in question, it is very clear that the Act is merely directory to the officer appointing the court, and that his decision as to the number which can be convened without manifest injury to the service, being in a matter submitted to his sound discretion, must be conclusive. But the present avowry goes farther, and alleges, not only that the court-martial was appointed by a general officer commanding an army, that it was composed of militia officers, naming them, but it goes on to assign the reason why a number short of thirteen composed the court, in the very terms of the 64th Article; and the truth of this allegation is admitted by the demurrer. Tried, therefore, by the very test which has been resorted to in support of the objection, it utterly fails....

The rules and Articles of War, by the very terms of the statute of 1806, are those "by which the armies of the United States shall be governed;" and the Act of 1795 has only provided "that the militia employed in the service of the United States "not the militia ordered into the service of the United States) shall be subject to the same rules and Articles of War as the troops of the United States;" and this is, in substance, re-enacted by the 97th of the rules and Articles of War....

The Act of the 18th of April, 1814, ch. 141, which expired at the end of the late war, was, in a great measure, intended to obviate difficulties arising from the imperfection of the provisions of the Act of 1795, and especially to aid court-martial in exercising jurisdiction over cases like the present. But whatever may have been the legislative intention, its terms do not extend to the declaration of the number of which such courts-martial shall be composed. The first section provides "that courts-martial to be composed of militia officers alone, for the trial of militia drafted, detached and called forth (not or called forth), for the service of the United States, whether acting in conjunction with the regular forces or otherwise, shall, when necessary, be appointed, held, and conducted, in the manner described by the rules and Articles of War, for appointing, holding, and conducting, court-martials for the trial of delinquents in the army of the United States." This language is obviously confined to the militia in the actual service of the United States, and does not extend to such as are drafted and refuse to obey the call; so that the court are driven back to the Act of 1795 as the legitimate source for the ascertainment of the organization and jurisdiction of the court-martial in the present case. And we are of opinion that nothing appears on the face of the avowry to lead to any doubt that it was a legal court-martial, organized according to military usage, and entitled to take cognizance of the delinquencies stated in the avowry....

Another objection to the proceedings of the court-martial is, that they took place, and the sentence was given, three years and more after the war was concluded, and in a time of profound peace. But the opinion of this court is, that a court-martial, regularly called under the Act of 1795, does not expire with the end of a war then existing, nor is its jurisdiction to try these offenses in any shape dependent upon the fact of war or peace. The Act of 1795 is not confined in its operation to cases of refusal to obey the orders of the President in times of public war. On the contrary, that Act authorizes the President to call forth the militia to suppress insurrections, and to enforce the laws of the United States, in times of peace. And court-martial are, under the 5th section of the act, entitled to take cognizance of, and to punish delinquencies in such cases, as well as in cases where the object is to repel invasion in times of war. It would be a strained construction of the act, to limit the authority of the court to the mere time of the existence of the particular exigency, when it might be there by unable to take cognizance of, and decide upon a single offense. It is sufficient for us to say that there is no such limitation in the Act itself....

Upon the whole, it is the opinion of the court that the judgment of the court for the trial of impeachments, and the correction of errors ought to be reversed, and that the cause be remanded to the same court, with directions to cause a judgment to be entered upon the pleadings in favor of the avowant.

Notes

1. Citations are found in Leonard Levy, Kenneth Kasst, and Dennis Mahoney. *American Constitutional History* (New York: Collier Macmillan Publishers, 1989), p. 49.
2. 3 Dall. 54. Justice William Paterson viewed the matter differently. While agreeing that the war powers were placed in Congressional hands, he believed that sovereignty in the field of foreign affairs was transferred from Great Britain to the United States after the Declaration of Independence. Justice Sutherland would support Paterson's contention nearly a century and a half later.
3. 4 Dall. at 40.
4. 1 Cr. 1 (1800) at 27.

5. Corwin. *The President: Office and Powers, 1789-1884*, 5th Edition (New York: New York University Press, 1984) p. 208. Hamilton, writing as "Pacificus" in a series of articles appearing in the *Gazette of the United States*, did argue "that the direction of foreign policy is inherently an *"executive"* function; however, he limited this function to the power of negotiation and the operation of laws and treaties.

6. Ibid, pp. 209-210.

7. Adler, "The Constitution and Presidential Warmaking," *Political Science Quarterly* (1988) pp. 20-1.

8. 2 Cr. 170 (1804) at 177.

9. See *Panama Refining Company v. Ryan*, 293 U.S. 388 (1934). Although, the Supreme Court excoriated Abraham Lincoln's suspension of the writ of habeas corpus during the Civil War, it did so *safely* after the war had been successfully concluded and the President had been buried in his grave. *Ex Parte Milligan*, 4 Wall. 17 (1865).

10. *Foster v. Neilson*, 2 Pet. 253 (1829) at 307.

11. Taney went on to say that, "As Commander in chief, he is authorized to direct movements of the naval and military forces placed by law at his command, and to employ them in a manner he may deem most effectual to harass and conquer and subdue the military" but not "extend the operation of our institutions and laws beyond the limits before assigned to them by the legislative powers." Ibid, p. 614.

12. Randall W. Bland, Theodore T. Hindson (eds.) Corwin's *The President: Office and Power* (New York: New York University Press, 1984), p 450, fn. #66.

Chapter Three:
The Traditional Era of Shared Powers (1846-1916)

The War of 1812, declared by the United States Congress against Great Britain, had been precipitated by the resumption of Franco-British hostilities and the renewal of disruptive English naval policies. It was concluded with the approval by the United States Senate of the Treaty of Ghent on February 15, 1815. In the years that followed, the United States began a movement of westward internal expansion ("Manifest Destiny") and limited its foreign policy interests to the protection of the Western Hemisphere from European expansion under the Monroe Doctrine enforced, to a great extent, by England. With the presidential election of Democrat James K. Polk in 1844, further national expansion was assured by the new President's pledge to annex Texas as a state. Upon annexation by a joint resolution of Congress a year later, Mexico severed relations with the United States and on April 9, 1846, its troops attacked American forces on the Texas side of the Rio Grande River. Immediately, Polk asked for, and received, a declaration of war against Mexico in compliance with Article I, section 8. After General Winfield Scott captured Mexico City, the capital of Mexico, and several of its ports in September 1847, the Mexican government surrendered. On February 2, 1848, Mexico signed the Treaty of Guadalupe-Hidalgo, ceding California and New Mexico to the United States for $15 million.

Clearly, the Declarations of War issued in 1812 and 1846 were extremely important in *enhancing* the plenary war powers of Congress. For *if* it was assumed by the nation's Highest Court, as well as in keeping with the intention of the Framers of the Constitution, that the conduct of foreign policy was one of *mutual* participation by the President and Congress; *then*, just as positively, was the authority to declare war found *only* in the legislative domain. The two declarations also demonstrated, quite clearly, that the Constitution granted to the President the power to "*make*" war, once it was declared. Central to this grant was the command of Article II, section 2, that "The President shall be Commander in Chief of the Army and Navy of the United States, and of the militia of the several States, when called into the actual Service of the United States." By 1850, the Taney Court took a more *restricted* view of the presidential role than had the Court under Marshall. In the *Fleming v. Page*, the Court ruled that the American occupation of Tampico during the course of the Mexican War (1846-1848) did *not* result in an *annexation* of that port to the United States. President James K. Polk, in his message to Congress in December, 1846, had declared:

> by the law of nations a conquered territory is subject to be governed by the conquered during his military possession, and...by the establishment of temporary governments in some of the conquered provinces in Mexico, assimilating them as far as practicable to the free institutions of our own country.[1]

Chief Justice Roger B. Taney, true to the concept of judicial activism, avoided the "political question" doctrine and asserted:

> A war, therefore, declared by Congress can never be presumed to be waged for the purpose of conquest or the acquisition of territory; nor does the law declaring war imply an authority of the President to enlarge the limits of the United States by subjugating the enemy's territory. The United States, it is true, may extend its boundaries by conquest or treaty and may demand the cession of territory as the condition of peace...but this can be done *only* by the treaty-making power or the *legislative authority*, and is *not* a part of the power conferred

upon the President by the declaration of war. His duty and *his* power are *purely* military [emphases added][2]

The administration of William McKinley in 1898 seemed rather unrestrained by Taney's earlier admonitions when it leaped into war with Spain while, at the same time, casting hungry eyes toward the Spanish territories of Cuba, Guam, and the Philippines. Much later, during the undeclared Iraqi war, President Bush stated that he would not "tie the hands of the military behind their backs" in pursuing American objectives; however, in keeping with the spirit of *Fleming*, he did *not* assume to *claim* the territory of Southern Iraq occupied by Allied or American forces, thus attesting to the fact that the jurisprudential record of American "imperialism" has been relatively mixed since 1850.

The explosive nature of the Commander in Chief clause was not fully ignited until the Civil War, when President Lincoln *combined* it with his *other* duty "to take care that the laws be faithfully executed." During the ten-week period between the fall of Fort Sumpter and the convening of Congress on July 4, 1861, he had meshed these clauses into the "war power" in order to justify several extraordinary measures: the call for volunteers; the blockade of the Southern ports; and, the suspension of the writ of habeas corpus without *any* authorization from Congress.[3] Indeed, Abraham Lincoln assumed the mantle of a "constitutional dictator" throughout the conduct of the "rebellion"; however, his actions did *not* go unchallenged in the federal courts.

In *Brig Amy Warwick* (1863), the Supreme Court met head-on the question of the President's proclamation of April, 1861, calling for a naval blockade of the Southern States.[4] Upholding the authority of Lincoln's action, Justice Robert C. Grier explained:

By the Constitution, Congress *alone* has the power to declare a national or foreign war. It *cannot* declare war against a State, or any number of States, by virtue of any clause in the Constitution. The Constitution confers on the President the whole Executive power. He is bound to take care that the laws be faithfully executed. He is Commander in chief.... He has *no* power to initiate or *declare* a war either against a foreign nation or a domestic State. But by the Acts of Congress, [February 28, 1795 and March 3, 1807] he is *authorized* to call out the militia and use the military and naval forces of the United States in case of invasion by foreign nations and to *suppress* insurrection against the government of a State or of the United States...[emphases added]

JUSTICE GRIER then forcefully concluded:

If a war be made by invasion of a foreign nation, the President is not only authorized but *bound* to resist by force. He does *not* initiate the war, but is bound to accept the challenge *without waiting* for any special legislative authority. And whether the hostile party be a foreign invader or States organized in rebellion, it is none the less a *war*, although the declaration of it be 'unilateral'. [Some Emphasis Added].[5]

A clearer, more *perceptive* view of the President's role as "initiator" would be most difficult to make! Uniformly, most constitutional scholars today would *agree* with Grier's statement.

The second significant decision of the Court growing out of the Civil War involved Lincoln's suspension of the writ of habeas corpus and the establishing of martial law even in "friendly" states which were not in the actual "theatre of war." Asked the President: "Are all the laws but one to go unexecuted and the Government itself go to pieces lest that one be violated?" In the view of one commentator, Lincoln was implying that "the President may in an emergency, thought by him to require it, partially *suspend* the Constitution."[6] Eighteen months after the President's action, an Act of Congress confirmed the suspension on March 3, 1863. Conveniently, it was not until the cessation of hostilities and Lincoln's death that the Supreme Court of the United States, in *ex post facto* fashion, declared the whole arrangement unconstitutional. Lambdin P. Milligan was a civilian and citizen of Indiana where no hostilities took place during the War. He was a "Copperhead" and, as such, sympathetic towards the Southern Cause. For this, Milligan was tried by a military commission and sentenced to be hanged. Noting that the proceedings "had the fullest sanction of the Executive Department of the government," Chief Justice Salmon P. Chase nonetheless held that the prisoner must be discharged since the commission did *not* have "jurisdiction to try and sentence" him.[7] Chase continued to elaborate:

Congress has the power not only to raise and support and govern armies, but to declare war. *It has, therefore, the power to provide by law for carrying on war.* This power necessarily extends to all legislation *essential* to the prosecution of war with vigor and success, *except* such as interferes with the command of the forces and conduct of campaigns. That power and duly belong to the President as Commander in Chief.... The power to *make* the necessary laws is in Congress; the power to *execute* in the President.[emphases added][8]

Reminding us that *both* branches are responsible for the formulation of war policy, Chase concluded his argument:

Both are servants of the people whose will is expressed in the fundamental law. Congress cannot direct the conduct of campaigns, nor can the President, or any commander under him, without the sanction of Congress, institute tribunals for the trial and punishment of offenses...unless in cases or *compelling necessity*, which justifies what it compels....[9]

There was not an important decision by the Supreme Court on the matter of foreign affairs for nearly two years, until the Chinese Exclusion Cases. Both *Chae Chan Ping v. United States* (1889)[10] and *Fong Yue Ting v. United States* (1893)[11] concerned the power of Congress to *invite* and to *exclude* aliens from the country; however, more generally, the Justices discussed the role of Congress in the shaping of foreign policy. In the former case, the treaty involved was one arranged in 1868 between the United States and China. In it, the United States conferred "most favored nation" status on China and welcomed her subjects to this country. Many Chinese immigrated to the West Coast at the time of the California "gold rush" and later the opportunity to work on the transcontinental railroad. In response to outcries of "an Oriental invasion" by many citizens of California, Congress negotiated a supplementary treaty with China in 1880 which further empowered the United States to limit, *or* exclude altogether, future Chinese immigration of laborers. On May 6, 1882, an Act of Congress was approved to carry this treaty into effect. It stipulated that "for the period of ten years from its date, the coming of Chinese laborers to the United States is *suspend-*

ed, and that it shall be *unlawful* for any such laborer to come, or, having come, to remain within the United States."[12]

In 1888, the restriction was strengthened by another Act of Congress which *deported* alien Chinese "who shall at any time heretofore have been...resident within the United States."[13] Chae was such a laborer who brought suit to challenge the validity of the law on the ground that it was an illegal abrogation of the Treaty of 1868. Holding that the question of whether the Act of 1888 superseded the treaty was a "political" one to be decided by the political departments, for only the second time since 1790, Mr. Justice Stephen J. Field ruled that:

> A treaty, it is true, is in its nature a contract between nations and is often merely promissory in its character, requiring legislation to carry its stipulations into effect. Such legislation will be open to *future* repeal or *amendment*. If the treaty operates on its own force, and relates to a subject within the power of Congress, it can be deemed in that particular only the equivalent of a legislature act, to be repealed or modified at the pleasure of Congress. In either case, the *last expression* of the sovereign *must control*. [emphases added][14]

As to the matter of the war power, Justice Field intimated:

> Congress has the power under the Constitution to declare war, and in two instances where the power has been exercised—in the War of 1812 against Great Britain, and in 1846 against Mexico—the propriety and wisdom and justice of its action were vehemently assailed by some of the ablest and best men in the country, but no one doubted the legality of the proceeding and any imputation by this or any other court of the United States upon the motives of the members of Congress who in either case voted for the declaration, would have been justly the cause of animadversion.[15]

Field concluded his commentary by emphasizing that the "sovereign powers" relating to the *conduct* of foreign policy are ones that invoke the joint participation of the political branches:

The power of exclusion of foreigners being an incident of sovereignty belonging to the government of the United States, as a part of those sovereign powers delegated by the Constitution, the right to its exercise at any time when, in the judgment of the government, the interests of the country require it, *cannot* be granted away or restrained on behalf of anyone. [They] are delegated in trust to the United States and are incapable of transfer to other parties. They *cannot* be abandoned or surrendered. Nor can their exercise be hampered, when needed for the public good, by any considerations of private interest. The exercise of these public trusts is *not* the subject of barter or *contract*. [emphasis added][16]

In the matter of *Fong Yue Ting*, which arose four years later, a challenge was made against the Renewal Treaty of May 5, 1892 extending the deportation of Chinese laborers for yet another ten years. The Court agreed that the authority to exclude or expel aliens is "an inherent and inalienable right of every sovereign and independent nation." Mr. Justice Horace Gray reiterated what the Court had always insisted upon rather consistently, in case after case, during this period:

...a power affecting international relations, is vested in the political departments of the government and is to be regulated by treaty or Act of Congress and to be executed by the executive authority according to regulations so established, except so far as the judicial department has been authorized by treaty or statute, or is required by the paramount law of the Constitution, to intervene.[17]

Central to the case, once again, was the supremacy of more recent laws versus earlier ratified treaties. Justice Gray responded to those who would side with the primacy of treaties:

In our jurisprudence, it is well settled that the provisions of an Act of Congress, passed in the exercise of its constitutional authority, on this as on any other subject, if clear and explicit, must be upheld by the courts, even in contravention of express stipulations in an earlier treaty.[18]

It is instructive to note that Justice Stephen Field, the author of the *Chae* opinion, *dissented* in this case. He made a distinction between the *exclusion*, or banning of Chinese persons into this country (Chae), and the *deportation* of resident aliens *(Fong)*. In the latter case, deportation "has never been asserted by the legislative or executive deportments except for crime, or as an act of war in view of the existing of anticipated hostilities."[19] Regarding the rights of legal aliens, thus abridged, Justice Field concluded:

> Aliens from countries at peace with us, domiciled within our country by its consent, are entitled to all the guarantees for the protection of their persons and property which are secured to native-born citizens. The moment any human being...comes within the jurisdiction of the United States, with their consent...he becomes subject to all laws, is amenable to their punishment and entitled to their protection. arbitrary and despotic power can no more be exercised over them...than over the persons and property of native-born citizens.[20]

Few students of the Constitution would agree with Justice Field's atrophied interpretation of the national deportation power, but at the same time, they probably would *not* differ with his views of the rights of legal resident aliens.

A final and extremely important note to be made in the history of the Civil War Court is reflected in the case of *Ex Parte McCardle* 74 U.S. 506 (1869). The decision in this case created a bulwark from which Congress may exercise its greatest and most controversial "check" over the judicial branch—the *limiting* of the Supreme Court's *appellate* jurisdiction, under Article III, from *any* topic which shall fall properly within *legislative*, not judicial, authority. Even though the congressional statute challenged in the case clearly involved domestic Reconstruction policies implemented by Congress after President Lincoln's death, and the cessation of internal hostilities, the rule was not limited by the language of the Justices to domestic affairs *alone*. If Congress wished to exclude judicial participation from a specific area of foreign policy there is *nothing* limiting congressional discretion from doing so.

In another decision carrying implications for future foreign policy questions, the Supreme Court allowed the President to possess a formalized tool in the exercise of purely executive policy-making. *In re Neagle* (1890) involved the validity of executive orders issued by the President to the ministerial officials within his administration that require them to perform a particular act or implement a specific policy. The Court upheld the use of such orders as being consistent with the command of Article II, Section 3, that "he shall take Care that the Laws be faithfully executed...." Despite the *Neagle* decision, it would be Congress, not the presidency, that would be the *prime* recipient of judicial grants of power during the remainder of the Nineteenth Century.

On the latter point, the Supreme Court turned to congressional participation in the treaty-making power given the President's authority to negotiate them. In *Geofrey v. Riggs* (1890), the Court clearly anticipated, by nearly seventy years, *Reid v. Covert* (1957) by surmising that *only* a violation of the rights of *American* citizens could negate the terms of a treaty. After Lincoln's death, a succession of relatively *weak* Presidents—Andrew Johnson, U. S. Grant, Chester A. Arthur, and Benjamin Harrison among them—gave rise to congressional *domination* in policy-making that, during its apex, seemed to control our tripartite system of constitutional government. Under the guise of "congressional government," as Woodrow Wilson then referred to it, the national legislature began to experiment in the delegation in legislative authority and responsibility. A weakened presidency obviously served no one's interest! Accordingly, Congress created a procedural mechanism by which a certain amount of its own *policy-making* could be legally shifted to the President; it allowed him to effectively *execute* the laws it had enacted.

The first case decided by the Supreme Court relating to a grant of legislative power from the legislative to the executive branch was *United States v. Brig Aurora* in 1812.[21] The litigation was based on the Non-Intercourse Act of 1809 which, in forbidding trade with France and Great Britain, granted President James Madison the power to either suspend or revive its terms depending upon the occurrence of certain events. Obviously, the case was not dissimilar from *Curtiss-Wright* over a century later. The *Aurora* was seized by the United States for violating the prohibition established earlier by the President. The defendants argued that since the presidential proclamation had the "force of law," it transgressed the principle that "Congress cannot transfer the legislative power to the President." The Court rejected this argument and held: "We see no sufficient reason why the legislature should not exercise its discretion in reviewing the Act of 1809, either expressly or conditionally as its judgment should direct."[22] Over eighty years would pass before the Court again reviewed a case involving such a delegation.

In 1891, the Supreme Court handed down its decision in *Marshall Field & Co. v. Clark* and, in effect, reaffirmed *Brig Aurora*.[23] The case arose out of the Tariff Act of 1890 which empowered President Benjamin Harrison to suspend certain provisions of the statue and spelled out the instances to be determined at his discretion. The Act was challenged, *inter alia,* as an illegal transfer by Congress of legislative and treaty-making power to chief executive. Nevertheless, the Court upheld the Tariff provision. Speaking for seven members of the Court, Associate Justice John M. Harlan said:

> That Congress cannot delegate legislative power to the President is a principal universally recognized as vital to the integrity and maintenance of the system of government ordained by the Constitution. The Act...under consideration, is not inconsistent with that principle. It does *not*, in any real sense, invest in the President power of legislation.[24]

He then turned to the matter or presidential authority:

> He had *no* discretion in the [policy] except as to the duration of the suspension which was absolutely required when the President ascertained the existence of a particular fact. It cannot be said...in issuing his proclamation, in obedience to the legislative will, [that] he exercised the function of making laws. He was the mere *agent* of the law making department to ascertain and declare the event upon which its expressed will was to take effect.[25] (some emphasis added)

In other words, the Court made a legal distinction between the power to *make* laws and the discretion to *execute* laws that pre-exist. presidential discretion in the enforcement of the legislative will is not, of itself, "lawmaking" of the kind prohibited by the doctrine of separated powers. Justice Harlan concluded his argument by completely dismissing the charge that the law delegated treaty-making power to the President,

without comment. The precedent having been established in *Fields,*
Congress, in later years, gave the President even *greater* latitude in the
execution of tariffs; however, the constitutional barrier against the
validity of yielding such authority did not cease.[26]

Nevertheless, the era of congressional "supremacy" or domination
proved to be relatively short-lived for, as events were to later dictate, the
dawn of the twentieth century brought with it a shift in America's
national priorities from immigration, taxation, trade, the growing labor
movement, the value of the tariff, and other *domestic* concerns, to the
entry of the United States onto the stage of *world* politics—a dramatic
change of focus that would increasingly necessitate strong leadership and
an inspired initiative that *only* a single leader or President, not a
multitude of legislators, could provide! The expansionist-inspired
Republican administrations and the easily convenient Spanish-American
War, near the end of the Nineteenth Century, increased the hegemony of
the United States over Puerto Rico and Guam as new territories.
Moreover, the United States also grabbed the Philippine Islands, using
it to serve as its foothold in the Pacific rim. Nevertheless, America's
western "imperialism" or exercise of "the white man's burden," and its
long-term importance, would become a secondary or even a minor
consideration when *contrasted* with American interests and intervention
in Europe during the First World War.

FLEMING v. PAGE
50 U.S. 602 (1850)

*On July 30, 1846, Congress passed an Act which set out the rates of duty to be collected on goods imported from the Mexican port of Tampico to the port of Philadelphia that increased on two different occasions in 1847. Upon entering Philadelphia harbor the second time, the captain of an American merchant ship was charged duties for goods imported on both voyages and he paid them under protest. Captain Fleming contended that the port from which he sailed was not a foreign port because it was under the domination and control of the U.S. military; his goods, therefore, should not have been subject to import duties under the aforementioned act. He received a favorable ruling from the U.S. Circuit Court in the Eastern District of Pennsylvania, and the case was brought before the Supreme Court on a certificate of division among the judges in the lower court. **Note:** Contrast Chief Justice Taney's reasoning on the relationship between the President and the British Crown with Justice Sutherland's argument in the **Curtiss-Wright** opinion in 1936. See, particularly, the last paragraph of **Fleming**.*

[excerpts]

MR. CHIEF JUSTICE ROGER B. TANEY delivered the opinion of the Court:

The port of Tampico,...was in the exclusive and firm possession of the United States, and governed by its military authorities, acting under the orders of the President. But it does not follow that it was a part of the United States...

The country in question had been conquered in war...A war, therefore, declared by Congress, can never be presumed to be waged for the purpose of conquest or the acquisition of territory; nor does the law declaring the war imply an authority of the President to enlarge the limits of the United states by subjugating the enemy's country. The United States, it is true, may extend its boundaries by conquest or treaty, and may demand the cession of territory as the condition of peace, in order to indemnify its citizens for the injuries they have suffered, or to re-imburse the government for the expenses of the war. But this can be done *only* by the treaty-making power or the *legislative authority*, and is *not* a part of the power conferred upon the President by the declaration of war. His duty and his power are purely military. As Commander in Chief, he is authorized to direct the movements of the naval and military forces placed by law at his command, and to employ them in the manner he may deem most effectual to harass and conquer and subdue the enemy. He may invade the hostile country, and subject it to the sovereignty and authority of the United States. But his conquests do not enlarge the boundaries of this Union, nor extend the operation of our institutions and laws beyond the limits before assigned to them by the legislative power.

...The department, in no instance that we are aware of, since the establishment of the government, has ever recognized a place in a newly acquired country as a domestic port, from which the coasting trade might be carried on, unless it had been previously made so by Act of Congress...under our revenue laws every port is regarded as a foreign one, unless the custom-house from which the vessel clears is within a collection district established by Act of Congress, and the officers granting the clearance exercise their functions under the authority and control of the laws of the United States...

Neither is it necessary to examine the English decisions which have been referred to by counsel. It is true that most of the States have adopted the principles of English jurisprudence, so far as it concerns private and individual rights. And when such rights are in question, we habitually refer to the English decisions, not only with respect, but in many cases as authoritative. *But in the distribution of political power between the great departments of government, there is such a wide difference between the power conferred on the President of the United States, and the authority and sovereignty which belong to the English crown, that it would be altogether unsafe to reason from any supposed resemblance between them, either as regards conquest in war, or any other subject where the rights and powers of the executive arm of the government are brought into question. Our own Constitution and form of government must be our only guide.* And we are entirely satisfied that, under the Constitution and laws of the United States, Tampico was a foreign port, within the meaning of the Act of 1846, when these goods were shipped, and that the cargoes were liable to the duty charted upon them. And we shall certify accordingly to the Circuit Court.

MR. JUSTICE MCLEAN dissented.

BRIG AMY WARWICK
67 U.S. 635 (1836)

On July 10, 1861, the **Brig Amy Warwick,** *a merchant vessel whose owners were Virginians, was captured by a Union ship of war, the* **Quaker City.** *The ship and her cargo were libeled as "enemy property" and were thereby forfeited to the Union. At the time of her capture, the* **Warwick** *was returning from Rio de Janeiro with a load of coffee. She was sailing under American colors, and her commander was ignorant of both the ongoing Civil War and the blockade of Southern ports. The owners denied any hostility on their part toward the government or laws of the United States, and therefore, they claimed that the seizure and forfeiture of their vessel was unlawful. The district court issued a decree of condemnation, and the claimants appealed to the Supreme Court.*

[excerpts]

MR. JUSTICE ROBERT C. GRIER gave the opinion of the Court:

There are certain propositions of law which must necessarily affect the ultimate decision...They are, 1st. Had the President a right to institute a blockade of ports in possession of persons in armed rebellion against the Government, on the principles of international law, as known and acknowledged among civilized States?

2d. Was the property of persons domiciled or residing within those States a proper subject of capture on the sea as "enemies' property?"

I. Neutrals have a right to challenge the existence of a blockade *de fact,* and also the authority of the party exercising the right to institute it. They have a right to enter the ports of a friendly nation for the purposes of trade and commerce, but are bound to recognize the rights of a belligerent engaged in actual war, to use this mode of coercion, for the purpose of subduing the enemy.

That a blockade *de facto* actually existed, and was formally declared and notified by the President on the 27th and 30th of April, 1861, is an admitted fact in these cases.

That the President, as the Executive Chief of the Government and Commander in Chief of the Army and Navy, was the proper person to make such notification, has not been, and cannot be disputed...

The laws of war, as established among nations, have their foundation in reason, and all tend to mitigate the cruelties and misery produced by the scourge of war. Hence the parties to a civil war usually concede to each other belligerent rights. They exchange prisoners, and adopt the other courtesies and rules common to public or national wars.

By the Constitution, Congress alone has the power to declare a national or foreign war. It cannot declare war against a State, or any number of States, by virtue of any clause in the Constitution. *The Constitution confers on the President the whole Executive power.* He is bound to take care that the laws be faithfully executed. He is Commander in Chief of the Army and Navy of the United States, and of the militia of the several States when called into the actual service of the United States. *He has no power to initiate or declare a war either against a foreign nation or a domestic State.* But by the *Acts of Congress* of February 28th, 1795, and 3d of March, 1807, *he is authorized* to call out the militia and use the military and naval forces of the United States in case of invasion by foreign nations, and to suppress insurrection against the government of a State or of the United States.

If a war be made by invasion of a foreign nation, the President is not only authorized but bound to resist force by force. He does *not* initiate the war, but is bound to accept the challenge without waiting for any special legislative authority. And whether the hostile party be a foreign invader, or States organized in rebellion, it is none the less a war, although the declaration of it be "*unilateral.*"

However long may have been its previous conception, it nevertheless sprung forth suddenly from the parent brain, a Minerva in the full panoply of *war.* The President was bound to meet it in the shape it presented itself, without waiting for Congress to baptize it with a name; and no name given to it by him or them could change the fact.

The law of nations is also called the law of nature; it is founded on the common consent as well as the common sense of the world. It contains no such anomalous doctrine as that which this Court are now for the first time desired to pronounce, to wit: That insurgents who have risen in rebellion against their sovereign, expelled her Courts, established a revolutionary government, organized armies, and commenced hostilities, are not *enemies* because they are *traitors*; and a war levied on the Government by traitors, in order to dismember and destroy it, is not a *war* because it is an "insurrection."

Whether the President in fulfilling his duties, as Commander in Chief, in suppressing an insurrection, has met with such armed hostile resistance, and a civil war of such alarming proportions as will compel him to accord to them the character of belligerents, is a question to be decided by him, and this Court must be governed by the decisions and acts of the political department of the Government to which this power was entrusted. "He must determine what degree of force the crisis demands." The proclamation of blockade is itself official and conclusive evidence to the Court that a state of war existed which demanded and authorized a recourse to such a measure, under t he circumstances peculiar to the case.

The correspondence of Lord Lyons with the Secretary of State admits the fact and concludes the question.

If it were necessary to the technical existence of a war, that it should have a legislative sanction, we find it in almost every Act passed at the extraordinary session of the Legislature of 1861, which was wholly employed in enacting laws to enable the Government to prosecute the war with vigor and efficiency. And finally, in 1861, we find Congress "ex majore cautela" and in anticipation of such astute objections, passing an Act "approving, legalizing, and making valid all the acts, proclamations, and orders of the President...as if they had been issued and done under the previous express authority and direction of the Congress of the United States."

The objection made to this act of ratification, that it is ex post facto, and therefore unconstitutional and void, might possibly have some weight on the trial of an indictment in a criminal Court. But precedents from that source cannot be received as authoritative in a tribunal administering public and international law.

On this first question therefore we are of the opinion that the President had a right, *jure belli*, to institute a blockade of ports in possession of the States in rebellion, which neutrals are bound to regard.

II. We come now to the consideration of the second question. What is included in the term "enemies' property?"

Is the property of all persons residing within the territory of the States now in rebellion, captured on the high seas, to be treated as "enemies' property" whether the owner be in arms against the Government or not?

The right of one belligerent not only to coerce the other by direct force, but also to cripple his resources by the seizure or destruction of his property, is a necessary result of a state of war. Money and wealth, the products of agriculture and commerce, are said to be the sinews of war, and as necessary in its conduct as numbers and physical force. Hence it is, that the laws of war recognize the right of a belligerent to cut these sinews of the power of the enemy, by capturing his property on the high seas.

Under the very peculiar Constitution of this Government, although the citizens owe supreme allegiance to the Federal Government, they owe also a qualified allegiance to the State in which they are domiciled. Their persons and property are subject to its laws. Hence, in organizing this rebellion, they have acted as States claiming to be sovereign over all persons and property within their respective limits, and asserting a right to absolve their citizens from their allegiance to the Federal Government.

All persons residing within this territory whose property may be used to increase the revenues of the hostile power are, in this contest, liable to be treated as enemies, though not foreigners.

Whether property be liable to capture as "enemies' property" does not in any manner depend on the personal allegiance of the owner. "It is the illegal traffic that stamps it as 'enemies' property.' It is of no consequence whether it belongs to an ally or a citizen. 8 Cr., 384. The owner, *pro hac vice*, is an enemy." 3 Wash. C. C. R., 183.

The produce of the soil of the hostile territory, as well as other property engaged in the commerce of the hostile power, as the source of its wealth and strength, are always regarded as legitimate prize, without regard to the domicile of the owner, and much more so if he reside and trade within their territory.

All the claimants at the time of the capture, and for a long time before, were residents of Richmond, Va., and were engaged in business there. Consequently, their property was justly condemned as "enemies' property."

The claim of Phipps & Co. for their advance was allowed by the Court below. That part of the decree was not appealed from and is not before us. The case presents no question but that of enemies' property.

The decree below is affirmed with costs.

EX PARTE MILLIGAN
4 Wall. 2; 18 L.Ed. 281 (1866)

On March 3, 1863, Congress enacted a law which, post facto, authorized President Abraham Lincoln to suspend the writ of habeas corpus and directed federal courts to discharge prisoners in instances where the grand jury had failed to take action. In 1864, Lambdin P. Milligan, an admitted "copperhead" and citizen of Indiana, was arrested by the military for conspiracy against the United States, for giving aid and comfort to the Confederacy and other charges. Brought before a military commission he was tried, convicted and sentenced to death by hanging. Thereafter, Milligan petitioned a U.S. circuit court for a writ of habeas corpus arguing that, as a civilian, he could not be tried by the military since the civilian courts were still open in Indiana. The court empaneled a grand jury following Milligan's conviction but it failed to bring an indictment. The circuit court then certified the questions before them to the Supreme Court.

[excerpts]

MR. JUSTICE DAVIS delivered the opinion of the Court:

The controlling question in the case is this: Upon the facts stated in Milligan's petition, and the exhibits filed, had the military commission mentioned in its jurisdiction, legally, to try and sentence him? Milligan, not a resident of one of the rebellious states, or a prisoner of war, but a citizen of Indiana for twenty years past, and never in the military or naval service, is, while at his home, arrested by the military power of the United States, imprisoned, and, on certain criminal charges preferred against him, tried, convicted, and sentenced to be hanged by a military commission, organized under the direction of the military commander of the military district of Indiana. Had this tribunal the *legal* power and authority to try and punish this man?

...The Constitution of the United States is a law for *rulers* and *people*, equally in war and in peace, and covers with the shield of its protection *all classes* of men, at *all times*, and under *all circumstances*. No doctrine involving more pernicious consequences was ever invented by the wit of man than that any of its provisions can be suspended during any of the great exigencies of government. Such a doctrine leads directly to anarchy or despotism, but the theory of necessity on which it is based is false; for the government, within the Constitution, has all the powers granted to it which are necessary to preserve its existence; as has been happily proved by the result of the great effort to throw off its just authority.

Have any of the rights guaranteed by the Constitution been violated in the case of Milligan? and if so, what are they?

Every trial involves the exercise of judicial power; and from what source did the military commission that tried him derive their authority? Certainly no part of the judicial power of the country was conferred on them; because the Constitution expressly vests it "in our supreme court and such inferior courts as the Congress may from time to time ordain and establish," and it is not pretended that the commission was a court ordained and established by Congress. *They cannot justify on the mandate of the President; because he is controlled by law, and has his appropriate sphere of duty, which is to execute, not to make, the laws; and there is "no unwritten criminal code to which resort can be had as a source of jurisdiction."*...

It can serve no useful purpose to inquire what those laws and usages are, whence they originated, where found and on whom they operate; they can never be applied to citizens in states which have upheld the authority of the government, and where the courts are open and their process unobstructed. This court has judicial knowledge that in Indiana the Federal authority was always unopposed, and its courts always open to hear criminal accusations and redress grievances; and no usage of war could sanction a military trial there for any offense whatever of a citizen in civil life, in nowise connected with the military service. *Congress could grant no such power*; and to the honor of our national legislature be it said, it has never been provoked by the state of the country even to attempt its exercise. One of the plainest constitutional provisions was, therefore, infringed when Milligan was tried by a court *not* ordained and established by Congress, and *not* composed of judges appointed during good behavior.

Why was he not delivered to the Circuit Court of Indiana to be proceeded against according to law? No reason of necessity could be urged against it; because Congress had declared penalties against the offenses charged, provided for their punishment, and directed that court to hear and determine them. And soon after this military tribunal was ended, the Circuit Court met, peacefully transacted its business, and adjourned. It needed no bayonets to protect it, and required no military aid to execute its judgments. It was held in a state, eminently distinguished for patriotism, by judges commissioned during the Rebellion, who were provided with juries, upright, intelligent, and selected by a marshal appointed by the President. The government had no right to conclude that Milligan, if guilty, would not receive in that court merited punishment; for its records disclose that it was constantly engaged in the trial of similar offenses, and was never interrupted in its administration of criminal justice. If it was dangerous, in the distracted condition of affairs, to leave Milligan unrestrained of his liberty, because he "conspired against the government, afforded aid and comfort to rebels, and incited the people to insurrection." The *law* said arrest him. confine him closely. render him powerless to do further mischief; and then present his case to the grand jury of the district, with proofs of his guilt, and, if indicted, try him according to the course of the common law....

Another guaranty of freedom was broken when Milligan was denied a trial by jury.... The Sixth Amendment affirms that "in all criminal prosecutions the accused shall enjoy the right to a speedy and public trial by an impartial jury," language broad enough to embrace all persons and cases; but the Fifth recognizes the necessity of an indictment, or presentment, before any one can be held to answer for high crimes, "*except* casing arising in the land or naval forces, or in the militia, when in actual service, in time of war or public danger"; and the Framers of the Constitution, doubtless, meant to limit the right of trial by jury, in the Sixth Amendment, to those persons who were subject to indictment or presentment in the Fifth....

It is claimed that martial law covers with its broad mantle the proceedings of this military commission. The proposition is this: that in a time of war the commander of an armed force (if in his opinion the exigencies of the country demand it, and of which he is to judge), has the power, within the lines of his military district, to suspend all civil rights and their remedies, and subject citizens as well as soldiers to the rule of *his will*; and in the exercise of his lawful authority cannot be restrained, except by his superior officer or the President of the United States.

If this position is sound to the extent claimed, then when war exists, foreign or domestic, and the country is sub-divided into military departments for mere convenience, the commander of one of them can, if he chooses, within his limits, on the plea of necessity, with the approval of the Executive, substitute military force for and to the exclusion of the laws, and punish all persons as he thinks right and proper without fixed or certain rules.

The statement of this proposition shows its importance; for, if true, republican government is a failure, and there is an end of liberty regulated by law. *Martial law, established on such a basis, destroys every guaranty of the Constitution, and effectually renders the "military independent of and superior to the civil power"—the attempt to do which by the King of Great Britain was deemed by our fathers such an offense, that they assigned it to the world as one of the causes which impelled them to declare their independence.* Civil liberty and this kind of martial law cannot endure together; the antagonism is irreconcilable; and, in the conflict, one or the other must perish.... But, it is insisted that the safety of the country in time of war demands that this broad claim for martial law shall be sustained. If this were true, it could be well said that a country preserved at the sacrifice of all the cardinal principles of liberty, is not worth the cost of preservation. Happily, it is not so.

It will be borne in mind that this is not a question of the power to proclaim martial law, when war exists in a community and the courts and civil authorities are overthrown. Nor is it a question what rule a military commander, at the head of his army, can impose on states in rebellion to cripple their resources and quell the insurrection. The jurisdiction claimed is much more extensive. The necessities of the service, during the late Rebellion, required that the loyal states should be placed within the limits of certain military districts and commanders appointed in them; and, it is urged, that this, in a military sense, constituted them the theater of military operations; and, as in this case, Indiana had been and was again threatened with invasion by the enemy, the occasion was furnished to establish martial law. The conclusion does not follow from the premises. If armies were collected in Indiana, they were to be employed in another locality, where the laws were obstructed and the national authority disputed. On *her* soil there was no hostile foot; if once invaded, that invasion was at an end, and with it all pretext for martial law. Martial law cannot arise from a *threatened* invasion. The necessity must be actual and present; the invasion real, such as effectually closes the courts and deposes the civil administration.

It is difficult to see how the *safety* of the country required martial law in Indiana. If any of her citizens were plotting treason, the power of arrest could secure them until the government was prepared for their trial, when the courts were open and ready to try them. It was as easy to protect witnesses before a civil as a military tribunal; and as there could be no wish to convict, except on sufficient legal evidence, surely an ordained and established court was better able to judge of this than a military tribunal composed of gentlemen not trained to the profession of the law.

It follows, from what has been said on this subject, that there are occasions when martial rule can be properly applied. If, in foreign invasions or civil war, the courts are actually closed, and it is impossible to administer criminal justice according to law, then, in the theater of active military operations, where war really prevails there is a necessity to furnish a substitute for the civil authority, thus overthrown, to preserve the safety of the army and society; and as no power is left but the military, it is allowed to govern by martial rule until the laws can have their free course. *As necessity creates the rule, so it limits its duration; for, if this government is continued after the courts are reinstated, it is a gross usurpation of power.* Martial rule can never exist where the courts are open, and in the proper and unobstructed exercise of their jurisdiction. It is also confined to the locality of actual war....

But it is insisted that Milligan was a prisoner of war, and, therefore, excluded from the privileges of the statute. It is not easy to see how he can be treated as a prisoner of war, when he lived in Indiana for the past twenty years, was arrested there, and had not been, during the late troubles, a resident of any of the states in rebellion. If in Indiana he conspired with bad men to assist the enemy, he is punishable for it in the courts of Indiana; but, when tried for the offense, he cannot plead the rights of war; for he was not engaged in legal acts of hostility against the government, and only such persons, when captured, are prisoners of war. If he cannot enjoy the immunities attaching to the character of a prisoner of war, how can he be subject to their pains and penalties?...

MR. CHIEF JUSTICE CHASE, joined by MR. JUSTICES WAYNE, SWAYNE and MILLER, dissented.

EX PARTE McCARDLE
74 U.S. 506 (1869)

*In March 1868, Congress enacted legislation to protect its Reconstruction Acts from unfriendly challenges by restricting the use of the writ of habeas corpus to "remove" from the jurisdiction of the state court to, inevitably, the appellate jurisdiction of the Supreme Court of the United States. Article III, section 2, clause 2 provides that the Court "shall have appellate jurisdiction, both as to law and fact, with such exceptions, and under such regulations as the Congress shall make." McCardle was a Southern newspaper editor who had been convicted of sedition and appealed to the Supreme Court under an earlier Act of 1867 which had been intended to aid the newly freed slaves in obtaining the protection of the federal Courts. The "exceptions" law, it should be noted, was passed over the veto of President Andrew Johnson and served as one of the "obstructions" for which the President was later impeached but not **removed** from office.*

[excerpts]

THE CHIEF JUSTICE [CHASE] delivered the opinion of the Court:

...[T]he appellate jurisdiction of this Court is not derived from acts of Congress. It is, strictly speaking, conferred by the Constitution. But it is conferred "with such exceptions and under such regulations as Congress shall make."

It is unnecessary to consider whether, if Congress had made no exceptions and no regulations, this court might not have exercised general appellate jurisdiction under rules prescribed by itself. From among the earliest acts of the first Congress [was the Judiciary Act of 1789 which] provided for the organization of this court, and prescribed regulations for the exercise of its jurisdiction.

[In] *Durousseau v. United States* [6 Cranch, 307 (1810)], particularly, the whole matter was carefully examined, and the court held, that [the] judicial Act was an exercise of the power given by the Constitution to Congress "of making exceptions to the appellate jurisdiction of the Supreme Court." "They have described affirmatively," said the court, "its jurisdiction, and this affirmative description has been understood to imply a negation of the exercise of such appellate power as is not comprehended within it."

The principle [thus] established, it was an almost necessary consequence that *acts of Congress*, providing for the exercise of jurisdiction, should come to be spoken of as acts *granting* jurisdiction and *not* as acts *making exceptions* to the constitutional grant of it.

The exception to appellate jurisdiction in the case before us, however, is not an inference from the affirmation of other appellate jurisdiction. It is made in terms.

We are not at liberty to inquire into the motives of the legislature. We can only examine into its power under the Constitution...

What, then, is the effect of the repealing act upon the case before us?...Jurisdiction is power to declare the law, and when it ceases to exist the only function remaining to the court is that of announcing the fact and dismissing the cause. And this is not less clear upon authority than upon principle. [J]udicial duty is not less fitly performed by declining ungranted jurisdiction any cases but appeals from Circuit Courts under the Act of 1867. It does not affect the jurisdiction which was previously exercised.

The appeal [must] be dismissed for want of jurisdiction.

IN RE. NEAGLE
135 U.S. 1 (1890)

Associate Justice Field was serving as Circuit Justice in the U.S. Circuit Court of California when a disturbing incident occurred. After the determination of a particular case, one Mrs. Terry accused Field of "selling" justice and was immediately warned to remain quiet. Thereupon, a fight took place and Mrs. Terry, as well as her husband, were cited for contempt. Sentenced to six months of confinement, Mrs. Terry swore to kill Justice Field if he should ever return to the state.

*Months later, Justice Field returned to California. Considering the threats made on his life, President Benjamin Harrison had issued an executive order to provide the jurist the protection of a United States Marshal. The bodyguard, Neagle, in carrying out his assignment shot and killed Mr. Terry after the latter threatened and assaulted Field in a railroad restaurant. Subsequently, Neagle was arrested by local authorities for murder; however, he was released by a writ of habeas corpus issued by the Circuit Court on the grounds that he was complying with an executive order and as such was pursuing the "law of the United States." Note: It is essential to observe the President's discretion to issue executive orders is **not** limited by the Court's opinion in **Neagle** to domestic policy and may well apply to foreign affairs as well.*

[excerpts]

MR. JUSTICE MILLER delivered the opinion of the Court, saying in part:

...Without a more minute discussion of this testimony, it produces upon us the conviction of a settled purpose on the part of Terry and his wife, amounting to a conspiracy, to murder Justice Field. And we are quite sure that if Neagle had been merely a brother or a friend of Judge Field, traveling with him, and aware of all the previous relations of Terry to the judge—as he was—of his bitter animosity, his declared purpose to have revenge even to the point of killing him, he would have been justified in what he did in defense of Mr. Justice Field's life, and possibly of his own.

But such a justification would be a proper subject for consideration on a trial of the case for murder in the courts of the State of California, and there exists no authority in the courts of the United States to discharge the prisoner while held in custody by the state authorities for this offense, unless there be found in aid of the defense of the prisoner some element of power and authority asserted under the government of the United States.

This element is said to be found in the facts that Mr. Justice Field, when attacked, was in the immediate discharge of his duty as judge of the Circuit Courts of the United States within California; that the assault upon him grew out of the animosity of Terry and wife. arising out of the previous discharge of his duty as Circuit Justice in the case for which they were committed for contempt of court; and that the deputy marshal of the United States, who killed Terry in defense of Field's life, was charged with a duty under the law of the United States to protect Field from the violence which Terry was inflicting, and which was intended to lead to Field's death.

To the inquiry whether this proposition is sustained by law and the facts which we have recited, we now address ourselves....

We have no doubt that Mr. Justice Field when attacked by Terry was engaged in the discharge of his duties as Circuit Justice of the Ninth Circuit, and was entitled to all the protection under those circumstances which the law could give him.

It is urged, however, that there exists no statute authorizing any such protection as that which Neagle was instructed to give Judge Field in the present case, and indeed no protection whatever against a vindictive or malicious assault growing out of the faithful discharge of his official duties; and that the language of section 753 of the Revised Statutes, that the party seeking the benefit of the writ of habeas corpus must in this connection show that he is "in custody for an act done or committed in pursuance of a law of the United States," makes it necessary that upon this occasion it should be shown that the act for which Neagle is imprisoned was done by virtue of an Act of Congress. It is not supposed that any special Act of Congress exists which authorizes the marshals or deputy marshals of the United States in express terms to accompany the judges of the Supreme Court through their circuits, and act as a body-guard to them, to defend them against malicious assaults against their persons. But we are of opinion that this view of the statute is an unwarranted restriction of the meaning of a law designed to extend in a liberal manner the benefit of the writ of habeas corpus to persons imprisoned for the performance of their duty. And we are satisfied that if it was the *duty of Neagle*, under the circumstances, a duty which could *only arise under the laws of the United States, to defend Mr. Justice Field* from a murderous attack upon him, he brings himself within the meaning of the section we have recited. This view of the subject is confirmed by the alternative provision, that he must be in custody "for an act done or committed in pursuance of a law of the United States or of an order, process, or decree of a court or judge thereof, or is in custody in violation of the Constitution or of a law or treaty of the United States."

In the view we take of the Constitution of the United States, any obligation fairly and properly inferable from that instrument, or any duty of the marshal to be derived from the general scope of his duties under the laws of the United States, is "a law" within the meaning of this phrase. It would be a great reproach to the system of government of the United States, declared to be within its sphere sovereign and supreme, if there is to be found within the domain of its powers no means of protecting the judges, in the conscientious and faithful discharge of their duties, from the malice and hatred of those upon whom their judgments may operate unfavorably ....

Where, then, are we to look for the protection which we have shown Judge Field was entitled to when engaged in the discharge of his official duties? Not to the courts of the United States; because, as has been more than once said in this court, in the division of the powers of government between the three great departments, executive, legislative and judicial, the judicial is the weakest for the purposes of self-protection and for the enforcement of the powers which it exercises. The ministerial officers through whom its commands must be executed are marshals of the United States, and belong emphatically to the executive department of the government. They are appointed by the President, with the advice and consent of the Senate. They are removable from office at his pleasure. They are subjected by Act of Congress to the supervision and control of the Department of Justice, in the hands of one of the cabinet officers of the President, and their compensation is provided by Acts of Congress. The same may be said of the district attorneys of the United States, who prosecute and defend the claims of the government in the courts.

The legislative branch of the government can only protect the judicial officers by the enactment of laws for that purpose, and the argument we are now combating assumes that no such law has been passed by Congress.

If we turn to the Executive Department of the government, we find a very different condition of affairs. The Constitution, section 3, Article II, declares that the President "shall take care that the laws be faithfully executed," and he is provided with the means of fulfilling this obligation by his authority to commission all the officers of the United States, and, by and with the advice and consent of the Senate, to appoint the most important of them and to fill vacancies. He is declared to be Commander in Chief of the army and navy of the United States. The duties which are thus imposed upon him he is further enabled to perform by the recognition in the Constitution, and the creation by Acts of Congress, of executive departments, which have varied in number from four or five to seven or eight, the heads of which are familiarly called cabinet ministers. These aid him in the performance of the great duties of his office, and represent him in a thousand acts to which it can hardly be supposed his personal attention is called, and thus he is enabled to fulfill the duty of his great department, expressed in the phrase that "he shall take care that the laws be faithfully executed." Is this duty limited to the enforcement of Acts of Congress or of treaties of the United States according to their express terms, or does it include the rights, duties and obligations growing out of the Constitution itself, *our international relations*, and all the protection implied by the nature of the government under the Constitution?...

We cannot doubt the power of the President to take measures for the protection of a judge of one of the courts of the United States, who, while in the discharge of the duties of his office, is threatened with a personal attack which may probably result in his death, and we think it clear that where this protection is to be afforded through the civil power, the Department of Justice is the proper one to set in motion the necessary means of protection. The correspondence already recited in this opinion between the marshal of the Northern District of California, and the Attorney-General, and the district attorney of the United States for that district, although prescribing no very specific mode of affording this protection by the Attorney-General. is sufficient, we think, to warrant the marshal in taking the steps which he did take, in making the provisions which he did make, for the protection and defense of Mr. Justice Field.

But there is positive law investing the marshals and their deputies with powers which not only justify what Marshal Neagle did in this matter, but which imposed it upon him as a duty. In chapter fourteen of the Revised Statutes of the United States, which is devoted to the appointment and duties of the district attorneys, marshals and clerks of the courts of the United States, section 788 declares:

"The marshals and their deputies shall have, in each State, the same powers, in executing the laws of the United States, as the sheriffs and their deputies in such State may have, by law, in executing the laws thereof."

If, therefore, a sheriff of the State of California was authorized to do in regard to the laws of California what Neagle did, that is, if he was authorized to keep the peace, to protect a judge from assault and murder, then Neagle was authorized to do the same thing in reference to the laws of the United States ....

That there is a peace of the United States; that a man assaulting a judge of the United States while in the discharge of his duties violates that peace; that in such case the marshal of the United States stands in the same relation to the peace of the United States which the sheriff of the county does to the peace of the State of California: are questions too clear to need argument to prove them. That it would be the duty of a sheriff. If one had been present at this assault by Terry upon Judge Field, to prevent this breach of the peace. to prevent this assault, to prevent the murder which was contemplated by it, cannot be doubted. And if, in performing this duty, it became necessary for the protection of Judge Field, or of himself, to kill Terry, in a case where, like this, it was evidently a question of the choice of who should be killed, the assailant and violator of the law and disturber of the peace, or the unoffending man who was in his power, there can be no question of the authority of the sheriff to have killed Terry. So the marshal of the United States, charged with the duty of protecting and guarding the judge of the United States court against this special assault upon his person and his life, being present at the critical moment, when prompt action was necessary, found it to be his duty, a duty which he had no liberty to refuse to perform, to take the steps which resulted in Terry's death. This duty was imposed on him by the section of the Revised Statutes which we have recited, in connection with the powers conferred by the State of California upon its peace officers, which become, by this statute, in

proper cases, transferred as duties to the marshals of the United States
....

The result at which we have arrived upon this examination is, that
in the protection of the person and the life of Mr. Justice Field while in
the discharge of his official duties, Neagle was authorized to resist the
attack of Terry upon him; that Neagle was authorized to resist the attack
of Terry upon him; that Neagle was correct in the belief that without
prompt action on his part the assault of Terry upon the judge would have
ended in the death of the latter; that such being his well-founded belief,
he was justified in taking the life of Terry, as the only means of
preventing the death of the man who was intended to be his victim; that
in taking the life of Terry, under the circumstances, he was acting under
the authority of the law of the United States, and was justified in so
doing; and that he is not liable to answer in the courts of California on
account of his part in that transaction. *We therefore affirm the judgment
of the Circuit Court authorizing his discharge from the custody of the
sheriff of San Joaquin County.*

MR. JUSTICE LAMAR delivered a dissenting opinion in which MR.
CHIEF JUSTICE FULLER concurred. MR. JUSTICE FIELD did not
sit in this case.

CHAE CHAN PING v. UNITED STATES
130 U.S. 581 (1889)

Chae Chan Ping was a subject of the Emperor of China. He had worked as a laborer in San Francisco, California for some twelve years until June 2, 1887 when he left the U.S. to return to China. Before departing on his voyage, the appellant procured a certificate entitling him to return to the U.S.: the certificate was issued by the collector of customs for the port of San Francisco pursuant to the restriction Act of May 6, 1882 as amended by the Act of July 5, 1884.

Upon returning to San Francisco on October 8, 1888, the appellant was denied entry by the collector of the port by virtue of a congressional Act which had been approved only one week prior (October 1, 1888). This latest Act was supplementary to the two earlier restriction acts, supra; it prohibited Chinese laborers who had departed the United States before its passage from re-entering the country—even if they had already received a certificate of entry.

The appellant demanded entry, and upon refusal, he was detained by the captain of the ship on which he had traveled. Chae brought suit, challenging the 1888 Act in the federal courts.

[excerpts]

MR. JUSTICE FIELD delivered the opinion of the Court.

It will serve to present with greater clearness the nature and force of the objections to the act, if a brief statement be made of the general character of the treaties between the two countries and of the legislation of Congress to carry them into execution.

The first treaty between the United States and the Empire of China was concluded on the 3d of July, 1844, and ratified in December of the following year. S Stat. 592. Previous to that time there had been an extensive commerce between the two nations, that to China being confined to a single port. It was not, however, attended by any serious disturbances between our people there and the Chinese...Congress placed at the disposal of the President the means to enable him to establish future commercial relations between the two countries "on terms of national equal reciprocity." Act of March, 1843, c. 90, 5 State. 624. A mission was accordingly sent by him to China, at the head of which was placed Mr. Caleb Cushing, a gentleman of large experience in public affairs. He found the Chinese government ready to concede by treaty to the United States all that had been reluctantly yielded to England through compulsion. As the result of his negotiations the treaty of 1844 was concluded. It stipulated, among other things, that there should be a "perfect, permanent and universal peace, and a sincere and cordial amity" between the two nations; that the five principal ports of the empire should be opened to the citizens of the United States, who should be permitted to reside with their families and trade there, and to proceed with their vessels and merchandise to and from any foreign port and either of said five ports; and while peaceably attending to their affairs should receive the protection of the Chinese authorities....

The discovery of gold in California in 1848, as is well known, was followed by a large immigration thither from all parts of the world, attracted not only by the hope of gain from the mines, but form the great prices paid for all kinds of labor. The news of the discovery penetrated China, and laborers came from there in great numbers, a few with their own means, but by far the greater number under contract with employers, for whose benefit they worked. These laborers readily secured employment, and, as domestic servants, and in various kinds of out-door work, proved to be exceedingly useful. For some years little opposition was made to them except when they sought to work in the mines, but, as their numbers increased, they began to engage in various mechanical pursuits and trades, and thus came in competition with our artisans and mechanics, as well as our laborers in the field....

The differences of race added greatly to the difficulties of the situation. Notwithstanding the favorable provisions of the new articles of the treaty of 1868, by which all the privileges, immunities, and exemptions were extended to subjects of China in the United States which were accorded to citizens or subjects of the most favored nation, they remained strangers in the land, residing apart by themselves, and adhering to the customs and usages of their own country. It seemed impossible for them to assimilate with our people or to make any change in their habits or modes of living. As they grew in numbers each year the people of the coast saw, or believed they saw, in the facility of immigration, and in the crowded millions of China, where population presses upon the means of subsistence, great danger that at no distant day that portion of our country would be overrun by them unless prompt action was taken to restrict their immigration. The people there accordingly petitioned earnestly for protective legislation....

So urgent and constant were the prayers for relief against existing and anticipated evils, both from the public authorities of the Pacific Coast and from private individuals, that Congress was impelled to act on the subject. Many persons, however, both in and out of Congress, were of opinion that so long as the treaty remained unmodified, legislation restricting immigration would be a breach of faith with China. A statute was accordingly passed appropriating money to send commissioners to China to act with our minister there in negotiating and concluding by treaty a settlement of such matters of interest between the two governments as might be confided to them...The treaty of November 17, 1880, was concluded and ratified in May of the following year...It declares in its first article that "Whenever, in the opinion of the Government of the United States, or their residence therein, affects of threatens to affect the interests of that country, or to endanger the good order of the said country or of any locality within the territory thereof, the Government of China agrees that the Government of the United States may regulate, limit, or suspend such coming or residence, but may not absolutely prohibit it. The limitation or suspension shall be reasonable and shall apply only to Chinese who may go to the United States as laborers, other classes not being included in the limitations. Legislation taken in regard to Chinese laborers will be of such a character only as is necessary to enforce the regulation, limitation, or suspension of immigration, and immigrants shall not be subject to personal maltreatment or abuse." In its second article it declares that "Chinese subjects, whether proceeding to the United States as teachers, students, merchants, or from curiosity, together with their body and household servants, and Chinese laborers who are now in the United States shall be allowed to go and come of their own free will and accord, and shall be accorded all the rights, privileges, immunities and exemptions which are accorded to the citizens and subjects of the most favored nation."....

It must be conceded that the Act of 1888 is in contravention of express stipulations of the treaty of 1868 and of the supplemental treaty of 1880, but it is not on that account invalid or to be restricted in its enforcement. The treaties were of no greater legal obligation than the Act of Congress. By the Constitution, laws made in pursuance thereof and treaties made under the authority of the United States are both declared to be the supreme law of the land, and no paramount authority is given to one over the other. A treaty, it is true, is in its nature a contract between nations and is often merely promissory in its character, requiring legislation to carry its stipulations into effect. Such legislation will be open to future repeal or amendment. If the treaty operates by its own force, and relates to a subject within the power of Congress, it can be deemed in that particular only the equivalent of a legislative act, to be repealed or modified at the pleasure of Congress. In either case the last expression of the sovereign will must control....

Congress has the power under the Constitution to declare war, and in two instances where the power has been exercised—in the War of 1812 against Great Britain, and in 1846 against Mexico—the propriety and wisdom and justice of its actions were vehemently assailed by some of the ablest and best men in the country, but no one doubted the legality of the proceeding, and any imputation by this or any other court of the United States upon the motives of the members of Congress who in either case voted for the declaration, would have been justly the cause of animadversion....

There being nothing in the treaties between China and the United States to impair the validity of the Act of Congress of October 1, 1888, was it on any other ground beyond the competency of Congress to pass it? If so, it must be because it was not within the power of Congress to prohibit Chinese laborers who had at the time departed from the United States, or should subsequently depart, from returning to the United States. Those laborers are not citizens of the United States; they are aliens. That the government of the United States, through the action of the legislative department, can exclude aliens from its territory is a proposition which we do not think open to controversy. Jurisdiction over its own territory to that extent is an incident of every independent nation. It is a part of its independence. If it could not exclude aliens it would be to that extent subject to the control of another power....

While under our Constitution and form of government the great mass of local matters is controlled by local authorities, the United States, in their relation to foreign countries and their subjects or citizens are one nation, invested with powers which belong to independent nations, the exercise of which can be invoked for the maintenance of its absolute independence and security throughout its entire territory. The powers to declare war, make treaties, suppress insurrection, repel invasion, regulate foreign commerce, secure republican governments to the States, and admit subjects of other nations to citizenship, are all sovereign powers, restricted in their exercise only by the Constitution itself and considerations of public policy and justice which control, more or less, the conduct of all civilized nations....

The control of local matters being left to local authorities, and national matters being entrusted to the government of the Union, the problem of free institutions existing over a widely extended country, having different climates and varied interests, has been happily solved. For local interests the several States of the Union exist, but for national purposes, embracing our relations with foreign nations, we are but one people, one nation, one power....

The power of the government to exclude foreigners from the country whenever, in its judgment, the public interests require such exclusion, has been asserted in repeated instances, and never denied by the executive or legislative departments....

The power of exclusion of foreigners being an incident of sovereignty belonging to the government of the United States, as a part of those sovereign powers delegated by the Constitution, the right to its exercise at any time when, in the judgment of the government, the interests of the country require it, cannot be granted away or restrained on behalf of any one. The powers of government are delegated in trust to the United States, and are incapable of transfer to any other parties. They cannot be abandoned or surrendered. Nor can their exercise be hampered, when needed for the public good, by any considerations of private interest. The exercise of these public trusts is not the subject of barter or contract....

Judgment affirmed.

GEOFREY v. RIGGS
133 U.S. 642 (1890)

A treaty between the United States and France signed in 1800, permitted French citizens to inherit property from citizens of the United States who reside in the District of Columbia. On January 19, 1888, one such American citizen, T. Lawson Riggs, a resident of the District, died intestate. George Louis Dominique Antoine De Geofrey filed a claim to the property since his wife was Mr. Riggs' sister, the former Kate S. Riggs. A counterclaim was filed by the decedent's only brother, E. Francis Riggs, on the grounds that the Treaty of 1800 was invalid and therefore violated his property rights. An interesting factor is that Congress enacted a statute on March 3, 1887 reinforcing the intent and quantities on behalf of French citizens. The case was appealed to the Supreme Court of the United States from the D. C. Court.

[excerpts]

MR. JUSTICE FIELD delivered the opinion of the Court:

The complainants are both citizens of France. The fact that one of them was born in Peking, China, does not changed his citizenship. His father was a Frenchman, and by the law of France a child of a Frenchman, though born in a foreign country, retains the citizenship of his father....

On the 30th of September, 1800, a Convention of Peace, Commerce and Navigation was concluded between France and the United States, the 7th article of which provided that "the citizens and inhabitants of the United States shall be at liberty to dispose by testament, donation or otherwise, of their goods, movable and immovable, holden in the territory of the French Republic in Europe, and the citizens of the French Republic shall have the same liberty with regard to good, movable and immovable, holden in the territory of the United States, in favor of such persons as they shall think property. The citizens and inhabitants of either of the two countries, who shall be heirs of goods, movable or immovable, in the other, shall be able to succeed *ab intestato*, without being obliged to obtain letters of naturalization, and without having the effect of this provision contested or impeded under any pretext whatever." (8 Stat. 182.)

This article, by its terms, suspended, during the existence of the treaty, the provisions of the common law of Maryland and of the Statutes of that State of 1780 and of 1791, so far as they prevented citizens of France from taking by inheritance from citizens of the United States, property, real or personal, situated therein.

MARSHALL FIELD & CO. v. CLARK
143 U.S. 294 (1892)

On October 1, 1890, Congress passed the Tariff Act which allowed, after certain conditions were met, the President to have the discretion to impose a federal tariff on the importation into the United States of certain foreign goods. Marshall Field & Company had imported woolen clothing which was subjected to the law. Refusing to pay the tariff, the Company challenged the constitutional validity of the Act on the grounds that Congress had violated the separation of powers doctrine by delegating legislative authority to the President. The case was appealed from the U.S. Circuit Court of Appeals in Illinois to the Supreme Court. It is interesting to note that William Howard Taft, later to be first President, and then Chief Justice, served as Solicitor General of the United States and argued the case for John M. Clark, tax collector for the Port of Chicago.

[excerpts]

MR. JUSTICE HARLAN delivered the opinion of the Court:

Duties were assessed and collected, according to the rates established by what is known as the Tariff Act of October 1st, 1890, on woolen dress goods, woolen wearing apparel, and silk embroideries, imported by Marshall Field & Co.; on silk and cotton leis imported by Boyd, Sutton & Co.; and on colored cotton cloths imported by Herman, Sternbach & Co....

That Congress cannot delegate legislative power to the President is a principle universally recognized as vital to the integrity and maintenance of the system of government ordained by the Constitution. The Act of October 1st, 1890, in the particular under consideration, is not inconsistent with that principle. It does not, in any real sense, invest the President with the power of legislation...Congress itself prescribed, in advance, the duties to be levied, collected, and paid, on sugar, molasses, coffee, tea, or hides, produced by or exported from such designated country, while the suspension lasted. Nothing involving the expediency or the just operation of such legislation was left to the determination of the President. The words, "he may deem," in the third section, of course, implied that the President would examine the commercial regulations of other countries producing and exporting sugar, molasses, coffee, tea and hides, and form a judgment as to whether they were reciprocally equal and reasonable, or the contrary, in their effect upon American products. But when he ascertained the fact that duties and actions, reciprocally unequal and unreasonable, were imposed upon the agricultural or other products of the United States by a country producing and exporting sugar, molasses, coffee, tea, or hides, it became his duty to issue a proclamation declaring the suspension, as to that country, which Congress had determined should occur...*It was not the making of law. He was the mere agent of the law making department to ascertain and declare the event upon which its expressed will was to take effect.....*

What has been said is equally applicable to the objection that the third section of the Act invests the President with treaty making power.

The court is of opinion that the third section of the Act of October 1st, 1890, is not liable to the objection that is transfers legislative and treaty making power to the President. Even if it were, it would not by any means follow that other parts of the Act, those which directly imposed duties upon articles imported, would be inoperative. But we need not in this connection enter upon the consideration of that question....

The question of constitutional power thus raised depends principally, if not altogether, upon the scope and effect of that clause of the Constitution giving Congress power "to lay and collect taxes, duties, imposts and excises, to pay the debts and provide for the common defense and general welfare of the United States." Art. 1, sec. 8. It would be difficult to suggest a question of larger importance, or one the decision of which would be more far-reaching. But the argument that the validity of the entire Act depends upon the validity of the bounty clause is so obviously founded in error that we should not be justified in giving the question of constitutional power, here raised, that extended examination which a question of such gravity would, under some circumstances demand. Even if the position of the appellants with respect to the power of Congress to pay these bounties were sustained, it is clear that the parts of the Act in which they are interested, namely, those laying duties upon articles imported, would remain in force. "It is an elementary principle," this court has said, "that the same statute may be in part constitutional and in part unconstitutional, and that if the parts are wholly independent of each other, that which is constitutional may stand while that which is unconstitutional will be rejected.".... It cannot be said to be evident that the provisions imposing duties on imported articles are so connected with or dependent upon those giving bounties upon the production of sugars in this country that the former would not have been adopted except in connection with the latter. Undoubtedly the object of the Act was not only to raise revenue for the support of the government, but to so exert the power of laying and collecting taxes and duties as to encourage domestic manufactures and industries of different kinds, upon the success of which, the promoters of the Act claimed, materially depended the national prosperity and the national safety. But it cannot be assumed, nor can it be made to appear from the act, that the provisions imposing duties on imported articles would not have been adopted except in connection with the clause giving bounties on the production of sugar in this country. These different parts of the Act, in respect to their operation, have no legal connection whatever with each other. They are entirely separable in their nature, and in law, are wholly independent of each other. One relates to the imposition of duties upon imported articles; the other, to the appropriation of money from the treasury for bounties on articles produced in this country. While, in a general sense, both may be said to be parts of a system, neither the words nor the general scope of the Act justifies the belief that Congress intended they should operate as a whole, and not separately for the purpose of accomplishing the objects for which they were respectively designed. Unless it be impossible to avoid it, a general revenue statute should never be declared inoperative in all its parts because a particular part relating to a distinct subject may be invalid. A different rule might be disastrous to the financial operations of the government, and produce the utmost confusion in the business of the entire country.

We perceive no error in the judgments below, and each is affirmed.

MR. JUSTICE LAMAR joint by MR. CHIEF JUSTICE FULLER, dissenting:

The Chief Justice and myself concur in the judgment just announced. But the proposition maintained in the opinion, that the third section, known as the reciprocity provision, is valid and constitutional legislation, does not command our assent, and we desire to state very briefly the ground of our dissent from it. We think that this particular provision is valid and constitutional legislation does not command our assent, and we desire to state very briefly the ground of our dissent form it. We think that this particular provision is repugnant to the first section of the first article of the Constitution of the United States, which provides that "all legislative powers herein granted shall be vested in a Congress of the United States, which shall consist of a Senate and House of Representatives." That no part of this legislative power can be delegated by Congress to any other department of the government, executive or judicial, is an axiom in constitutional law, and is universally recognized as a principle essential to the integrity and maintenance of the system of government ordained by the Constitution. The legislative power must remain in the organ where it is lodged by that instrument. We think that the section in question does delegate legislative power to the executive department, and also commits to that department matters belonging to the treaty making power, in violation of paragraph two of the second section of Article II of the Constitution.

FONG YUE TING v. UNITED STATES
149 U.S. 698 (1893)

Fong Yue Ting serves as the title for three Chinese deportation cases that were simultaneously argued and decided before the Supreme Court.

In another attempt to minimize the perceived deluge of Chinese subjects into the United States, Congress passed an Act on May 5, 1892 requiring all Chinese laborers to apply to a collector of internal revenue for a certificate of residence. They had one year to do this. According to the act, persons found to be without the required certificate after the grace period expired would be deemed to be illegally in the United States and therefore subject to deportation.

The petitioners were arrested and scheduled for deportation for failure to comply with this act. A writ of habeas corpus was denied by the U.S. Circuit Court for the Southern District of New York Subsequently, the petitioners appealed to the Supreme Court for a ruling on the constitutionality of the statute.

[excerpts]

MR. JUSTICE GRAY, after stating the facts, delivered the opinion of the court:

The general principles of public law which lie at the foundation of these cases are clearly established by previous judgments of this court, and by the authorities therein referred to....

The same views were more fully expounded in the earlier case of *Chae Chan Ping v. United States*, 130 U. S. 581, in which the validity of a former Act of Congress, excluding Chinese laborers from the United States, under the circumstances therein stated, was affirmed....

The right to exclude or to expel all aliens, or any class of aliens, absolutely or upon certain conditions, in war or in peace, being an inherent and inalienable right of every sovereign and independent nation, essential to its safety, its independence and its welfare, the question now before the court is whether the manner in which Congress has exercised this right in sections 6 and 7 of the Act of 1892 is consistent with the Constitution.

The United States are a sovereign and independent nation, and are vested by the Constitution with the entire control of international relations, and with all the powers of government necessary to maintain that control and to make it effective. The only government of this country, which other nations recognize or treat with, is the government of the Union; and the only American flag known throughout the world is the flag of the United States.

The Constitution of the United States speaks with no uncertain sound upon this subject....

In exercising the great power which the people of the United States, by establishing a written Constitution as the supreme and paramount law, have vested in this court, of determining, whenever the question is properly brought before it, whether the acts of the legislature or of the executive are consistent with the Constitution; it behooves the court to be careful that it does not undertake to pass upon political questions, the final decision of which has been committed by the Constitution to the other departments of the government....

The power to exclude or to expel aliens, being a power affecting international relations, is vested in the political departments of the government, and is to be regulated by treaty or by Act of Congress, and to be executed by the executive authority according to the regulations so established, except so far as the judicial department has been authorized by treaty or by statute, or is required by the paramount law of the Constitution, to intervene...

The power to exclude aliens and the power to expel them rest upon one foundation, are derived from one source, are supported by the same reasons , and are in truth but parts of one and the same power.

The power of Congress, therefore, to expel, like the power to exclude aliens, or any specified class of aliens, from the country, may be exercised entirely through executive officers; or Congress may call in the aid of the judiciary to ascertain any contested facts on which an alien's right to be in the country has been made by Congress to depend.

Congress, having the right, as it may see fit, to expel aliens of a particular class, or to permit them to remain, has undoubtedly the right to provide a system of registration and identification of the members of that class within the country, and to take all proper means to carry out the system which it provides.

It is no new thing for the law-making power, acting either through treaties made by the President and Senate, or by the more common method of acts of Congress, to submit the decision of questions, not necessarily of judicial cognizance, either to the final determination of executive officers, or to the decision of such officers in the first instance, with such opportunity for judicial review of their action as Congress may see fit to authorize or permit.

For instance, the surrender, pursuant to treaty stipulations, of persons residing or found in this country, and charged with crime in another, may be made by the executive authority of the President alone, when no provision has been made by treaty or by statute for an examination of the case by a judge or magistrate.... Under those acts, this court held, in *Chew Heong v. United States*, 112 U.S. 536, that the clause of section 4 of the Act of 1884, making the certificate of identity the only evidence to establish a right to reenter the United States was not applicable to a Chinese laborer who resided in the United States until after the passage of the Act of 1884, and then returned by sea; and in *United States v. Yung Ah Lung*, 124 U.S. 621, that a Chinese laborer, who resided in the United States at the date of the treaty of 1880, and until 1883, when he left San Francisco for China, taking with him a certificate of identity from the collector of the port in the form provided by the Act of 1882, which was stolen from him in China, was entitled to land again in the United States in 1885, on proving by other evidence these facts, and his identity with the person described in the register kept by the collector of customs as the one to whom that certificate was issued....

In our jurisprudence, it is well settled that the provisions of an Act of Congress, passed in the exercise of its constitutional authority, on this, as on any other subject, if clear and explicit, must be upheld by the courts, even in contravention of express stipulations in an earlier treaty....

In *Yick Wo v. Hopkins*, the point decided was that the Fourteenth Amendment of the Constitution of the United States, forbidding any State to deprive any person of life, liberty or property without due process of law, or to deny to any person within its jurisdiction the equal protection of the laws, was violated by municipal ordinance of San Francisco, which conferred upon the board of supervisors arbitrary power, without regard to competency of persons or to fitness of places, to grant or refuse licenses to carry on public laundries, and which was executed by the supervisors by refusing licenses to all Chinese residents, and granting them to other persons under like circumstances. The question there was of the power of a State over aliens continuing to reside within its jurisdiction, not of the power of the United States to put an end to their residence in the country....

Upon careful consideration of the subject, the only conclusion which appears to us to be consistent with the principles of international law, with the Constitution and laws of the United States, and with the previous decisions of this court, is that in each of these cases the judgment of the Circuit Court, dismissing the writ of *habeas corpus*, is right and must be *Affirmed*....

CHIEF JUSTICE FULLER and MR. JUSTICE BREWER dissented. MR. JUSTICE FIELD also dissented:

I also wish to say a few words upon these cases and upon the extraordinary doctrines announced in support of the orders of the court below.

With the treaties between the United States and China, and the subsequent legislation adopted by Congress to prevent the immigration of Chinese laborers into this country, resulting in the Exclusion Act of October 1, 1888, the court is familiar. They have often been before us and have been considered in almost every phase. The Act of 1888 declared that after its passage it should be unlawful for any Chinese laborer—who might then or thereafter be a resident of the United States, who should depart therefrom and not return before the passage of the act—to return or remain in the United States. The validity of this Act was sustained by this court. 130 U.S. 581. In the opinion announcing the decision we considered the treaties with China, and also the legislation of Congress and the causes which led to its enactment. The court cited numerous instances in which statesmen and jurists of eminence had held that it was the undoubted right of every independent nation to exclude foreigners from its limits whenever in its judgment the public interests demanded such exclusion....

I had the honor to be the organ of the court in announcing this opinion and judgment. I still adhere to the views there expressed in all particulars; but between legislation for the exclusion of Chinese persons — that is, to prevent them from entering the country — and legislation for the deportation of those who have acquired a residence in the country under a treaty with China, there is a wide and essential difference. The power of the government to exclude foreigners from this country, that is, to prevent them from entering it, whenever the public interests in its judgment require such exclusion, has been repeatedly asserted by the legislative and executive departments of our government and never denied; but its power to deport from the country persons lawfully domiciled therein by its consent, and engaged in the ordinary pursuits of life, has never been asserted by the legislative or executive departments except for crime, or as an act of war in view of existing or anticipated hostilities.... Aliens from countries at peace with us, domiciled within our country by its consent, are entitled to all the guaranties for the protection of their persons and property which are secured to native-born citizens. The moment any human being from a country at peace with us comes within the jurisdiction of the United States, with their consent—and such consent will always be implied when not expressly withheld, and in the case of the Chinese laborers before us was in terms given by the treaty referred to—he becomes subject to all their laws, is amenable to their punishment and entitled to their protection. Arbitrary and despotic power can no more be exercised over them with reference to their persons and property, than over the persons and property of native-born citizens....

The Act provides for the seizure of the person without oath or affirmation or warrant, and without showing any probable cause by the officials mentioned. The arrest, as observed by counsel, involves a search of his person for the certificate which he is required to have always with him. Who will have the hardihood and effrontery to say this is not an "unreasonable search and seizure of the person"? Until now it has never been asserted by any court or judge of high authority that foreigners domiciled in this country by the consent of our government could be deprived of the securities of this amendment; that their persons could be subjected to unreasonable searches and seizures, and that they could be arrested without warrant upon probable cause supported by oath or affirmation.

I will not pursue the subject further. The decision of the Court and the sanction it would give to legislation depriving resident aliens of the guaranties of the Constitution fills me with apprehensions. Those guaranties are of priceless value to every one resident in the country, whether citizen or alien. I cannot but regard the decision as a blow against constitutional liberty, when it declares that Congress has the right to disregard the guaranties of the Constitution intended for the protection of all men, domiciled in the country with the consent of the government, in their rights of person and property.

How far will this legislation go? The unnaturalized resident feels it to-day, but if Congress can disregard the guaranties with respect to any one domiciled in this country with its consent, it may disregard the guaranties with respect to naturalized citizens. What assurance have we that it may not declare that naturalized citizens of a particular country cannot remain in the United States after a certain day, unless they have in their possession a certificate that they are of good moral character and attached to the principles of our Constitution, which certificate they must obtain from a collector of internal revenue upon the testimony of at least one competent witness of a class or nationality to be designated by the government?

What answer could the naturalized citizen in that case make to his arrest for deportation, which cannot be urged in behalf of the Chinese laborers of today?

I am of the opinion that the orders of the court below should be reversed, and the petitioners should be discharged.

Notes

1. 9 How. 602 (1850) at 607
2. Taney went on to say that, "As commander in chief, he is authorized to direct movements of the naval and military forces placed by law at his command, and to employ them in a manner he may deem most effectual to harass and conquer and subdue the military" but not "extend the operation of our institutions and laws beyond the limits before assigned to them by the legislative powers" Ibid., p. 614.
3. See Corwin, *The President: Office and Powers*, Fifth Edition, p. 264. For other challenges to the president's legal authority during the Civil War and Reconstruction (1861-1877) see *ex parte Merryman* F. Cas. 9487 (1861); *Mississippi v. Johnson* 71 U.S. 475 (1867); and *Springer v. U.S.* 102 U.S. 586 (1881).
4. This is one of several cases in which certain vessels—The Schooner Crenshaw, The Barque Hiawatha, and the Schooner Brilliante—together with their cargoes, were captured and brought in as "prizes" by Union ships. *The Prize Cases*, 67 US 635.
5. 67 US 668.

6. Corwin, *The President*, p. 265. Also see Justice Tom Clark's concurring opinion in *Youngstown Sheet and Tube Company v. Sawyer*, 343 US 579 (1952).
7. *Ex Parte Milligan*, (4 Wall. 2) 71 US 281 (1866) at 299, 300. Mr. Justice David Davis delivered a majority opinion largely consumed by his concern for individual rights.
8. 71 US at 301.
9. The Court ruled that Congress in the Act of 1863 did not intend to apply martial law to Indiana. Ibid., p. 302.
10. 130 US 581.
11. 149 US 698.
12. 22 Stat. 58, c. 126.
13. 25 Stat. 504, c. 1064.
14. 130 US 581 at 600. Also see *Whitney v. Robertson*, 124 US 190 (1887).
15. Ibid. p. 603. The Court during this period consistently ruled that decisions affecting foreign affairs, effectively excluded the state and local governments. See *The Exchange*, 7 Cr. 116 (1812), *Cohens v. Virginia*, 6 Wheat. 264 (1821) and *Knox v. Lee*, 12 Wall. 457 (1871).
16. Ibid. p. 609.
17. 149 US 698 at 713. Also see *Chew Heong v. United States*, 112 US 536 (1884) and *United States v. Yung Ah Lung* 124 US 621 (1888).
18. Ibid. p. 720.
19. Ibid. p. 746. Mr. Chief Justice Melville W. Fuller and Mr. Justice David J. Brewer dissented also.
20. Ibid. p. 754.
21. 17 Cr. 382. Also see Edward Corwin. The President, Fifth Edition, pp. 145-147; 245-247.
22. See *Wayman v. Southard*, 10 Wheat 1 (1825), in which the Court upheld a delegation by Congress to the federal courts the power to formulate rules of procedure under the Judiciary Act of 1789. Chief Justice John Marshall made a salient distinction between this kind of policy-making authority and the other that is "strictly and exclusively *legislative*." The intentions of the Framers encourages the former and condemns the latter. Also see *Springer v. Philippine Islands*, 277 U.S. 189 (1928).
23. 143 U.S. 294.
24. Ibid., p. 310.
25. Ibid.
26. For example, see the Tariff Acts of 1922, 1930, and 1963 ("The Kennedy Round").

Chapter Four:
The United States Steps Onto the World Stage (1901-1935)

As noted, the United States successfully concluded its war with Spain and an armistice between the two countries was signed on August 12, 1898. The armistice assigned terms of peace under the Paris Treaty on December 10, which included the Spanish evacuation of Cuba, the ceding of Puerto Rico and Guam to the United States, and the sale by Spain of the Philippine islands to the victor for $20 million. President William McKinley, who felt inspired by the Lord, adopted this policy of territorial acquisition in the name of "shouldering the White Man's burden." The President was twice blessed by the fact that, at home, the United States also enjoyed increased industrial growth and prosperity to fuel its spread of imperialism abroad.

In November of 1900, the American people overwhelmingly supported the Republican ticket of McKinley and Theodore Roosevelt, the Rough Riding hero of San Juan hill; however, McKinley's good fortune came to an end when he was mortally wounded by an assassin's bullet at the Buffalo Exhibition in September 1901. Succeeding to the presidency, Theodore Roosevelt gladly accepted his predecessor's foreign policies but pledged economic and social reforms in domestic affairs.

The Supreme Court, also affected by progressism, was not reluctant in placing limitations on the "legal niceties and raw excesses" of

American expansionism during the turn of the Century. In the *Insular Cases*, 190 U. S. 197, (1903), the Court concluded that the "Constitution does not follow the flag," *necessarily*, in attempting to determine the legal status of the peoples in the new American possessions.[1] As with statehood, *only* Congress has the authority to legislate for the inclusion of territories. Since these newly-acquired lands are not an integral part of the United States, declared Justice Brown, they enjoy *only* those statutory and constitutional privileges that are spelled out in accompanying legislation; therefore, the citizens of Puerto Rico and Guam, as "constitutional" territories, *must* enjoy the same rights as other American citizens except the right to vote in federal elections. President Roosevelt added to McKinley's foreign largess by taking up unfinished business on a two-ocean canal in this hemisphere.

The Administration negotiated the Hay-Herman Treaty with Columbia and had it approved by the Senate in March, 1903; however, the Colombian Senate *rejected* the treaty which would have allowed the United States to construct and then lease a canal for an annual fee of $250,000 per year after an initial down payment of $10 million. Thereafter, with the complicity of the administration, a province of Columbia-Panama, revolted against its motherland; on November 6, 1903, it was recognized as independent by the United States under the *Hay-Bumak-Vanilla Treaty*. Moreover, under the terms of the Treaty, the American construction of the Panama Canal began in 1907. In other hemispheric action, a problem for the United States arose over Venezuela's failure to pay its international debts to Great Britain, Germany and Italy. The latter governments sent ultimatums to, and severed diplomatic relations with, Venezuela; they also seized her ships and blockaded her ports of call. Finally, Roosevelt strongly suggested that the European nations submit the problem to international arbitration and proclaimed his own corollary to the Monroe Doctrine: If offenses by Latin American countries threaten the security of either European or American nationals, the United States will intervene militarily if necessary. Therefore, the United States would assume the uniform of "policeman" of the Western Hemisphere. The debt crisis in Santo Domingo, similar to that of Venezuela earlier, brought about the Treaty of 1907 which codified in law, America's *right* of intervention.

Thereafter, President Roosevelt called for an international conference of forty-four countries—known as the Second Hague Conference—to lessen the possibility of on-going warfare within the hemisphere or elsewhere. The Conference adopted guidelines for the settlement of disputes, increased the authority of the Permanent Court of arbitration, and adopted the Calvo-Drago Doctrine of using a non-military method of collecting international debts.

For the next decade, the United States under the succeeding administrations of Republican William Howard Taft and Democratic Woodrow Wilson, enjoyed a relatively peaceful period except for Wilson's war with Mexico and his sending the Marines into Santa Domingo in 1916. Nevertheless, a new and more ominous war had broken out among the "Old Regimè" expansionist powers of Europe that had arisen from events two years earlier. While President Wilson sympathized with Great Britain and the Allied powers against Germany and Austria-Hungary, American public opinion was deeply divided. In the 1916 presidential election, Wilson barely eked out a victory over his Republican challenger Charles Evans Hughes, on the Democratic slogan, "He kept us out of war!" However, the continued use of submarine warfare against American and Allied ships by Imperial Germany, in defiance of Wilson's warnings, resulted in a declaration of war enacted by Congress on April 6, 1917.

Prior to America's entry into the First World War, albeit as early as three years after its inception, the Republic had been an agricultural nation primarily concerned with possible European intervention in our own Western Hemisphere. After the Civil War, and with the advent of industrial expansion, such leaders as McKinley and Teddy Roosevelt had begun to expand our foreign policy interests *beyond* hemispheric concerns. Because of German intrigue and the unrestricted sinking of American ships, President Wilson led his country into the European War of 1914. During this initial entry of the United States onto the stage of world affairs, only a few cases were brought before the Supreme Court relating to the war powers or Wilson's shaping of foreign policy. Article I, section 8, clauses 12-13 of the Constitution informs us that Congress is "to raise and support armies... [and] to provide and maintain a navy." Accordingly, Congress enacted the Selective Draft Law of World War I on June 15, 1917, which was the second national conscription law since the Civil War. The Act was challenged as a violation of the Thirteenth Amendment's prohibition of "involuntary servitude" but the Court rejected that argument and upheld the Act as a "necessary and proper" power of Congress.[2] Another case centered on the question of which government has the authority to extend the diplomatic recognition of the United States, whether *de jure* or *de facto*, to another sovereign government. The Constitution is silent on this point except to say that the President "shall have power, by and with the advice and consent of the Senate to...appoint Ambassadors, other public Ministers, and Consuls" (Article II, section 2, clause 2), and on his *own* authority to "receive Ambassadors and other public Ministers" (section 30). In *Oetjen v. Central Leather Company* (1918), the Court decided that under the above Article, *only* the national government, primarily the President, has the power to recognize another government, not the individual states since it would "vex the peace of nations."[3]

Throughout the conduct of the War, President Wilson viewed the presidential office, and his role in it, as being that of a "prime minister" within a parliamentary system. On several occasions, the President asked Congress and the voters to support his positions with a "vote of confidence." During his second term of office, he appealed directly to the people, over the heads of Senator Henry Cabot Lodge and other Senate opponents, to encourage the approval by the Upper House of the Treaty of Versailles (1919); it was worth the risk, in order to make his dream of a League of Nations a reality. Despite Woodrow Wilson's failure in this regard, the United States had reached the level of a *world* power and, with the exception of the isolationist policies of the President's Republican successors, Warren G. Harding, Calvin Coolidge, and Herbert Hoover, a period of only twelve years, this country would *not* retreat from that responsibility.

After the War, the last of the Supreme Court decisions specifically aimed at the carrying out of foreign policy focused on the treaty power. In *Missouri v. Holland* (1920), the Court noted the important distinction made by the Framers in Article IV: *ordinary* legislation must be made "in pursuance of the Constitution," while *treaties* must only be made "under the authority of the United States."[4] Thus, domestic legislation must have inherent and obvious *constitutional roots*—a requirement *not* so applied to treaties! The case involved a 1916 Treaty with Great Britain under which the United States and Canada were to foster policies to protect migratory birds. Two years later, Congress enacted enforcement or accompanying legislation forbidding the capturing, selling or killing of birds, except those exempted by the Secretary of Agriculture.

Missouri brought suit to enjoin the enforcement of the Act on the grounds that her "reserved powers" under the Tenth Amendment were violated. Justice Oliver Wendell Holmes, speaking for the Court, rejected Missouri's contention:

> ...it is not enough to refer to the 10th Amendment, reserving the power not delegated to the United States, because by Article 2, section 2, the power to make treaties is delegated expressly, and by Article 6, treaties make under the authority of the United States...are the supreme law of the land . If the treaty is valid, there can be no dispute about the validity of the statue under Article 1, section 8, as a necessary and proper means to execute the powers of the government.[5]

Although, Holmes did not refer to the war power in *specific* terms, he did adhere to the well-established principle that the treaty-making aspect of foreign affairs was a plenary one entrusted to the political branches:

> It is open to question whether the authority of the United States means more than the formal acts prescribed to make the convention.... [It] is obvious that there may be matters of the sharpest exigency for the national well being that an Act of Congress could not deal with, but that a treaty followed by such an act could, and it is not lightly to be assumed that, in matters requiring national action, "a power must belong to and somewhere reside in every civilized government" is not to be found.[6]

The related practical question of what is required by the phrase "the authority of the United States," and what is not, was left unanswered; however, as to whether a treaty could withstand a challenge that its terms violated the rights of United States citizens was answered much later and, not surprisingly, in the negative by the High Court in *Reid v. Covert* (1957).[7]

The remaining five decisions during this period, at first blush, seem consumed with purely *domestic* concerns, but to accept such an appraisal would be purblind. For the principles involved were to have a tremendous impact on both the formalities and the process of foreign diplomacy.

In *J. W. Hampton & Co. v. United States* (1928), a challenge was made against an increase in the tariff by President Calvin Coolidge on certain shipments of chemicals as, *inter alia*, an illegal delegation of authority to the President by Congress.[8] The President was assisted in making such rate determinations by an advisory Tariff Commission. Citing the maxim *"delegate potestas non protest delegari"* (delegated power may *not* be redelegated) Chief Justice Howard Taft, himself a former President, nevertheless pointed out that:

> Congress may feel itself unable conveniently to determine exactly when its exercise of the legislative power should become effective, because, dependent on future conditions, and it may leave the determination of such time to the decision of an executive....[9]

The Chief Justice then introduced the following comment:

> If Congress shall lay down by legislative Act an intelligible principle to which the person or body authorized to fix such rates is directed to conform, such legislative action is *not* a forbidden *delegation* of legislative power. If it is thought wise to vary the customs duties according to changing conditions of production at home and abroad, it may *authorize* the Chief Executive to *carry out* this purpose, with the advisory assistance of a Tariff commission appointed under Congressional authority. [emphases added][10]

In Taft's mind, the authority to discern tariff rates was in no sense different than allowing Congress the flexibility to create commissions to determine rates in interstate commerce; both were *equally* constitutional!

Years later, despite the Hughes Court's decisions in the *Schechter case* and *Panama Refining Co. v. Ryan* (1935), the majority of the Court led by George Sutherland was more than willing to create a "transubstantiation" in the law when it was applied to foreign policy-making ; the seeds planted in *Field* and *Hampton* were to finally take root in *Curtiss-Wright*.[11]

Returning to the internal policies, the Supreme Court carefully fashioned certain of the inherent powers of the two political branches. In *Myers v. United States* (1927), Chief Justice Taft forcefully enunciated that the plenary nature of the President's removal powers extended over purely *executive* officers. Without consulting Congress, the chief executive may remove any official with executive functions, from bureau chief to cabinet minister or department secretary, *without* cause. Such discretionary authority also extends to officials within the State and Defense Departments, the armed forces, and other facilitators of foreign policy; this becomes particularly cogent on those occasions in which an officer takes a *divergent* public stance on policy than that of the President. As civilian head, this is certainly true within the ranks of the armed forces. President Harry Truman's removal of General Douglas MacArthur in 1952 during the height of the Korean War is an outstanding example. With respect to officials within the executive branch of government whose responsibilities are *not* executive in nature, it is Congress, not the President, that wields the final exercise of discretion.

In *Humphrey's Executor v. United States* 295 U. S. 602 (1935), the Court severely limited the President's influence over members of those independent agencies that were created by Congress and whose members' tenure was made immune by it. Specifically, members of independent regulatory boards or commissions who possess *quasi-legislative, quasi-judicial* functions are usually protected within the terms of the creating statute from the President's arbitrary or political removal *except* "for inefficiency, neglect of duty, or malfeasance in office." The decision enhances congressional authority to create such commissions affecting foreign affairs, as well, and, of course, restraining the President's unilateral discretion. Later, as will be discussed in Volume II of this study [forthcoming], the Supreme Court further decreased executive authority over such "political" removals in the *Wiener* decision.[12]

On the other hand, Congress has experienced similar "give and take" treatment from the Court regarding its implied power to *investigate* economic, social and political problems which may necessitate remedial legislation to provide uniform, national oversight. In *McGrain v. Daughety*, 273 U. S. 135 (1927), the Court proclaimed that the power of Congress to investigate is inherent in its power to legislate. Each house may create committees, either standing or temporary (*AD HOC*), to inquire of witnesses those questions that may shed light on some area that relates to the legislative process. A "necessary and proper" component of the investigating machinery includes the committee's use of court-ordered subpoena to force hostile witnesses to appear before it and to give whatever relevant testimony they may possess. Twenty-seven years later, the Court also upheld the ancillary authority of congressional investigating committees to seek from the federal court a limited grant of "use" *immunity* to require testimony from hostile witnesses. Modern history is replete with cogent examples of such committees investigating particular aspects of presidential policies affecting other nations, executive agreements, treaty negotiations, military commitments, our involvement in regional and international organizations, and the like. It would not be until the nadir of the Cold War Years, that the Supreme Court finally curbed the apparent excesses of such free-wheeling investigations as those conducted by the House on Un-American Activities Committee (HUAC).[13]

The first decision to be examined involved the purely domestic question of the contract clause and, on its face, bore no relation to the subject of our study; however, a closer analysis of the majority opinion, in *Home Building & Loan Association v. Blaisdell* (1934) reveals that Hughes cited critical *foreign policy* questions to reach his conclusion.[14] Essential to the Court's reasoning in this 5-4 decision which upheld the Minnesota Mortgage Moratorium Law, in the face of Article I, &10 and its expressed prohibition, was the following passage by Chief Justice Charles E. Hughes:

> While emergency does not *create* power, Emergency may *furnish* the occasion for the exercise of power.... The constitutional question presented in the light of an emergency is whether the power possessed embraces the particular conditions. Thus, the war power of the *federal government* is not created by the emergency of war, but it is a power given to *meet* that emergency.[15] [emphases added]

The Chief Justice could well have stopped with citing the war power as an example of readily-available authority to be tapped—a "kinetic" source of constitutional energy! Yet, Hughes continued in his analysis aided by the Constitution's most extreme grant within the realms of international relations:

It is a power to wage war *successfully*, and thus it permits the
harnessing of the entire energies of the people in a supreme
cooperative effort to *preserve* the nation. But even the war
power does not *remove* constitutional limitations safeguarding
essential liberties. [emphases added]

As always, the words chosen by the author of the Court's opinion
carry great legal, historical, and cultural weight. Hughes focused on the
fact that the execution of war is a "cooperative effort," not only on the
part of the American people, but the two political branches as well.
There is no reason to assume that a majority of the members of the
Court, as late as 1934, had shifted from the traditional view: that the
conduct of foreign policy was a bi-lateral responsibility and not *solely* a
presidential prerogative. On the other hand, the history of law in the
United States does not support the Chief Justice's dictum that the
exercise of the war power "does *not* remove constitutional limitations
safeguarding essential liberties." During wartime, our freedoms are much
more limited than during times of peace—freedom of speech, the right
to travel. True, in the past the Supreme Court has sometimes vindicated
persons who had their rights of citizenship denied. There were even rare
cases where Congress made reparations to persecuted victims. However,
notable cases such as *Milligan* and *Korematsu* were hard-fought and
vindication came only years *after* the successful conclusion of the wars.
   Home Building & Loan and a majority of the cases decided during
the 1901-1935 era were clearly examples of judicial law-making or, if
you will, judicial activism.[16] Certain of the justices at the time readily
admitted that this *was* the case. In 1907, the Governor of New York told
an audience that law and politics are intrinsically intertwined. "We are
under a Constitution," said Charles Evans Hughes, "but the Constitution
is what the judges *say* it is."
   As products of activism or not, by the mid-1930's the Supreme
Court of the United States, from *Penhallow* to *Humphrey's Executor*, had
provided in writing, a *model* of consistency. It would not be until a controversial "watershed" case involving Curtiss-Wright Export Corporation
in 1936 that students of the Court would witness a dramatic *shift* in this
traditional evolution of legal philosophy on American foreign policy: The
spirit of cooperation and constitutional "harmony" would be sacrificed

on the altar of "progressive reform"—the single leader theory, the myth of the "nuclear button" and the rise of presidential supremacy.

To reiterate the evolving legal principles of the period, and thus conclude this section, the Supreme Court of the United States since 1789, while occasionally recognizing the existence of "political questions," did not seem reluctant to make *regular* pronouncements on either the responsibility or the conduct of foreign policy. To be sure, these rules have a constitutional basis, but it was the Supreme Court that *first* gave them "life." These rules are as follows: First, the sovereign power over foreign affairs is vested in *both* Congress and the President, and the states play *no* role in the matter; second, the war powers—except for the Commander in Chief and the "faithfully execute" clauses—are placed by the Constitution in the hands of Congress *exclusively*; third, the President *alone* negotiates treaties, but their going effect usually *requires* legislation that *only* Congress can stipulate; and fourth, the supercessation of laws or of treaties, both being the "supreme law of the land," rests with the political branches, but particularly with *Congress* as "the 1st expression of the sovereign [peoples'] will."

As a matter of constitutional law, the Congress is most *representative* of popular sentiment and, as such (despite the directives of Article II), it holds the *controlling* hand. This legal picture was to change—and change *drastically*—during the period between 1936 and 1945.

ARVEN v. U.S.
245 U.S. 316 (1918)

From the beginning of American involvement in World War I, it soon became evident that Allied victory was predicated on the fact that the United States needed to dramatically increase the number of its military personnel. A congressional answer was given to this pressing need in an Act entitled, "An Act to Authorize the President to Increase Temporarily the Military Establishment of the United States," dated May 18, 1917. The Act had several provisions, but the major point of contention revolved around the constitutionality of the system of compelled selective service (draft). Mr. Joseph F. Arven, plaintiff in error, failed to register for this "draft" and was subsequently prosecuted under the statute for the penalties that it provided. The lower court rendered conviction based on instruction that Arven's legal defense was without merit and that the statute was constitutional.

[excerpts]

MR. CHIEF JUSTICE WHITE delivered the opinion of the court:

We are here concerned with some of the provisions of the *Act of May 28, 1917* (public No. 12, 65th Congress, chap. 15, 40 Stat. at L. 76, Comp. Stat. -,§ 2044a), entitled, "*An Act to Authorize the President to Increase Temporarily the Military Establishment of the United States.*" The law, as its opening sentence declares, was *intended to supply temporarily* the increased military force which was required by the *existing emergency*, the war then and now flagrant. The clauses we must pass upon and those which will throw light on their significance are briefly summarized.

The Act proposed to raise a national army, first by increasing the regular force to its maximum strength and there maintaining it; second, by incorporating into such army the members of the National Guard and National Guard Reserve already in the service of the United States (Act of Congress of June 3, 1916, chap. 134, 39 Stat. at L. 211), and maintaining their organizations to their full strength; third, by giving the President power in his discretion to organize by volunteer enlistment four divisions of infantry; fourth, by *subjecting all male citizens between the ages of twenty-one and thirty* to duty in the national army after the proclamation of the President announcing the necessity for their service;

and fifth, by providing for selecting from the body so called, on the further proclamation of the President, 500,000 enlisted men, and a second body of the same number should the President, in his discretion, deem it necessary. To carry out its purposes the Act made it the duty of those liable to the call to present themselves for registration on the proclamation of the President so as to subject themselves to the terms of the act, and provided full Federal means for carrying *out the selective draft.* It gave the *President in his discretion, power to create local boards to consider claims of redemption for physical disability* or otherwise made by those called. The Act exempted from subjection to the draft designated United States and state officials as well as those already in the military or naval service of the United States, regular or duly ordained ministers of religion and theological students under the conditions provided for, and while relieving from military service in the strict sense the members of religious sects as enumerated whose tenets excluded the moral right to engage in war, nevertheless subjected such persons to the performance of *service of a noncombatant character*, to be *defined by the President.*

The proclamation of the President calling the persons designated within the ages described in the statute was made, and the plaintiffs in error, who were in the class, and, under the statue, were obliged to present themselves for registration and subject themselves to the law, *failed to do so and were prosecuted under these statue for the penalties for which it provided.* They all defended by *denying* that there had been *conferred* by the *Constitution upon Congress* the power to *compel military* service by a *selective draft*, and if such power had been given by the Constitution to Congress, the terms of the particular act, for various reasons, caused it to be beyond the power and repugnant to the Constitution. The cases are here for review because of the constitutional questions thus raised, convictions having resulted from instructions of the courts that the legal defenses were without merit and that the statute was constitutional.

The possession of authority to enact the statute must be found in the clauses of the of the Constitution giving Congress power "to declare war;...to raise and support armies, but no appropriation of money to that use shall be for a longer term than two years;...to make rules for the government and regulation of the land, and naval forces." Article 1, § 8. And, of course, the powers conferred by these provisions, like all other powers given, carry with them as provided by the Constitution the authority "to make all laws which shall be necessary and proper for carrying into execution the foregoing powers." Article 1, § 8.

As the mind cannot conceive an army without the men to compose it, on the face of the Constitution the objection that it does not give power to provide for such men would seem to be too frivolous for further notice. it is said, however, that since under the Constitution as originally framed state citizenship was primary and United States citizenship but derivative and dependent thereon, therefore the power conferred upon Congress to raise armies was only coterminous with United states citizenship and could not be exerted so as to cause that citizenship to lose its dependent character and dominate state citizenship. But the proposition simply denies to Congress the power to raise armies which the Constitution gives. That power, by the very terms of the Constitution being delegated, is supreme. Article 6. In truth, the contention simply assails the wisdom of the framers of the Constitution in conferring authority on Congress, and in not retaining it, as it was under the Confederation, in the several states. Further, it is said, the right to provide is not denied by calling for volunteer enlistment's, but it does not and cannot include the power to exact enforced military duty by the citizen. This, however, but challenges the existence of all power, for a governmental power which has no sanction to it and which therefore can only be exercised provided the citizens consents to its exertion is in no substantial sense a power. it is argues however, that although this is abstractly true, it is not concretely so because, as compelled military service is repugnant to a free government and in conflict with all the great guaranties of the Constitution as to individual liberty, it must be assumed that the authority to raise armies was intended to be limited to the right to call an army into existence counting alone upon the willingness of the citizen to do his duty in time of public need; that is. in time of war. But the premise of this proposition is so devoid of foundation that it leaves not even a shadow of ground upon which to base the conclusion.

In the Colonies before the separation from England there cannot be the slightest doubt that the right to enforce military service was unquestioned and that practical effect was given to the power in many cases. Indeed, the brief of the government contains a list of colonial acts manifesting the power and its enforcement in more than two hundred cases. And this exact situation existed also after the separation. Under the Articles of Confederation, it is true, Congress had no such power, as its authority was absolutely limited to making calls upon the states for the military forces needed to create and maintain the army, each state being bound for its quota as called. But it is indisputable that the states, in response to the calls made upon them, met the situation when they deemed it necessary by directing enforced military service and the power to compel him against his consent to do so was expressly sanctioned by the constitutions of at least nine of the states, an illustration being afforded by the following provisions of the Pennsylvania Constitution of 1776: "That every member of society that a right to be protected in the enjoyment of life, liberty and property and therefore is bound to contribute his proportion toward the expense of that protection, and yield his personal service when necessary, or an equivalent thereto." Art. 8 (5 Thorpe, American Charters, Constitutions, and Organic Laws, pp. 3081, 3083). While it is true that the states were sometimes slow in exerting the power in order to fill their quotas—a condition shown by resolutions of Congress calling upon them to comply by exerting their compulsory power to draft, and by earnest requests by Washington to Congress that a demand be made upon the states to resort to drafts to fill their quotas—that fact serves to demonstrate instead of to challenge the existence of the authority. A default in exercising a duty may not be resorted to as a reason for denying its existence.

When the Constitution came to be formed it may not be disputed that one of the recognized necessities for its adoption was the want of power in Congress to raise an army and the dependence upon the states for their quotas. In supplying the power it was manifestly intended to give it all and leave none to the states, since, besides the delegation to Congress of authority to raise armies, the Constitution prohibited the states, without the consent of Congress, from keeping troops in time of peace or engaging in war. Article 1, § 10.

The fallacy of the argument results from confounding the constitutional provisions concerning the militia with that conferring upon Congress the power to raise armies. It treats them as one while they are different. This is the militia clause: "The Congress shall have power...[t]o provide for calling forth the militia to execute the laws of the Union, suppress insurrections and repel invasions; to provide for organizing, arming and disciplining, the militia, and for governing such

draft at a very critical moment of the civil strife which obviated a disaster which seemed impending and carried that struggle to a complete and successful conclusion.

In reviewing the subject we have hitherto considered it as it has been argued from the point of view of the Constitution as it stood prior to the adoption of the 14th Amendment. But, to avoid all misapprehension, we briefly direct attention to that amendment for the purpose of pointing out, as has been frequently done in the past, how completely it broadened the national scope of the government under the Constitution by causing *citizenship of the United States to be paramount and dominant instead of being subordinate and derivative,* and therefore operating, as it does, upon all the powers conferred by the Constitution, leaves no possible support for the contentions made, if their want of merit was otherwise not so clearly made manifest.

Finally, as we are unable to conceive upon what theory the exaction by government from the citizen of the performance of his supreme and noble duty of contributing to the defense of the rights and honor of the nation as the result of a war declared by the great representative body of the people can be said to be the imposition of involuntary servitude, in violation of the prohibitions of the 13th Amendment, we are constrained to the conclusion that the contention to that effect is refuted by its mere statement.

Affirmed.

OETJEN v. CENTRAL LEATHER CO.
246 U. S. 297 (1918)

On February 23, 1913, the President of the Republic of Mexico (Madero) was assassinated. This event served as the impetus for the Mexican Civil War. General Huerta declared himself to be the provisional President of the Republic. A month later, General Carranza, governor of the state of Coahuila and future President of the Republic, started a revolution against Huerta's "claimed" authority, and he commissioned General Francisco "Pancho" Villa as the "Commander of the North" for his "Constitutionalist" forces. By the autumn of 1913, Carranza's forces were in possession of two thirds of the country. After capturing a city or town, it was common practice for the army under General Villa to levy a military contribution on the inhabitants.

Mr. Oetjen is the assign for the plaintiff in error, who as a resident of one of these captured cities, supra, had two large consignments of animal hides confiscated by General Villa. These goods were thereafter sold to a company in Texas who then sold the goods to the defendant. The plaintiff filed a suit of replevin (i.e., a writ to reclaim title of property which has been wrongfully seized) in a New Jersey Court of Errors and Appeals. Both that court and the Circuit Court from Hudson County in the same state ruled in favor of the defendant. It should be noted that the United States government recognized the government of Carranza as the de facto government of Mexico on October 19, 1915, and as the de jure government on August 31, 1917.

[excerpts]

MR. JUSTICE CLARKE delivered the opinion of the court:

These two cases, involving the same question, were argued and will be decided together. They are *suits in replevin* and involve the title to two large consignments of hides, which the plaintiff in error claims to own as assignee of Martinez & Company, a partnership engaged in business in the city of Torreon, Mexico, but which the defendant in error claims to own by purchase from the Finnegan-Brown Company, a Texas corporation, which it is alleged purchased the hides in Mexico from *General Francisco Villa*, on January 3, 1914.

The cases were commenced in a circuit court of New Jersey, in which judgments were rendered for the defendants, which were affirmed by the court of errors and appeals, and they are brought to this court on the theory that the claim of title to the hides by the defendant in error is invalid because based upon a purchase from General Villa, who it is urged, confiscated them contrary to the provisions of the *Hague Convention of 1907* respecting the laws and customs of war on land; that the judgment of the state court denied to the plaintiff in error this right which he "set up and claimed" under the Hague Convention or Treaty; and that this denial gives him the right of review in this court.

A somewhat detailed description will be necessary of the political conditions in Mexico prior to and at the time of the seizure of the property ii controversy by the military authorities. It appears in the record, and is a matter of general history, that on February 23, 1913, *Madero, President of the Republic of Mexico, was assassinated*; that immediately thereafter *General Huerta declared* himself *Provisional President* of the Republic and took the oath of office as such; that on the 26th day of March following *General Carranza*, who was then *governor of* the state of *Coahuila*, inaugurated a revolution against the claimed authority of Huerta and in a "Manifesto addressed to the Mexican Nation" proclaimed the organization of a *constitutional government* under *"The Plan of Guadalupe,"* and that civil war was at once entered upon between the followers and forces of the two leaders. When General Carranza assumed the leadership of what were called the Constitutionalist forces he commissioned General Villa his representative, as "Commander of the North," and assigned him to an independent command in that part of the country. Such progress was made by the *Carranza forces* that in the *autumn of 1913* they were in military *possession*, as the record shows of approximately *two thirds* of the area *of the entire country*, with the exception of a few scattered towns and cities, and after a battle lasting several days the city of *Torreon* in the state of *Coahuila* was captured by General Villa on *October 1* of that year. Immediately after the capture of Torreon, Villa proposed *levying a military contribution on the inhabitants*, for the support of his army, and thereupon influential citizens, preferring to provide the required money by an assessment upon the community, to having their property forcibly seized , called together a largely attended meeting and after negotiations with General Villa as to the amount to be paid, an *assessment was made on the men of property* of the city, which was in large part promptly paid. *Martinez*, the *owner* from whom the plaintiff in error reclaims title to the property involved in this case, was a *wealthy resident of Torreon* and was a *dealer in hides* in a large way. Being an adherent of Juerta, when Torreon was captured Martinez fled the city and failed to pay the assessment imposed upon him, and it was to satisfy this assessment that by order of General Villa, the hides in controversy were seized and on January 3, 1914, were sold in Mexico to the Finnegan-Brown Company. They were paid for in Mexico, and were thereafter shipped into the United States and were *replevied*, as stated.

This court will take judicial notice of the fact that since the transactions thus detailed and since the trial of this case in the lower courts, the governments of the United States recognized the government of Carranza as the *de facto* government on *August 31, 1917.*

On this state of fact the plaintiff in error argues that the "regulations" annexed to the Hague Convention of 1907 *"respecting Laws and Customs of War on Land" constitute a treaty* between the United States and Mexico; that these "regulations" forbid such seizure and sale of property as we are considering in this case; and that, therefore, somewhat vaguely, no title passed by the sale made by General Villa, and the property may be recovered by the Mexican owner or his assignees when found in this country.

It would, perhaps, be sufficient answer to this contention to say that the *Hague Conventions* are international in character, designed and adapted to *regulate international warfare*, and that *they do not, in terms or in purpose, apply to a civil war*. Were it otherwise, however, it might be effectively argued that the declaration relied upon that "private property cannot be confiscated," contained in Article 46 of the regulations, does not have the scope claimed for it, since Article 49 provides that "money contributions...for the needs of the army" may be levied upon occupied territory, and Article 52 provides that "requisitions in kind and services may be demanded for the needs of the army of occupation," and that contributions in kind shall, as far as possible, be paid for in cash, and when not so paid for a receipt shall be given and payment of the amount due shall be made as soon as possible. And also for the reason that the "Convention" to which the "regulations" are annexed, recognizing the incomplete charter of the results arrived at, expressly provides that until a more complete code is agreed upon, cases not provided of in the "regulations" shall be governed by the principles of the law of nations.

But, since claims similar to the one before us are being made in many cases in his and in other courts, we prefer to place our decision upon the application of three clearly settled principles of law to the facts of this case as we have stated them.

The conduct of the foreign relations of our government is committed by the Constitution to the executive and legislative—"the political"—departments of the government, and the property of what may be done in the exercise of this political power is not subject to judicial inquiry or decision. It has been specifically decided that "who is the sovereign de jure or de facto of a territory is not a judicial but a political question, the determination of which by the legislative and executive departments of any government conclusively binds the judges, as well as all of the officers, citizens, and subjects of that government. This principle has always been affirmed under a great variety of circumstances."

It is also the result of the interpretation by this court of the principles of international law that when a government which originates in revolution or revolt is recognized by the political department or our government as the de jure government of the country in which it is established, such recognition is retroactive in effect and validates all the actions and conduct of the government so recognized from the commencement of it existence.

To these principles we must add that "every sovereign state is bound to respect the independence of every other sovereign state, and the courts of one country will not sit in judgment on the acts of the government of another, done within its own territory. Redress of grievances by reason of such acts must be obtained through the means open to be themselves."

Applying these principles of law to the case at bar, we have a duly commissioned military commander of what must be accepted as the legitimate government of Mexico, in the progress of a revolution, and when conducting active independent operations, seizing and selling in Mexico, as a military contribution, the property in controversy, at the time owned and in the possession of a citizen of Mexico, the assignor of the plaintiff in error. Plainly this was the action, in Mexico when dealing with a Mexican citizen, and, as we have seen, for the soundest reasons, and upon repeated decisions of this court, such action is not subject to re-examination and modification by the courts of this country.

The principle that the conduct of one independent government cannot be successfully questioned in the courts of another is applicable to a case involving the title to property brought within the custody of a court, such as we have here, as it was held to be to the cases cited, in which claims for damages were based upon acts done in a foreign country; for it rests at last upon the highest considerations of international comity and expediency. To permit the validity of the acts of one sovereign state to be re-examined and perhaps condemned by the courts of another would very certainly "imperil the amicable relations between governments and vex the peace of nations."

It is not necessary to consider, as the New Jersey court did, the validity of the levy of the contribution made by the Mexican commanding general, under rules of international law applicable to the situation, since the subject is not open to re-examination by this or any other American court.

The remedy of the former owner, or of the purchaser from him, of the property in controversy, if either has any remedy, must be found in the courts of Mexico or through the diplomatic agencies of the political department of our government. The judgments of the Court of Errors and Appeals of New Jersey must be affirmed.

MISSOURI v. HOLLAND, UNITED STATES GAME WARDEN

252 US. 346; 40 sup. Ct. 382; 64L. Ed. 641 (1920)

In 1916, the United States signed a treaty with Great Britain (within whose commonwealth Canada resided) called the Migratory Bird Treaty. Two years later, Congress enacted legislation to enforce its terms. The law prohibited killing, capturing, or selling certain migratory birds in this country which were considered endangered species. Missouri challenged the enforcement of the Act as an unconstitutional interference with "states' rights" under the Tenth Amendment. After the federal district court declined relief, Missouri appealed to the Supreme Court. The main questions presented were: (1) was the Act of Congress considered a part of the treaty or was it ordinary legislation, and (2) to which test of validity under Article VI was the law subject—the more difficult substantive test of being "made in pursuance of the Constitution" or the loose procedural requirement of being "made under the authority of the United states"?

[excerpts]

MR. JUSTICE HOLMES delivered the opinion of the Court:

This is a bill in equity, brought by the state of Missouri to prevent a game warden of the United States from attempting to enforce the Migratory Bird Treaty Act of July 3, 1918, Fed. Stat. Anno. Supp. 1918, p. 196, and the regulations made by the Secretary of Agriculture in pursuance of the same. The ground of the bill is that the statue is an unconstitutional interference with the rights reserved to the states by the 10th amendment, and that the acts of the defendant, done and threatened under that authority, invade the sovereign right of the state and contravene its will manifested in statutes. The state also alleges a pecuniary interest, as owner of the wild birds within its borders and otherwise, admitted by the government to be sufficient, but it is enough that the bill is a reasonable and proper means to assert the alleged quasi-sovereign rights of a state. A motion to dismiss was sustained by the district court on the ground that the Act of Congress is constitutional.

On December 8, 1916, a treaty between the United states and Great Britain was proclaimed by the President. It recited that many species of birds in their annual migrations traversed many parts of the United States and of Canada, and that they were of great value as a source of food and in destroying insects injurious to vegetation, but were in danger of extermination through lack of adequate protection. It therefore provided for specified close seasons and protection in other forms, and agreed that the two powers would take or propose to their lawmaking bodies the necessary measures for carrying the treaty out.

To answer this question it is not enough to refer to the 10th Amendment, reserving the powers not delegated to the United States, *because by Article 2, § 2 , the power to make treaties is delegated expressly, and by Article 6, treaties made under the authority of the United States,* along with the Constitution and laws of the United States, made in pursuance thereof, *are declared the supreme law of the land. If the treaty is valid, there can be no dispute about the validity of the statue* under Article 1, § 8, as a necessary and proper means to execute the powers of the government. The language of the Constitution as to the supremacy of treaties being general, the question before us is narrowed to an inquiry into the ground upon which the present supposed exceptions is placed.

It is said that a treaty cannot be valid if it infringes the Constitution; that there are limits, therefore, to the treaty-making power; and that one such limit is that what an Act of Congress could not do unaided, in derogation of the powers reserved to the states, a treaty cannot do.

Acts of Congress are the supreme law of the land *only* when made in *pursuance* of the *Constitution*, while *treaties are* declared to be so *when made under the authority of the United States.* It is open to question whether the authority of the United states means *more than* the formal *acts* prescribed to make the convention. We do not mean to imply that there are no qualifications to the treaty-making power; but they must be ascertained in a different way. It is obvious that there may be matters of the sharpest exigency for the national well-being that an Act of Congress could not deal with, but that a treaty followed by such an act could, and it is not lightly to be assumed that, in matters requiring national action, "a power which must belong to and somewhere reside in every civilized government" is not to be found. The case before us *must* be considered in the light of our *whole experience*, and not merely in that of what was said a hundred years ago. The treaty in question does *not* follow that its authority is exclusive of paramount powers. To put the claim of the state upon title is to lean upon a slender reed. Wild birds are *not* in the possession of *anyone*; and possession is the beginning of ownership. The whole foundation of the state's right is the presence within their jurisdiction of birds that yesterday had not arrived, tomorrow may be in another state, and in a week a thousand miles away. If we are to be accurate, we cannot put the case of the state upon higher ground than that the treaty deals with creatures that for the moment are within the state borders, that it must be carried out by officers of the United states within the same territory, and that, but for the treaty, the state would be free to regulate this subject itself.

Valid treaties, of course, "are as binding within the territorial limits of the states as they are effective throughout the dominion of the United States." No doubt the great body of private relations usually falls within the control of the state, but a treaty may *override* its power. We do not have to invoke the later developments of constitutional law for this proposition.

Here a national interest of very nearly the first magnitude is involved. It can be protected only by national action in concert with that of another power. The subject-matter is only transitory within the state, and has no permanent habitat therein. But for the treaty and the statute, there soon might be *no* birds for any powers to deal with. We see nothing in the Constitution that compels the government to sit by while a food supply is cut off and the protectors of our forests and of our crops are destroyed. It is *not* sufficient to *rely* upon the *states*. The reliance is vain, and were it otherwise, the question is whether the United States is forbidden to act. we are of opinion that the treaty and statute must be upheld.

Decree affirmed.

MR. JUSTICE VAN DEVANTER and MR. JUSTICE PITNEY dissented.

MYERS v. UNITED STATES
272 U. S. 52 (1926)

In 1917, President Woodrow Wilson appointed Myers to the position of postmaster of Portland which had a tenure of four years. However, in 1920 the President removed him under the terms of a congressional statute (1876), providing for such executive removal "by and with the advice and consent of the Senate." Nevertheless, Wilson did not refer the matter to the upper house for its consent. Myers sued the administration in the United States Court of Claims for the unpaid salary denied him during the eighteen months remaining in his term of office—roughly $8,840. The Court of Claims denied relief; the question then proceeded to the Supreme Court of the United States.

[excerpts]

MR. CHIEF JUSTICE TAFT delivered the opinion of the Court, saying in part:

The question where the power of removal of executive officers appointed by the President by and with the advice and consent of the Senate was vested, was presented early in the first session of the First Congress. There is no express provision respecting removals in the Constitution, except as § 4 of Article 2 provides for removal from office by impeachment. The subject was not discussed in the Constitutional Convention....

In the House of Representatives of the First Congress, on Tuesday, May 18, 1789, Mr. Madison moved in the Committee of the Whole that there should be established three executive departments-one of Foreign Affairs, another of the Treasury, and a third of War, at the head of each of which there should be a Secretary to be appointed by the President by and with the advice and consent of the Senate, and to be removable by the President. The committee agreed to the establishment of a Department of Foreign Affairs, but a discussion ensued as to making the Secretary removable by the President....

On June 16, 1789, the House resolved itself into a Committee of the Whole on a bill proposed by Mr. Madison of reestablishing an executive department to be denominated the Department of Foreign Affairs, in which the first clause, after stating the title of the officer and describing his duties had these words "to be removable from office by the President of the United States."...

On June 22, in the renewal of the discussion, Mr. Benson moved to amend the bill, by altering the second clause, so as to imply the power of removal to be in the President alone....

Mr. Benson stated that his objection to the clause to be removable by the President hereafter might appear to be exercised by virtue of a legislative grant only, and consequently be suggested to legislative instability, hen he was well satisfied in his own mind that it was fixed by a fair legislative construction of the Constitution....

Mr. Benson's first amendment to alter the second clause by the insertion of the italicized words made that clause to read as follows:

"That there shall be in the State Department an inferior officer to be appointed by the said principal officer, and to be employed therein as he shall deem proper, to be called the Chief Clerk in the Department of Foreign Affairs, *and who, whenever the principal officer shall be removed from office by the President of the United States,* or in any other case of vacancy, shall, during such vacancy, have charge and custody of all records, books and papers appertaining to said department."

The first amendment was then approved by a vote of thirty to eighteen.... Mr. Benson then moved to strike out in the first clause the words "to be removable by the President," in pursuance of the purpose he had already declared, and this second motion of his was carried by a vote of thirty-one to nineteen.... It is very clear from this history that the exact question which the House voted upon was whether it should recognize and declare the power of the President under the Constitution to remove the Secretary of Foreign affairs without the advice and consent of the Senate. That was what the vote was taken for. Some effort has been made to question whether the decision carries the result claimed for it, but there is not the slightest doubt, after an examination of the record, that the vote was, and was intended to be, a legislative declaration that the power to remove officers appointed by the President and the Senate vested in the President alone, and until the Johnson impeachment trial in 1868, its meaning was not doubted even by those who questioned its soundness....

The bill was discussed in the House at length and with great ability.... James Madison was then a leader in the House, as he had been in the Convention. His arguments in support of the President's constitu-

tional power of removal independently of Congressional provision, and
without the consent of the Senate, were masterly, and he carried the
House.

It is convenient in the course of our discussion of this case to review
the reasons advanced by Mr. Madison and his associates of their
conclusion, supplementing them, so far as may be, by additional
considerations which lead this Court to concur therein.

First, Mr. Madison insisted that Article 2 by vesting the executive
power in the President was intended to grant to him the power of
appointment and removal of executive officers except as thereafter
expressly provided in that Article. He pointed out that one of the chief
purposes of the Convention was to separate the legislative from the
executive functions. He said: "If there is a principle in our Constitution,
indeed in any free Constitution more sacred than another, it is that which
separates the legislative, executive and judicial powers. If there is any
point, in which the separation of the legislative and executive powers
ought to be maintained with great caution, it is that which relates to
officers and offices."...

Mr. Madison and his associates in the discussion in the House dwelt
at length upon the necessity there was of reconstructing Article 2 to give
the President the sole power of removal in his responsibility of the
conduct of the executive branch, and enforced this by emphasizing his
duty expressly declared in the third section of the Article to "take care
that the laws be faithfully executed."...

The vesting of the executive power in the President was essentially
a grant of the power to execute the laws. But the President alone and
unaided could not execute the laws. But the President alone and unaided
could not execute the laws. He must execute them by the assistance of
subordinates.... As he is charged specifically to take care that they be
faithfully executed, the reasonable implication, even in the absence of
express words, was that as part of his executive power he should select
those who were to act for him under his direction in the execution of the
laws. The further implication must be, in the absence of any express
limitation respecting removals, that as his selection of administrative
officers is essential to the execution of the laws by him, so must be his
power of removing those for whom he cannot continue to be responsible.... It was urged that the natural meaning of the term "executive
power" granted the President included the appointment and removal of

executive subordinates. If such appointments and removals were not an exercise of the executive power, what were they? They certainty were not the exercise of legislative or judicial power in government as usually understood....

Second. The view of Mr. Madison and his associates was that not only did the grant of executive power to the President in the first section of Article 2 carry wit it the power of removal, but the express recognition of the power of appointment in the second section enforced this view on the well approved principle of constitutional and statutory construction that the power of removal of executive officers was incident to the power of appointment. It was agreed by the opponents of the bill, with only one or two exceptions, that as a constitutional principle the power of appointment carried with it the power of removal.... This principle as a rule of constitutional and statutory construction, then generally conceded, has been recognized ever since.... The reason for the principle is that those in charge of and responsible for administering functions of government who select their executive subordinates need in meeting their responsibility to have the power to remove those whom they appoint.

Under § 2 of Article 2, however, the power of appointment by the Executive is restricted in its exercise by the provision that the Senate, a part of the legislative branch of the government, may check the action of the Executive by rejecting the officers he selects. Does this make the Senate part of the removing power? And this, after the whole discussion in the House is read attentively, is the real point which was considered and decided in the negative by the vote already given.

The history of the clause by which the Senate was given a check upon the President's power of appointment makes it clear that it was not prompted by any desire to limit removals. As already pointed out, the important purpose of those who brought about the restriction was to lodge in the Senate, where the small states had equal representation with the larger states, power to prevent the President from making too many appointments from the larger states....

It was pointed out in this great debate that the power of removal. though equally essential to the executive power is different in its nature from that of appointment.... A veto by the Senate-a part of the legislative branch of the government-upon removals is a much greater limitation upon the executive branch and a much more serious blending of the legislative with the executive than a rejection of a proposed appointment.

It is not to be implied. The rejection of a nominee of the President for a particular office does not greatly embarrass him in the conscientious discharge of his high duties in the selection of those who are to aid him, because the President usually has an ample field from which to select for office, according to his preference, competent and capable men. The Senate has full power to reject newly proposed appointees whenever the President shall remove the incumbents. Such a check enables the Senate to prevent the filling of offices with bad or incompetent men or with those against whom there is tenable objection.

The power to prevent the removal of an officer who has served under the President is different from the authority to consent to or reject his appointment. When a nomination is made, it may be presumed that the Senate is, or may become, as well advised as to the fitness of the nominee as the President, but in the nature of things the defects in ability or intelligence or loyalty in the administration of the laws of one who has served as an officer under the President, are facts as to which the President, or his trusted subordinates, must be better informed than the Senate, and the power to remove him may, therefore, be regarded as confined, for very sound and practical reasons, to the governmental authority which has administrative control. The power of removal is incident to the power of appointment, not to the power of advising and consenting to appointment, and when the grant of the executive power is enforced by the express mandate to take care that the laws be faithfully executed, it emphasizes the necessity of including within the executive power as conferred the exclusive power of removal....

Third. Another argument urged against the constitutional power of the President alone to remove executive officers appointed by him with the consent of the Senate is that, in the absence of an express power of removal granted to the President, power to make provision of removal of all such officers is vested in the Congress by § 8 of Article 1....

The constitutional construction that excludes Congress from legislative power to provide for the removal of superior officers finds support in the second section of Article 2.... This is "but the Congress may by law vest the appointment of such inferior officers, as they think proper, in the President alone, in the courts of law, or in the heads of Departments." These words, it has been held by this court, give to Congress the power to limit and regulate removal of such inferior officers by heads of departments when it exercises its constitutional power to lodge the power of appointment with them. *United States v. Perkins* [1886]. Here, then, is an express provision introduced in words of exception of the exercise by Congress of legislative power in the matter of appointments and removals in the case of inferior executive officers. The phrase "But Congress may be law vest" is equivalent to "excepting that Congress may by law vest." By the plainest implication it excludes Congressional dealing with appointments or removals of executive officers not falling within the exception and leaves unaffected the executive power of the President to appoint and remove them....

It is reasonable to suppose that, had it been intended to give to Congress power to regulate or control removals in the manner suggested, it would have been included among the specifically enumerated legislative powers in Article 1, or in the specified limitations on the executive power in Article 2. The difference between the grant of legislative power under Article 1 to Congress which is limited to powers therein enumerated, and the more general grant of the executive power to the President under Article 2, is significant. The fact that the executive power is given in general terms strengthened by specific terms where emphasis is appropriate, and limited by direct expressions where limitation is needed and that no express limit is placed on the power of removal by the executive is a convincing indication that none was intended....

Fourth. Mr. Madison and his associates pointed out with great force the unreasonable character of the view that the convention intended, without express provision, to give to Congress or the Senate, in case of political or other differences, the means of thwarting the Executive in the exercise of his great powers and in the bearing of his great responsibility by fastening upon him, subordinate executive officers, men who by their inefficient service, or by their different views of policy might make his taking care that the laws be faithfully executed most difficult or impossible....

Made responsible under the Constitution of the effective enforcement of the law, the President needs as an indispensable aid to meet it the disciplinary influence upon those who act under him of a reserve power of removal....

In all such cases, the discretion to be exercised is that of the President in determining the national public interest and in directing the action to be taken by his executive subordinates to protect it. In this field his cabinet officers must do his will. He must place in each member of his official family, and his chief executive subordinates, implicit faith. The moment that he loses confidence in the intelligence, ability, judgment or loyalty of any one of them, he must have the power to remove him without delay. To require him to file charges and submit them to the consideration of the Senate might make impossible that unity and co-ordination in executive administration essential to effective action.

The duties of the heads of departments and bureaus in which the discretion of the President is exercised and which we have described are the most important in the whole field of executive action of the government. There is nothing in the Constitution which permits a distinction between the removal of the head of a department or a bureau, when he discharges a political duty of the President or exercises his discretion, and the removal of executive officers engaged in the discharge of their other normal duties. The imperative reasons requiring an unrestricted power to remove the most important of his subordinates in their most important duties must, therefore, control the interpretation of the Constitution as to all appointed by him.

But this is not to say that there are not strong reasons why the President should have a like power to remove his appointees charged with other duties than those above described. The ordinary duties of officers prescribed by statue come under the general administrative control of the President by virtue of the general grant to him of the executive power, and he may properly supervise and guide their construction of the statutes under which they act in order to secure that unitary and uniform execution of the laws which Article 2 of the Constitution evidently contemplated in vesting general executive power in the President alone. Laws are often passed with specific provision for the adoption of regulations by a department or bureau head to make the law workable and effective. The ability and judgment manifested by the official thus empowered, as well as his energy and stimulation of his subordinates, are subjects which the President must consider and supervise in is administrative control. Finding such officers to be negligent and inefficient, the President should have the power to remove them. Of course there may be duties so peculiarly and specifically committed to the discretion of a particular officer as to raise a question whether the President may overrule or revise the officer's interpretation of his statutory duty in a particular instance. Then there may be duties of a quasi-judicial character imposed on executive officers and members of executive tribunals whose decisions after hearing affect interests of individuals, the discharge of which the President cannot in a particular case properly influence or control. But even in such a case he may consider the decision after its rendition as a reason of removing the officer, on the ground that the discretion regularly entrusted to that officer by statute has not been on the whole intelligently or wisely exercised. Otherwise he does not discharge his own constitutional duty of seeing that the laws be faithfully executed.

Summing up then the facts as to acquiescence by all branches of the Government in the legislative decision of 1789 as to executive officers whether superior or inferior, we find that from 1789 until 1823, a period of seventy-four years, there was no Act of Congress, no executive act, and no decision of this court at variance with the declaration of the First Congress, but there was, as we have seen, clear affirmative recognition of it by each branch of the Government....

We come now to a period in the history of the Government when both Houses of Congress attempted to reverse this constitutional construction and to subject the power of removing executive officers appointed by the President and confirmed by the Senate to the control of the Senate, indeed finally to the assumed power in Congress to place the removal of such officers anywhere in the Government.

This reversal grew out of the serious political difference between the two Houses of Congress and President Johnson. There was a two-thirds majority of the Republican party in control of each House of Congress, which resented what it feared would be Mr. Johnson's obstructive course in the enforcement of the reconstruction measures in respect of the States whose people had lately been at war against the National Government.

...Without animadverting on the character of the measures taken, we are certainly justified in saying that hey should not be given the weight affecting proper constitutional construction to be accorded to that reached by the First Congress of the United States during a political calm and acquiesced in by the whole Government for three-quarters of a century, especially when the new construction contended for has never been acquiesced in by either the executive or the judicial departments. While this court has studiously avoided deciding the issue until it was presented in such a way that it could not be avoided, in the references it has made to the history of the question, and in the presumptions it has indulged in favor of a statutory construction not inconsistent with the legislative decision of 1789, it has indicated a trend of view that we should not and can not ignore. When on the merits we find our conclusion strongly favoring the view which prevailed in the First Congress, we have no hesitation in holding that conclusion to be correct; and it therefore follows that the Tenure of Office Act of 1867, in so far as it attempted to prevent the President from removing excessive officers who had been appointed by him by and with the advice and consent of the Senate, was invalid and that subsequent legislation of the same effect was equally so.

For the reasons given, we must therefore hold that the provision of the law of 1876 by which the unrestricted power of removal of first class postmasters is denied to the President is in violation of the Constitution and invalid. This leads to an affirmance of the judgment of the Court of Claims....

                                                              Judgment affirmed.

MR. JUSTICE HOLMES dissented and said in part:

The argument drawn from the executive power of the President and from his duty t appoint officers of the United States (when Congress does not vest the appointment elsewhere), to take care that the laws be faithfully executed, and to commission all officers of the United States, seem to me spiders' webs inadequate to control the dominant facts.

We have to deal with an office that owes its existence to Congress and that Congress may abolish tomorrow. Its duration and the pay attached to it while it lasts depend on Congress alone. Congress alone confers on the President the power to appoint to it and at any time may transfer the power to other hands. With such power over its own creation, I have no more trouble in believing that Congress has power to prescribe a term of life of it free from any interference that I have in accepting the undoubted power of Congress to decree its end. I have equally little trouble in accepting its power to prolong the tenure of an incumbent until Congress or the Senate shall have assented to his removal. The duty of the President to see that the laws be executed is a duty that does not go beyond the laws or require him to achieve more than Congress sees fit to leave within his power.

MR. JUSTICE McREYNOLDS also dissented and said in part:

The long struggle of civil service reform and the legislation designed to insure some security of official tenure ought not to be forgotten. Again and again Congress has enacted statutes prescribing restrictions on removals, and by approving them many Presidents have affirmed it power therein....

Nothing short of language clear beyond serious disputation should be held to clothe the President with authority wholly beyond congressional control arbitrarily to dismiss every officer whom he appoints except a few judges. There are no such words in the Constitution, and the asserted inference conflicts with the heretofore accepted theory that this government is one of carefully enumerated power under an intelligible charter....

If the phrase "executive power" infolds the one now claimed many others heretofore totally unsuspected may lie there awaiting future supposed necessity; and no human intelligence can define the field of the President's permissible activities. "A masked battery of constructive powers would complete the destruction of liberty."...

McGRAIN v. DOUGHERTY
273 U. S. 135 (1927)

During the administration of President Warren G. Harding, several national scandals were exposed involving certain presidential appointees. The most serious political problem centered on the granting of naval oil leases within the Attorney General's Office and the Veteran's Bureau. The so-called "Tea Pot Dome" scandal attracted the attention of the Senate which created an ad hoc committee of certain of its members to investigate the Department of Justice and to make more avcondiscent the activities of the Attorney General, Harry M. Dougherty. The latter's sole qualification for holding the position of the nation's highest legal authority seemed to be that he managed Harding's presidential campaign in 1920. During the investigation, the Senate committee subpoenaed his brother, "Molly" Dougherty, who refused to appear before the committee. Consequently, the committee ordered the deputy sergeant-at-arms, Mr. McGrain, to arrest Molly for contempt of Congress. The federal district court granted Mr. Dougherty habeas corpus relief and discharged him from custody. McGrain appealed to the Supreme Court.

[excerpts]

MR. JUSTICE VAN DEVANTER delivered the opinion of the Court, saying in part:

This is an appeal from the final order in a proceeding in habeas corpus discharging a recusant witness held in custody under process of attachment issued from the United States Senate in the course of an investigation which it was making of the administration of the Department of Justice....

The Constitution provides for a Congress consisting of a Senate and House of Representatives and invests it with "all legislative powers" granted to the United States, and with power "to make all laws which shall be necessary and proper" for carrying into execution these powers and "all other powers" vested by the Constitution in the United States or in any department or officer thereof. Art. 1, § 1, 8.... But there is no provision expressly investing either house with power to make investigations and exact testimony to the end that it may exercise its legislative function advisedly and effectively. So the question arises whether this power is so far incidental to the legislative function as to be implied.

In actual legislative practice power to secure needed information by such means has long been treated as an attribute of the power to legislate. It was so regarded in the British Parliament and in the colonial legislatures before the American Revolution; and a like view has prevailed and been carried into effect in both houses of Congress and in most of the state legislatures.

This power was both asserted and exerted by the House of Representatives in 1792, when it appointed a select committee to inquire into the St.Clair expedition and authorized the committee to send for necessary persons, papers, and records. Mr. Madison, who had taken an important part in framing the Constitution only five years before, and four of his associates in that work, were members of the House of Representatives at the time, and all voted for the inquiry.... Other exertions of the power by the House of Representatives, as also by the Senate, are shown in the citations already made. Among those by the Senate, the inquiry ordered in 1859 respecting the raid by John Brown and his adherents on the armory and arsenal of the United States at Harper's Ferry is of special significance. The resolution directing the inquiry authorized the committee to send for persons and papers, to inquire into the facts pertaining to the raid and the means by which it was organized and supported, and to report what legislation, if any, was necessary to preserve the peace of the country and protect the public property. The resolution was briefly discussed and adopted without opposition.... Later on the committee reported that Thaddeus Hyatt although subpoenaed to appear as a witness, had refused to do so; whereupon the Senate ordered that he be attached and brought before it to answer for his refusal. When he was brought in he answered by challenging the power of the Senate to direct the inquiry and exact testimony to aid it in exercising its legislative function. The question of power thus presented was thoroughly discussed by several senators—Mr. Sumner of Massachusetts taking the lead in denying the power, and Mr. Fessenden of Maine in supporting it. Sectional and party lines were put aside and the question was debated and determined with special regard to principle and precedent. The vote was taken on a resolution pronouncing the witness's answer insufficient and directing that he be committed until he should signify that he was ready and willing to testify. The resolution was adopted-forty-four senators voting for it and ten against....

The deliberate solution of the question on that occasion has been accepted and followed on other occasions by both houses of Congress, and never has been rejected or questioned by either.

The state courts quite generally have held that the power to legislate carries with it by necessary implication ample authority to obtain information needed in the rightful exercise of the power, and to employ compulsory process for the purpose....

Four decisions of this court are cited and more or less relied on, and we now turn to them.

The first decision was in *Anderson v. Dunn* [1821]. The question there was whether, under the Constitution, the House of Representatives has power to attach and punish a person other than a member for contempt of its authority-in fact, an attempt to bribe one of its members. The court regarded the power as essential to the effective exertion of other powers expressly granted, and therefore as implied.... The next decision was in *Kilbourn v. Thompson* [1881]. The question there was whether the House of Representatives had exceeded its power in directing one of its committees to make a particular investigation. The decision was that it had. The principles announced and applied in the case are-that neither house of Congress possesses a "general power of making inquiry into the private affairs of the citizen"; that the power actually possessed is limited to inquires relating to matters of which the particular house "has jurisdiction," and in respect of which the particular house "has jurisdiction," and in respect of which it rightfully may take other actions; that if the inquiry relates to "a matter wherein relief or redress could be had only by a judicial proceeding" it is not within the range of this power, but must be left to the courts, conformably to the constitutional separation of governmental powers; and that for the purpose of determining the essential character of the inquiry recourse may be had to the resolution or order under which it is made. The court examined the resolution which it is made. The court examined the resolution which was the basis of the particular inquiry, and ascertained therefrom that the inquiry related to a private real-estate pool or partnership in the District of Columbia. Jay Cook & Company had had an interest in the pool, but had become bankrupts, and their estate was in course of administration in a federal bankruptcy court in Pennsylvania. The United States was one of their creditors. The trustee in the bankruptcy proceeding had effected a settlement of the bankrupts' interest in the pool, and of course his action was subject to examination and approval or disapproval by the bankruptcy court. Some of the creditors, including the United States, were dissatisfied with the settlement. In these circumstances, disclosed in the preamble, the resolution directed the committee "to inquire into the matter and history of said real-estate pool and the character of said settlement, with the amount of property involved in which Jay Cook & Company were interested, and the amount paid or to be paid in said settlement, with power to send for persons and papers and report to the House." The court pointed out that the resolution contained no suggestion of contemplated legislation; that the matter was one in respect to which no valid legislation could be had; that the bankrupts' estate and the trustee's settlement were still pending in the bankruptcy court; and that the United States and other creditors were free to press their claims in that proceeding. And on these grounds the court held that in undertaking the investigation "the House of Representatives not only exceeded the limits of its own authority, but assumed power which could only be properly exercised by another branch of the government, because it was in its nature clearly judicial."...

While these cases are not decisive of the question we are considering, they definitely settle two propositions which we recognize as entirely sound and having a bearing on its solution: One, that the two houses of Congress, in their separate relations, possess not only such powers as are expressly granted to them by the Constitution, but such auxiliary powers as are necessary and appropriate to make the express powers effective; and, the other, that neither house is invested with "general" power to inquire into private affairs and compel disclosures, but only with such limited power of inquiry as is shown to exist when the rule of constitutional interpretation just stated is rightly applied....

We are of opinion that the power of inquiry—with process to enforce it—is an essential and appropriate auxiliary to the legislative function. it was so regarded and employed in American legislatures before the Constitution was framed and ratified. Both Houses of Congress took this view of it early in their history—the House of Representatives with the approving votes of Mr. Madison and other members whose service in the convention which framed the Constitution gives special significance to their action—and both houses have employed the power accordingly up to the present time. The Acts of 1798 and 1857, judged by their comprehensive terms, were intended to recognize the existence of this power in both houses and to enable them to employ it "more effectually" than before. So, when their practice in the matter is appraised according to the circumstances in which it was begun and to those in which it has been continued, it falls nothing short of a practical construction, long continued, of the constitutional provisions respecting their powers, and therefore should be taken as fixing the meaning of those provisions, if otherwise doubtful.

We are further of opinion that the provisions are not of doubtful meaning, but, as was held by this court in the cases we have reviewed, are intended to be effectively exercised, and therefore to carry with them such auxiliary powers, as are necessary and appropriate to that end. While the power to exact information in aid of the legislative function was not involved in those cases, the rule of interpretation applied there is applicable here. *A legislative body cannot legislate wisely or effectively in the absence of information respecting the conditions which the legislation is intended to affect or change; and where the legislative body does not itself possess the requisite information—which not infrequently is true—recourse must be had to others who do possess it.* Experience has taught that mere requests for such information often are unavailing, and also that information which is volunteered is not always accurate or complete; so some means of compulsion are essential to obtain what is needed....

The contention is earnestly made on behalf of the witness that this power of inquiry, if sustained, may be abusively and oppressively exerted. If this be so, it affords no ground for denying the power.... And it is a necessary deduction from the decisions in *Kilbourn v. Thompson* and re Chapman that a witness rightfully may refuse to answer where the bounds of the power are exceeded or the questions are not pertinent to the matter under inquiry.

We come now to the question whether it sufficiently appears that the purpose of which the witness's testimony was sought was to obtain information in aid of the legislative function. The court below answered the question in the negative, and put its decision largely on this ground, as is shown by the following excerpts from its opinion:

"It will be noted that in the second resolution the Senate has expressly avowed that the investigation is in aid of other action than legislation. Its purpose is to "obtain information necessary as a basis of such legislative and other action as the Senate may deem necessary and

proper." This indicates that the Senate is contemplating the taking of action other than legislative, as the outcome of the investigation; the spirit of hostility towards the then Attorney General which they breathe; that it was not avowed that legislative action of the Senate had been challenged; and that the avowal then was coupled with an avowal that other action had in view are calculated to create the impression that the idea of legislative action being in contemplation was an afterthought....

"That the Senate has in contemplation the possibility of taking action other than legislation as an outcome of the investigation, as thus expressly avowed, would seem of itself to invalidate the entire proceeding. But, whether so or not, the Senate's action is invalid and absolutely void, in that, in ordering and conducting the investigation, it is exercising the judicial function, and power to exercise that function, in such a case as we have here, has not been conferred upon it expressly or by fair implication. What it is proposing to do is to determine the guilt of the Attorney General of the shortcomings and wrongdoings set forth in the resolutions. It is "to hear, adjudge, and condemn." In so doing it is exercising the judicial function....

What the Senate is engaged in doing is not investigating the Attorney General's office; it is investigating the former Attorney General. What it has done is to put him on trial before it. In so doing it is exercising the judicial function. This it has no power to do."

We are of opinion that the court's ruling on this question was wrong, and that it sufficiently appears, when the proceedings are rightly interpreted, that the object of the investigation and of the effort to secure the witness's testimony was to obtain information for legislative purposes.

It is quite true that the resolution directing the investigation does not in terms avow that it is intended to be in aid of legislation; but it does show that the subject to be investigated was the administration of the Department of Justice—whether its functions were being properly discharged or were being neglected or misdirected, and particularly whether the Attorney General and his assistants were performing or neglecting their duties in respect of the institution and prosecution of proceedings to punish crimes and enforce appropriate remedies against the wrongdoers—specific instances of alleged neglect being recited. Plainly the subject was one on which legislation could be had and would be materially aided by the information which the investigation was calculated to elicit. This becomes manifest when it is reflected that the functions of the Department of Justice, the powers and duties of the Attorney General and the duties of his assistants, are all subject to regulation by congressional legislation, and that the department is maintained and its activities are carried on under such appropriations as in the judgment of Congress are needed from year to year.

The only legitimate object the Senate could have in ordering the investigation was to aid it in legislating; and we think the subject-matter was such that the presumption should be indulged that this was the real object. An express avowal of the object would have been better; but in view of the particular subject-matter was not indispensable....

We conclude that the investigation was ordered for a legitimate object; that the witness wrongfully refused to appear and testify before the committee and was lawfully attached; that the Senate is entitled to have him give testimony pertinent to the inquiry, either at its bar or before the committee; and that the district court erred in discharging him from custody under the attachment....

Final order reversed.

MR. JUSTICE STONE did not participate in the case.

J.W. HAMPTON, JR. & CO. v. U.S.
276 U.S. 624 (1928)

The petitioners, Hampton & Co., imported a load of barium dioxide into the Port of New York upon which the collector of customs assessed the dutiable rate of 6 cents per pound—a rate which was 2 cents more than that fixed by statute. The collector raised the rate of duty by virtue of a presidential proclamation issued under, and by the authority of, § 315 of title III of the Tariff Act of September 21, 1922. In this "flexible tariff provision," Congress gave the executive the power to investigate the manufacturing and trade practices of companies importing goods into the U.S.A. for purposes of assigning duties that would maintain a fair and competitive environment for American businesses.

The petitioners protested this assignment of a higher duty, and they requested a hearing before the U.S. Customs Court to determine the constitutionality of the statute. A majority of that court ruled the Act constitutional, and the petitioners subsequently appealed to the U.S. Court of Customs Appeals. The judgment was affirmed, and a writ of certiorari was granted by the Supreme Court.

[excerpts]

MR. CHIEF JUSTICE WILLIAM H. TAFT delivered the opinion of the court:

J.W. Hampton, Jr. & Company made an importation into New York of *barium dioxide* which the *collector of customs* as*sessed at the dutiable rate of 6 cents per pound.* This was *2 cents per pound more than that fixed by statute*, § 12, chap. 356, 42 Stat. at L. 858, 860, U.S. C. title 19, § 121. The rate was *raised by* the collector by *virtue* of the *proclamation of the President, 45 Treas. Dec. 669, T. D. 40, 216,* issued under, and by authority of § *315* of *title III.* of the *Tariff Act of September 21, 1922* (chap. 356, 42 Stat. at L. 858, 941, U.S.C. title 19, §154), which is the *so-called "flexible tariff provision."* Protest was made and an appeal was taken under § 514, Part 3, title IV. (chap. 356, 42 Stat. at L. 969, 970, U.S.C. title 19, § 398). The case came on for hearing before the United States customs court. *49 Treas. Dec. 593.* A majority held the *Act constitutional.* Thereafter the case was appealed to the United States court of customs appeals. On the 16th day of October, 1926, the *Attorney General certified* that in his opinion *the case was of*

such importance as to render expedient its review by this court.
Thereafter the judgment of the United States customs court was affirmed.
14 Ct. Cust. App. 350. On a petition to this court for certiorari, filed
May 10, 1927, the writ was granted June 6, 1927, 274 U.S. 735, 71 L.
ed. 1336, 47 Sup. Ct. Rep. 769. The pertinent parts of § *315 of title III.
of the Tariff Act* (chap. 356, 42 Stat. at L. 858, 941, U.S.C. title 19, §
154, 156) are as follows: Section 315 (a). That in order to regulate the
foreign commerce of the United States and to put into force and effect
the policy of the Congress by this act, intended, whenever the President,
upon investigation of the differences in costs of production of articles
wholly or in part the growth or product of the United States and of like
or similar articles wholly or in part the growth or product of competing
foreign countries, shall find it thereby shown that the duties fixed in this
Act do not equalize the said differences in costs of production in the
United States and the principal competing country he shall, by such
investigation, ascertain said differences and determine and proclaim the
changes in classifications or increases or decreases in any rate of duty
provided in this Act shown by said ascertained differences in such costs
of production necessary to equalize the same. Thirty days after the date
of such proclamations, such changes in classification shall take effect,
and such changes in classification shall take effect, and such increased or
decreased duties shall be levied, collected, and paid on such articles
when imported from any foreign country into the United States or into
any of its possessions (except the Philippine Islands, the Virgin Islands,
and the islands of Guam and Tutuila); Provided, That the total increase
or decrease of such rates of duty shall not exceed 50 per centum of the
rates specified in title I. of this act, or in any amendatory act....

(c). That in ascertaining the differences in costs of production, under
the provisions of subdivisions (a) and (b) of this section, the President,
in so far as he finds it practicable, shall take into consideration (1) the
differences in conditions [of] production, including wages, costs of
material, and other items in costs of production of such or similar
articles in the United States and in competing foreign countries; (2) the
differences in the wholesale selling prices of domestic and foreign
articles in the principal markets of the United States; (3) advantages
granted to a foreign producer by a foreign government, or by a person,
partnership, corporation, or association in a foreign country; and (4) any
other advantages or disadvantages in competition.

Investigations to assist the President in ascertaining differences in costs of production under this section shall be made by the United Sates Tariff Commission, and no proclamation shall be issued under this section until such investigation shall have been made. The commission shall give reasonable public notice of its hearings and shall give reasonable opportunity to parties interested to be present, to produce evidence, and to be heard. The commission is authorized to adopt such reasonable procedure, rules, and regulations as it may deem necessary.

The President, proceeding as herein, before provided for in proclaiming rates of duty, shall when he determines that it is shown that the differences in costs of production have changed or no longer exist which led to such proclamation, accordingly as so shown, modify or terminate the same. Nothing in this section shall be construed to authorize a transfer of an article from the dutiable list to the free list or from the free list to the dutiable list, nor a change in form of duty. Whenever it is provided in any paragraph of title I. of this act, that the duty or duties shall not exceed a specified ad valorem rate upon the articles provided for in such paragraph, no rate determined under the provision of this section upon such articles shall exceed the maximum ad valorem rate so specified.

The President issued his proclamation May 19, 1924. After reciting part of the foregoing from § 315, the proclamation continued as follows:

"Whereas, under and by virtue of said section of said act, the United States Tariff Commission has made an investigation to assist the President in ascertaining the differences in costs of production of and of all other facts and conditions enumerated in said section with respect to...*barium dioxide*,...

Whereas in the course of said investigation a hearing was held, of which *reasonable public notice* was given and at which parties interested were given a reasonable opportunity to be present, to produce evidence, and to be heard";

And whereas the President upon said investigation...has thereby found that the *principal competing country* is *Germany*, and that the duty fixed in said title and Act does not equalize the differences in sorts of production in the United States and in...Germany, and has ascertained and determined the increased rate of duty necessary to equalize the same.

Now; therefore, I, *Calvin Coolidge*, President of the United States of America, do hereby determine and proclaim that the increase in the rate of duty provided in said Act shown by said ascertained differences in said costs of production necessary to equalize the same is as follows:

An increase in said duty on barium dioxide (within the limit of total increase provided for in said Act from 4 cents per pound to 6 cents per pound.

In witness whereof, I have hereunto beset my hand and caused the seal of the United States to be affixed.

Done at the City of Washington this *ninetieth* day of May in the year of our Lord, *one thousand nine hundred and twenty-four,* and of the Independence of the United States of America the one hundred and forty-eighth.

Calvin Coolidge.

By the President: *Charles E. Hughes*, Secretary of State." [43 Stat. at L. 1951.]

The issue here is as to the constitutionality of § 315 upon which depends the authority for the proclamation of the President and for 2 of the 6 cents per pound duty collected from the petitioner. The contention of the taxpayers is twofold: First, they ague that the section is invalid in that it is a delegation to the President of the legislative power, which by Article 1, § 1 of the Constitution, is vested in Congress, the power being that declared in § 8 of Article 1, that the Congress shall have power to lay and collect taxes, duties, imposts, and excises. Their second objection is that, as § 315 was enacted with the avowed intent and for the purpose of protecting the industries of the United States, it is invalid because the Constitution gives power to lay such taxes only for revenue.

First. It seems clear what Congress intended by § 315. Its plan was to secure by law the imposition of customs duties on articles of imported merchandise which should equal the difference between the cost of producing in a foreign country the articles in question and laying them down for sale in the United States, so that the duties not only secure revenue by at the same time enable domestic producers to compete on terms of equality with foreign producers in the markets of the United States. It may be that it is difficult to fix with exactness this difference, but the difference which is sought in the statute is perfectly clear and perfectly intelligible. Because of the difficulty in practically determining what that difference is, Congress seems to have doubted that the information in its possession was such as to enable it to make the adjustment accurately, and also to have apprehended that with changing conditions the difference might vary in such a way that some readjustments would be necessary to give effect to the principle on which the statute proceeds. To avoid such difficulties, Congress adopted § 315 the method of describing with clearness what its policy and plan was and then authorizing a member of the executive branch to carry out its policy and plan and to find the changing difference from time to time and to make the adjustments necessary to conform the duties to the standard underlying that policy and plan. As it was a matter of great importance, it concluded to give by statute to the President, the chief of the executive branch, the function of determining the difference as it might vary. He was provided with a body of investigators who were to assist him in obtaining needed fact and ascertaining the facts justifying readjustments. There was no specific provision by which action by the President might be invoked under this act, but it was presumed that the President would through this body of advisers keep himself advised of the necessity for investigation or change and then would proceed to pursue his duties under the Act and reach such conclusion as he might find justified by the investigation, and proclaim the same if necessary.

The well-known maxim "delegata potestas non potest delegari," applicable to the common law, is well understood and has wider application in the construction of our Federal and state Constitutions than it has in private law. Our Federal Constitution and state Constitutions of this country divide the governmental power into three branches. This is not to say that the three branches are not co-ordinate parts of one government and that each in the field of its duties may not invoke the action of the two other branches in so far as the action invoked shall not be an assumption of the constitutional field of action of another branch. In determining what it may do in seeking assistance from another branch, the extent and character of that assistance must be fixed according to common sense and the inherent necessities of the governmental co-ordination.

The field of Congress involves all and many varieties of legislative action, and Congress has found it frequently necessary to use officers of the executive branch within defined limits, to secure the exact effect intended by its acts of legislation, by vesting discretion in such officers to make public regulations interpreting a statute and directing the details of its execution, even to the extent of providing of penalizing a breach of such regulations.

Congress may feel itself unable conveniently to determine exactly when its exercise of the legislative power should become effective, because dependent on future conditions, and it may leave the determination of such time to the decision of an executive, or, as often happens in matters of state legislation, it may be left to a popular vote of the residents of a district to be affected by the legislation. While in a sense one may say that such residents are exercising legislative power, it is not an exact statement, because the power has already been exercised legislatively by the body vested with that power under the Constitution, the condition of its legislation going into effect being made dependent by the legislature on the expression of the voters of a certain district.

Again, one of the great functions conferred on Congress by the Federal Constitution is the regulation of interstate commerce and rates to be exacted by interstate carriers for the passenger and merchandises traffic. The rates to be fixed are myriad. If Congress were to be required to fix every rate , it would be impossible to exercise the power at all. Therefore, common sense requires that i the fixing of such rates, Congress may provide a Commission, as it does, called the Interstate Commerce Commission, to fix those rates, after hearing evidence and argument concerning them from interested parties, all in accord with a general rule that Congress first lays down that rates shall be just and reasonable considering the service given and not discriminatory.

It is conceded by counsel that Congress may use executive officers in the application and enforcement of a policy declared in law by Congress and authorize such officers in the application of the congressional declaration to enforce it by regulation equivalent to law. But it is said that this never has been permitted to be done where Congress has exercised the power to levy taxes and fix customs duties. The authorities make no such distinction. The same principle that permits Congress to exercise its rate making power to in interstate commerce by declaring the rule which shall prevail in the legislative fixing of rates, and enables it to remit to a rate-making body created in accordance with its provisions the fixing of such rates, justifies a similar provision of the fixing of customs duties on imported merchandise. If Congress shall lay down by legislative action is not a forbidden delegation of legislative Act an intelligible principle to which the person or body authorized to fix such rates is directed to conform, such legislative action is not a forbidden delegation of legislative action is not a forbidden delegation of legislative power. If it is thought wise to vary the customs duties according to changing conditions of production at home and abroad, it may authorize the Chief Executive to carry out this purpose, with the advisory assistance of a Tariff Commission appointed under congressional authority. This conclusion is amply sustained by a case in which there was no advisory commission furnished the President-a case to which this court gave the fullest consideration nearly forty years ago. In *Marshall Field & Co. v. Clark*, 143 U.S. 649, the third section of the Act of October 1, 1890, contained this provision:

"That with a view to secure reciprocal trade with countries producing the following articles, and for this purpose, on and after the first day of January, eighteen hundred and ninety-two, whenever, and so often as the President shall be satisfied that the government of any country producing and exporting sugars, molasses, coffee, tea and hides, raw and uncured, or any of such articles, imposes duties or other exactions upon the agricultural or other products of the United States, which in view of the free introduction of such sugar, molasses, coffee, tea and hides into the United States he may deem to be reciprocally unequal and unreasonable, he shall have the power and it shall be his duty to suspend, by proclamation to that effect, the provisions of this Act relating to the free introduction of such country, for such times he shall deem just, and in such case and during such suspension duties shall be levied, collected, and paid upon sugar, molasses, coffee, tea and hides, the product of or exported from such designated country as follows, namely": [26 Stat. at L. 612, chap. 1244.]

Then followed certain rates of duty to be imposed. It was contended that this section delegated to the President both legislative and treaty-making powers and was unconstitutional. after an examination of all the authorities, the court said that while Congress could not delegate legislative power to the President, this Act did not in any way real sense invest the President with the power of legislation, because nothing involving the expediency or just operation of such legislation was left to the determination of the President; that the legislative power was exercised when Congress declared that the suspension should take effect upon a named contingency. What the President was required to do was merely in execution of the Act of Congress. It was not the making of law-making department to ascertain and declare the event upon which its expressed will was to take effect.

Second. The second objection to § 315 is that the declared plan of Congress, either expressly or by clear implication, formulates its rule to guide the President and his advisory Tariff Commission as one directed to a tariff system of protection that will avoid damaging competition to the country's industries by the importation of goods from other countries at too low a rate to equalize foreign an domestic competition the markets of the United States. It is contended that the only power of Congress i the levying of customs duties is to create revenue and that it is unconstitutional to frame the customs duties with any other view than that of revenue raising. It undoubtedly is true that during the political life of this country there has been much discussion between parties as to the wisdom of the *policy of protection* and we may go further and say as to its constitutionality, but o historian, whatever his view of the wisdom of the policy of protection, would contend that Congress since the first Revenue Act in 1789 has not assumed that it was within its power in making provision for the collection of revenue to put taxes upon importation's and to vary the subjects of such taxes or rates in an effort to encourage the growth of the industries of the nation by protecting home production against foreign competition. It is enough to point out that the second Act adopted by the Congress of the United States July 4, 1789 (chap. 2, 1 Stat. at L. 24), contained the following recital: "Sec. 1. Whereas it is necessary for the support of government, for the discharge of the debts of the United States, and the encouragement and protection of manufactures, that duties be laid on goods, wares and merchandises imported: "Be it enacted, etc."

In this first Congress sat many members of the Constitutional Convention of 1787. This court has repeatedly laid down the principle that a contemporaneous legislative exposition of the Constitution when the founders of our government and framers of our Constitution were actively participating in public affairs, long acquiesced in, fixes the construction to be given its provisions. The enactment and enforcement of a number of customs revenue laws drawn with a motive of maintaining a system of protection since the Revenue Law of 1789 are matters of history.

Whatever we may think of the wisdom of a protection policy, we can not hold it unconstitutional.

So long as the motive of Congress and the effect of its legislative action are to secure revenue for the benefit of the general government, the existence of other motives in the selection of the subjects of taxes cannot invalidate congressional action. As we said in the Child Labor Tax Case (*Bailey v. Drexel Furniture* Co.) 259 U. S. 20; "Taxes are occasionally imposed in the discretion of the legislature on proper subjects with the primary motive of obtaining revenue from them, and with the incidental motive of discouraging them by making their continuance onerous. They do not lose their character as taxes because of the incidental motive." And so here the fact that Congress declares that one of its motives in fixing the rates of duty is so to fix them that they shall encourage the industries of this country in the competition with producers in other countries in the sale of goods in this country can not invalidate a revenue Act so framed. Section 315 and its provisions are within the power of Congress. The judgment of the Court of Customs Appeals is affirmed.

HOME BUILDING & LOAN ASSOCIATION
v. BLAISDELL
290 U.S. 398 (1934)

During the Great Depression of the 1930's, it was common for banking, finance and trust companies to foreclose on the homes of those families whose mortgage payments were not being made. Mr. Blaisdell and his family experienced such a foreclosure. As a result, Blaisdell sought relief under the Minnesota Mortgage Moratorium Act of 1933 which temporarily extended the period of redemption of real property from foreclosure proceedings. A county court granted Blaisdell an extension and the Minnesota Supreme Court upheld that judgment and affirmed the validity of the statute. The Home Building Association moved the question for review by the U.S. Supreme Court.

[excerpts]

MR. CHIEF JUSTICE HUGHES delivered the opinion of the Court:

...The state court upheld the statute as an emergency measure. Although conceding that the obligations of the mortgage contract were impaired, the court decided that what it thus described as an impairment was, notwithstanding the contract clause of the Federal Constitution, within the police power of the State as that power was called into exercise by the public power of the State as that power was called into exercise by the public economic emergency which the legislature had found to exist. Attention is thus directed to the preamble and first section of the statute, which described the existing emergency in terms that were deemed to justify the temporary relief which the statute affords. The state court, declaring that it could not say that this legislative finding was without basis, supplemented that finding by its own statement of conditions of which it took judicial notice. The court said: "In addition to the weight to be given the determination of the legislature that an economic emergency exists which demands relief, the court must take notice of other considerations. The members of the legislature come from every community of the state and from all the walks of life. They are familiar with conditions generally in every calling, occupation, profession, and business in the state. Not only they, but the courts must be guided by what is common knowledge. It is common knowledge that in the last few years land values have shrunk enormously. Loans made a few years ago upon the basis of the then going values cannot possibly be replaced on the basis of present values. We all know that when this law was enacted the large financial companies, which had made it their business to invest in mortgages, had ceased to do so. No bank would directly or indirectly loan on real estate mortgages. Life-insurance companies, large investors in such mortgages, had even declared a moratorium as to the loan provisions of their policy contracts. The President had closed banks temporarily. The Congress, in addition to many extraordinary measures looking to the relief of the economic emergency, had passed an Act to supply funds whereby mortgagors may be able within a reasonable time to refinance their mortgages or redeem from sales where the redemption has not expired. With this knowledge the court cannot well hold that the legislature had no basis in fact for the conclusion that an economic emergency existed which called for the exercise of the police power to grant relief."

In determining whether the provision for this temporary and conditional relief exceeds the power of the State by reason of the clauses in the Federal Constitution are the obligations of contracts? What constitutes impairment of these obligations? What residuum of power is there still in the States in relation to the operation of contracts, to protect the vital interests of the community? Questions of this character, "of no small nicety and intricacy, have vexed the legislative halls, as well as the judicial tribunals, with an uncounted variety and frequency of litigation and speculation."

...Not only is the constitutional provision qualified by the measure of control which the State retains over remedial processes, but the state also continues to possess authority to safeguard the vital interests of its people. It does not matter that legislation appropriate to that end "has the result of modifying or abrogating contracts already in effect."... *Not only are existing laws read into contracts in order to fix obligations as between the parties, but the reservation of essential attributes of sovereign power is also read into contracts as a postulate of the legal order. The policy of protecting contracts against impairment presupposes the maintenance of a government by virtue of which contractual relations are worth while-a government which retains adequate authority to secure the peace and good order of society.* This principle of harmonizing the constitutional prohibition with the necessary residuum of state power has had progressive recognition in the decisions of this Court....

The legislature cannot "bargain away the public health or the public morals." Thus, the constitutional provision against the impairment of contracts was held not to be violated by an amendment of the state constitution which put an end to a lottery therefore authorized by the legislature. *Stone v. Mississippi*, 101 U.S. 814.... The lottery was a valid enterprise when established under express state authority, but the legislature in the public interest could put a stop to it. A similar rule has been applied to the control by the State of the sale of intoxicating liquors.... The States retain adequate power to protect the public health against the maintenance of nuisances despite insistence upon existing contracts.... Legislation to protect the public safety comes within the same category of reserved power.... This principle had recent and noteworthy application to the regulation of the use of public highways by common carriers and "contracts carriers," where the assertion of interference with existing contract rights has been without avail....

The argument is pressed that in the cases we have cited the obligation of contracts was affected only incidentally. This argument proceeds upon a misconception. The question is no whether the legislative action affects contracts incidentally, or directly or indirectly, but whether the legislation is addressed to a legitimate end and the measures taken are reasonable and appropriate to that end. Another argument, which comes more closely to the point, is that the state power may be addressed directly to the prevention of the enforcement of contracts only when these are of a sort which the legislature in its discretion may denounce as being in themselves hostile to public morals, or public health, safety, or welfare, or where the prohibition is merely of injurious practices; that interference with the enforcement of other and valid contracts according to appropriate legal procedure, although the interference is temporary and for a public purpose, is not permissible. This is but to contend that in the latter case the end is not legitimate in the view that it cannot be reconciled with a fair interpretation of the constitutional provision.

Undoubtedly, whatever is reserved of state power must be consistent with the fair intent of the constitutional limitation of that power. The reserved power cannot be construed so as to destroy the limitation, nor is the limitation to be construed in harmony with each other. This principle precludes a construction which would permit the State to adopt as its policy the repudiation of debts or the destruction of contracts or the denial of means to enforce them. But it does not follow that conditions may not arise in which a temporary restraint of enforcement may be consistent with the spirit and purpose of the constitutional provision and thus be found to be within the range of the reserved power of the State to protect the vital interest of the community. It cannot be maintained that the constitutional prohibition should be so construed as to prevent limited and temporary interpositions with respect to the enforcement of contracts if made necessary by a great public calamity such as fire, flood, or earthquake.... *The reservation of state power appropriate to such extraordinary conditions may be deemed to be as much a part of all contracts, as is the reservation of state power to protect the public interest in the other situations to which we have referred.* And if state power exists to give temporary relief from the enforcement of contracts in the presence of disasters due to *physical causes* such as fire, flood ,or earthquake, that power *cannot* be said to be nonexistent when the urgent public need demanding such relief is produced by other and *economic causes....*

It is manifest...that there has been a growing appreciation of public needs and of the necessity of finding ground for a rational compromise between individual right sand public welfare. The settlement and consequent contraction of the public domain, the pressure of a constantly increasing density of population, the interrelation of the activities of our people and the complexity of our economic interests, have inevitably led to an increased use of the organization of society in order to protect the very bases of individual opportunity. Where, in earlier days, it was thought that only the concerns of individuals or of classes were involved, and that those of the State itself were touched only remotely, it has later been found that the fundamental interests of the State are directly affected; and that the question is no longer merely that of one party to a contract as against another, but of the use of reasonable means to safeguard the economic structure upon which the good of all depends.

It is no answer to say that this public need was not apprehended a century ago, or to insist that what the provision of the Constitution meant to the vision of that day it must mean to the vision of our time. *If by the statement that what the Constitution meant at the time of its adoption it means today, it is intended to say that the great clauses of the Constitution must be confined to the interpretation which the framers, with the conditions and outlook of their time, would have placed upon them, the statement carrier its own refutation.* It was to guard against such a narrow conception that Chief Justice Marshall uttered the memorable warning-"We must never forget that it is a *constitution* we are expounding" (*McCulloch v. Maryland...*)—"a constitution intended to endure for ages to come, and consequently, to be adapted to the various *crises* of human affairs."... When we are dealing with the words of the Constitution, said this Court in *Missouri v. Holland,* "we must realize that they have called into life a being the development of which could not have been foreseen completely by the most gifted of its begetters.... The case before us must be considered in the light of our whole experience and not merely in that of what was said a hundred years ago."

Nor is it helpful to attempt to draw a fine distinction between the intended meaning of the words of the Constitution and their intended application. When we consider the contract clause and the decisions which have expounded it in harmony with the essential reserved power of the States to protest the security of their peoples, we find no warrant for the conclusion that the clause has been warped by these decisions from its proper significance or that the founders of our Government would have interpreted the clause differently had they had occasion to assume that responsibility in the conditions of the later day. The vast body of law which has been developed was unknown to the fathers, but it is believed to have preserved the essential content and the spirit of the Constitution. With a growing recognition of public needs and the relation of individual right to public security, the court has sought to prevent the perversion of the clause through its use as an instrument to throttle the capacity of the States to protect their fundamental interests. This development is a growth from the seeds which the fathers planted....

Applying the criteria established by our decision we conclude:

1. An emergency existed in Minnesota which furnished a proper occasion for the exercise of the reserved power of the State to protect the vital interests of the community. The declarations of the existence of this emergency by the legislature and by the Supreme Court of Minnesota cannot be regarded as a subterfuge or as lacking in adequate basis....

2. The legislation was addressed to a legitimate end, that is, the legislation was not for the mere advantage of particular individuals but of the protection of a basic interest of society.

3. In view of the nature of the contracts in question-mortgages of unquestionable validity -the relief afforded and justified by the emergen-

cy, in order not to contravene the constitutional provision, could only be of a character appropriate to that emergency and could be granted only upon reasonable conditions.

4. The conditions upon which the period of redemption is extended do not appear to be unreasonable. ....

5. The legislation is temporary in operation. It is limited to the exigency which called it forth....

We are of the opinion that the Minnesota statute as here applied does not violate the contract clause of the Federal Constitution. Whether the legislation is wise or unwise as a matter of policy is a question with which we are not concerned.

What has been said on that point is also applicable to the contention presented under the due process clause....

Nor do we think that the statute denies to the appellant the equal protection of the laws. The classification which the statute makes cannot be said to be an arbitrary one....

Judgment affirmed.

HUMPHREY'S EXECUTOR
v. UNITED STATES
295 U.S. 602 (1935)

As important as the Myers decision was for its time, it left unanswered the question of whether the Chief Executive has unlimited power of removal that extends to officials whose functions and responsibilities are not exclusively executive in nature. Most saliently, does the President have a free hand, unfettered by Congress, to remove members of independent regulatory boards and commissions whose functions are quasi-legislative and quasi-judicial? Mr. William Humphrey was nominated for membership on the Federal Trade Commission by President Herbert Hoover and he was confirmed by the U.S. Senate in 1931 for a term of seven years. On October 7, 1933, President Franklin Roosevelt removed Humphrey, a conservative Republican, from the Commission for purely political reasons. Four months later, Humphrey died; however, Mr. Rathbun, the executor of the former Commissioner's estate, brought suit against the government for his unpaid salary in the U.S. Court of Claims. After some deliberation, the Court of Claims certified the case to the U.S. Supreme Court:

[excerpts]

MR. JUSTICE SUTHERLAND delivered the opinion of the Court:

On July 25, 1933, President Roosevelt addressed a letter to the commissioner asking for his resignation, on the ground "that the aims and purposes of the Administration with respect to the work of the Commission can be carried out most effectively with personnel of my own selection," but disclaiming any reflection upon the commissioner personally or upon his services. The commissioner replied, asking time to consult his friends. After some further correspondence upon the subject, the President, on August 31, 1933, wrote the commissioner expressing the hope that the resignation would be forthcoming and saying: "You will, I know, realize that I do not feel that your mind and my mind go along together on either the policies or the administering of the Federal Trade Commission, and, frankly, I think it is best for the people of this country that I should have a full confidence."

The commissioner declined to resign, and on October 7, 1933, the President wrote him: "Effective as of this date, you are hereby removed from the office of Commissioner of the Federal Trade Commission."

Humphrey never acquiesced in this action, but continued thereafter to insist that he was still a member of the commission, entitled to perform its duties and receive the compensation provided by law at the rate of $10,000 per annum. Upon these and other facts set forth in the certificate, which we deem it unnecessary to recite.

In exercising this power the commission must issue a complaint stating its charges and giving notice of hearing upon a day to be fixed. A person, partnership, or corporation proceeded against is given the right to appear at the time and place fixed and show cause why an order to cease and desist should not be issued. There is provision for intervention by others interested. If the commission finds the method of competition is one prohibited by the act, it is directed to make a report in writing stating its findings as to the facts, and to issue and cause to be served a cease and desist order. If the order is disobeyed the commission may apply to the appropriate Circuit Court of Appeals for its enforcement. This party subject to the order may seek and obtain a review in the Circuit Court of Appeals in a manner provided by the act.

Section 6, among other things, gives the commission wide powers of investigation in respect of certain corporations subject to the act, and in respect of other matters, upon which it must report to Congress with recommendations. Many such investigations have been made, and some have served as the basis of congressional legislation.

Section 7 provides: "That in any suit in equity brought by or under the direction of the Attorney General, as provided in the anti-trust acts, the court may, upon the conclusion of the testimony therein, if it shall be then of opinion that the complaint is entitled to relief, refer said suit to the commission, as a master in chancery, to ascertain and report an appropriate form of decree therein. The commission shall proceed upon such notice to the parties and under such rules of procedure as the court may prescribe and upon the coming in of such report such exceptions may be filed and such proceedings had in relation thereto as upon the report of a master in other equity causes, but the court may adopt or reject such report, in whole or in part, and enter such decree as the nature of the case may in its judgment require."

First. The question first to be considered is whether, by the provisions of § 1 of the Federal Trade Commission Act already quoted, the President's power is limited to removal for the specific causes enumerated therein....

...The statute fixes a term of office in accordance with many precedents. The first commissioners appointed are to continue in office for terms of three, four, five, six, and seven years, respectively; and their successors are to be appointed for terms of seven years-any commissioner being subject to removal by the President for inefficiency, neglect of duty, or malfeasance in office. The words of the Act are definite and unambiguous.

The government says the phrase "continue in office" is of no legal significance, and, moreover, applies only to the first commissioners. We think it has significance. It may be that, literally, its application is restricted as suggested; but it, nevertheless, lends support to a view contrary to that of the government as to the meaning of the entire requirement in respect of tenure; for it is not easy to suppose that Congress intended to secure the first commissioners against removal except for the causes specified and deny like security to their successors. Putting this phrase aside, however, the fixing of a definite term subject to removal for cause, unless there be some countervailing provision or circumstance indicating the contrary, which here we are unable to find, is enough to establish the legislative intent that the term is not to be curtailed in the absence of such cause. But if the intention of Congress that no removal should be made during the specified term except for one or more of the enumerated causes were not clear upon the face of the statute, as we think it is, it would be made clear by a consideration of the character of the commission and the legislative history which accompanied and preceded the passage of the act.

The commission is to be nonpartisan; and it must, from the very nature of its duties, act with entire impartiality. It is charged with the enforcement of no policy except the policy of the law. Its duties are neither political nor executive, but predominantly quasi-judicial and quasi-legislative. Like the Interstate Commerce Commission, its members are called upon to exercise the trained judgment of a body of experts "appointed by law and informed by experience."...

The legislative reports in both houses of Congress clearly reflect the view that a fixed term was necessary to the effective and fair administration of the law....

Thus, the language of the act, the legislative reports and the general purposes of the legislation as reflected by the debates, all combine to demonstrate the Congressional intent to create a body of experts who shall gain experience by length of service—a body which shall be independent of Executive authority, *except in its selection*, and free to exercise its judgment without the leave or hindrance of any other official or any department of the government. To the accomplishment of these purposes it is clear that Congress was of opinion that length and certainty of tenure would vitally contribute. And to hold that, nevertheless, the members of the commission continue in office at the mere will of the President, might be to thwart, in large measure, the very ends which Congress sought to realize by definitely fixing the term of office.

We conclude that the intent of the Act is to limit the executive power of removal to the causes enumerated, the existence of none of which is claimed here.

The office of a postmaster is so essentially unlike the office now involved that the decision in the *Myers case* cannot be accepted as controlling our decision here. A postmaster is an executive officer restricted to the performance of executive functions. He is charged with no duty at all related to either the legislative or judicial power. The actual decision in the *Myers case* finds support in the theory that such an officer is merely one of the units in the executive department and hence inherently subject to the exclusive and illimitable power of removal by the chief executive, whose subordinate and aide he is. Putting aside dicta, which may be followed if sufficiently persuasive but which are not controlling, the necessary reach of the decision goes far enough to include all purely executive officers. It goes no farther; much less does it include an officer who occupies no place in the executive department and who exercises no part of the executive power vested by the Constitution in the President.

The Federal Trade Commission is an administrative body created by Congress to carry into effect legislative policies embodied in the statute, in accordance with the legislative standard therein prescribed, and to perform other specified duties as a legislative or as a judicial aid. Such a body cannot in any proper sense be characterized as an arm or an eye of the executive. Its duties are performed without executive leave and, in the contemplation of the statute in respect of "unfair methods of competition"—that is to say in filling in and administering the details embodied by the general standard-the commission acts in part quasi-legislatively and in part quasi-judicially. In making investigations and reports thereon for the information of Congress under § 6, in aid of the legislative power it acts as a legislative agency. Under § 7 which authorizes the commission to act as a master in chancery under rules prescribed by the court, it acts as an agency of the judiciary. To the extent that it exercises any executive power in the constitutional sense-it does so in the discharge and effectuation of its quasi-legislative or quasi-judicial powers, or as an agency of the legislative or judicial departments of the government.

If Congress is without authority to prescribe causes for removal of members of the Trade Commission and limit executive power of removal accordingly, that power at once becomes practically all inclusive in respect of civil officers, with the exception of the judiciary provided for by the Constitution.

We think it plain under the Constitution that illimitable power of removal is not possessed by the President in respect of officers of the character of those just named. The authority of Congress, in creating quasi-legislative or quasi-judicial agencies, to require them to act in discharge of their duties independently of executive control, cannot well be doubted and that authority includes, as an appropriate incident, power to fix the period during which they shall continue, and to forbid their removal except for cause in the meantime. For it is quite evident that one who holds his office only during the pleasure of another cannot be depended upon to maintain an attitude of independence against the latter's will.

The fundamental necessity of maintaining each of the three general departments of government entirely free from the control or coercive influence, direct or indirect, of either of the others, has often been stressed and is hardly open to serious question. So much is implied in the very fact of the separation of the powers of these departments by their Constitution, and in the rule which recognizes their essential co-equality. The sound application of a principle that makes one master in his own house precludes him from imposing his control in the house of another who is master there....

The power of removal here claimed for the President falls within this principle, since its coercive influence threatens the independence of a commission, which is not only wholly disconnected from the executive department, but which, as already fully appears, was created by Congress as a means of carrying into operation legislative and judicial powers, and as an agency of the legislative and judicial department.

The result of what we now have said is this: Whether the power of the President to remove an officer shall prevail over the authority of Congress to condition the power by fixing a definite term and precluding a removal except for cause will depend upon the character of the office. The *Myers* decision, affirming the power of the President alone to make the removal, is confined to purely executive officers. And as to officers of the kind here under consideration, we hold that no removal can be made during the prescribed term for which the officer is appointed, except for one or more of the causes named in the applicable statute.

To the extent that, between the decision in the Myers case, which sustains the unrestrictable power of the President to remove purely executive officers, and our present decision that such power does not extend to an office such as that here involved, there shall remain a field of doubt, we leave such cases as may fall within it for future consideration and determination as they may arise.

In accordance with the foregoing the questions submitted are answered.

Question No. 1, Yes.
Question No. 2, Yes.

Notes

1.   182 U.S. 1 (1901).
2.   See *Arven v. United States* 245 U.S. 366 (1918).
3.   246 U.S. 297 (1918)
4.   252 U.S. 416 (1920).
5.   Ibid., 419.
6.   Ibid., 420-421.
7.   354 U.S. 1 (1957).
8.   276 U.S. 394 (1928).
9.   Ibid., 402.
10.   Ibid., 404.
11.   299 U.S. 304 (1936).

12. 357 U.S. 349 (1958).
13. See, *Watkins v. United States*, 354 U.S. 178 (1957).
14. *Home Building & Loan Association v. Blaisdell*, 290 U.S. 398 (1934).
15. Ibid., p. 400.
16. See Bland, *Constitutional Law in the United States* (Austin & Winfield, 1993) pp. 26-27.

Chapter Five:
The Roosevelt Court and the Rise of Presidential Supremacy 1936-1945

In 1936, a dramatic transformation was brought about in judicial philosophy with respect to the conduct of foreign policy. The Supreme Court of the United States anointed the President as the "sole organ of foreign affairs." As David Adler has properly argued, "There can be little doubt that the opinion in *United States v. Curtiss-Wright Export Corp.* has been the Court's principal contribution to the growth of executive power over foreign affairs.... its spirit, indeed its talismanic aura, has provided a common thread in a pattern of cases that have exalted presidential power *above* constitutional norms."[1] An amazing aspect of this development was that the same conservative "Nine Old Men"—President Franklin Roosevelt's nemeses on the matter of New Deal *domestic* legislation—granted this expansive authority to the presidential office in *foreign* policy.[2] How did the Court knock into a "cocked hat," the 125 years old presidential-congressional partnership in formulating of American foreign policy, particularly since the *Curtiss-Wright* case involved the *narrow* question of whether Congress could, by a joint resolution, allow the President the authority to prohibit the sale of arms to Paraguay and Bolivia which were then fighting in the Chaco?[3]

Although scholars can cite a number of factors implicated in the decision, *two* are of primary significance: First, the question of a congressional delegation of purely legislative power to the President, which the *same* Court had held unconstitutional in domestic affairs.[4] Second, the language and the sweep of Justice George Sutherland's majority opinion, a great deal of which was merely *obiter dicta!*

On its face, *Curtiss-Wright* appeared to be an "open and shut" case, *not* demanding of a sweeping opinion from the Supreme Court of the United States. The latter company conspired to sell fifteen machine guns to Bolivia in violation of the Joint Resolution of Congress approved May 28, 1934 and the terms of a proclamation issued the same day by President Franklin Roosevelt pursuant to authority conferred on him by section one. *Curtiss-Wright* insisted that the Justice Sutherland, speaking for a seven man majority, assumed (but did *not* decide) that had the resolution applied "solely to internal affairs" it would be invalid.[5] He maintained:

> The two classes of power are different, both in respect of their *origin* and their *nature*. The broad statement that the federal government can exercise no powers except those specifically enumerated in the Constitution, and such implied powers are necessary and proper to carry into effect the enumerated powers, is categorically true *only* in respect of our *internal* affairs. [emphasis added][6]

But *was* this a correct, or even a consistent, statement on the part of this conservative Associate Justice? *Does* the talisman of "foreign affairs" immunize the President from the specific terms of Article II, section 2? *May* the President arrange treaties and translate them into law without the "advice and consent" of the Senate? *May* he appoint "officers of the United States" without Senate approval? More to the point, *may* the President of the United States commit American troops to an undeclared war in clear violation of the command of Article I? All of these questions are systemic to Sutherland's assumption and unfortunately, in spirit at least, the answers to them are positive! As we shall see, Congress may by legislative action, or inaction, grant nearly *any* legislative authority, with the absolution of the Supreme Court, *if* it is a matter affecting foreign policy. Even so, Sutherland further expanded the presidential prerogative:

> It is important to bear in mind that we are here dealing not alone with an authority vested in the President by an exertion of legislative power, but with such authority plus the very delicate, *plenary* and *exclusive* power of the President as the sole organ of the federal government in the field of international relations—a power which does *not* require as a basis for its exercise an Act of Congress, but which, of course, like every other governmental power, must be in subordination to the *applicable* provisions of the Constitution. [emphases added][7]

This olympian pronouncement immediately gives rise to additional important questions: what "plenary" and "exclusive" power does the Constitution yield to the President in the external policy of the nation? If such powers are indeed "plenary," are there any "applicable" provisions of that document that *limit* the President in this "exclusive" domain? Sutherland avoids these kinds of questions *entirely* and instead cites a litany of presidential indulgences: his need for "confidential sources of information"; support buttressed by a history of "legislative enactments" and "legislative practice"; sustenance from a "steady stream" of court precedents; and, of all things, the President's "inherited sovereignty from the British crown." The Associate Justice was reduced to vastly stretching his dicta to justify his long-held view that the presidential powers in this regard do not depend upon any direct grant of authority to the national government stemming from the Constitution.[8] It was such usage of *Sutherland's* imagination, rather than constitutional interpretation, that forces our attention on the second factor in the case: the "unhappy legacy" of his opinion having been relied upon, ever since, as the rule of *law*. By not adhering to the delegation question, George Sutherland's personal views unfortunately have placed this almost *unrestricted* power in the hands of the President.[9]

The Associate Justice's logic was, at best, *faulty!* From the outset, Justice Sutherland argued that "since the states severally never possessed international powers," that the authority to conduct foreign policy was obviously "transmitted to the United States from some other source."[10] Therefore, he concluded:

> As a result of the separation from Great Britain [in 1783] by
> the colonies acting as a unit, the powers of external sovereignty
> passed from the crown not to the colonies severally, but to the
> colonies in their collective and corporate capacity as the United
> States of America.

Sutherland's views on the subject were heavily influenced by Justice
Paterson's opinion in *Penhallow* (1795).[11] However, it is more important to note that this perception of external sovereignty is plainly *untrue!*
As the Articles of Confederation, ratified in 1781, stated clearly, "Each
state retains its sovereignty, freedom and independence and every power
[not] expressly delegated to the United States." Therefore, the "states, in
their highest sovereign capacity," yielded reluctantly, certain powers to
the Continental Congress including Article IX which contained the war
and treaty powers.[12] Students of American constitutionalism may well
agree with Professor Raoul Berger's contention that this grant of
authority "*alone* undermines Sutherland's central premise that these
powers were derived from 'some other source' than the several
states."[13] Even if one acceded to Sutherland's views on the subject, he
failed to explain *why* the power of external sovereignty was given to the
President. Was it the logical branch in which to vest such unbridled
authority?[14]

Professor Adler goes so far as to argue that "Sutherland was plainly
in error in his contention that the conduct of foreign policy is not
restricted by the Constitution" and he cites James Madison's The
Federalist #45: "the powers delegated by the proposed Constitution are
few and *defined...* [they] will be exercised principally on external objects
as war, place, negotiation and foreign commerce."[15] But even Adler is
partially *incorrect*, since Sutherland said, *supra*, that this power, like
other governmental powers, "*must* be in subordination to the applicable
provisions of the Constitution." The Associate Justice well deserves
legitimate criticism, but not on this point. Sutherland did, however, make
the following assertion:

> ...the investment of the federal government with the powers
> of external sovereignty did *not depend* on the *affirmative* grants
> of the Constitution. The powers to declare and wage war, to
> conclude peace, to make treaties, to maintain diplomatic

relations with other sovereignties, if they had never been mentioned in the Constitution, *would have* vested in the federal government as necessary concomitants of nationality [emphases added].[16]

No less a constitutional authority than Edward S. Corwin of Princeton strongly supported this line of argumentation by saying,

...that the Constitution, instead of being the *immediate* source of the external powers of the national government, is only their *mediate* source, confers them simply in consequence of having established a nation truly sovereign in relation to other nations. In other words, the power... while susceptible of limitation by the Constitution when the restrictions that it imposes on all powers apply, is an *inherent* power, *one that owes its existence to the fact that the American People are a sovereign entity at international law* [Corwin's emphasis].[17]

Nevertheless, most of Adler's criticisms are valid and no list of justifications—confidentiality, legislative practice, judicial precedent, and inherited sovereignty—can justify Sutherland's conclusion that the President *alone* is constitutionally responsible for the formulation *and* conduct of foreign policy. As we have witnessed, the intentions of the Framers, our constitutional history and judicial precedent *refute* this contention.

Finally, on the matter of an illegal congressional delegation, Mr. Justice Sutherland, who referred to such decisions as *Brig Aurora* and *Field v. Clark*, hinted that there were in existence no set limitations on what Congress could delegate to the President in this regard. He pointed out that many "acts or joint resolutions of Congress...either leave the exercise of the power to his *unrestricted* judgment or provide a standard far more general than that which has always been considered requisite with regard to domestic affairs."[18] Inherent in this reasoning is the suggestion that congressional inaction or "silence" would be translated into acquiescence; the President could under such circumstances exercise his unfettered judgment in foreign policy matters. If this be true, then we may conclude that the *only* possible road block to presidential mischief in foreign affairs would be a clear, *unmistakable restriction* or prohibition as expressed by Congress or in the Constitution itself. Thirty-seven years later, after every President from Franklin Roosevelt to Richard Nixon had relied on the Marshall-Sutherland "sole organ" concept, in one form or another, Congress finally attempted such "road blocks" and enacted the War Power Resolution—a law we shall examine later in Volume II [forthcoming].

With the advent of war in Europe, the Court continued to expand the presidential prerogative in foreign affairs and during the term following *Curtiss Wright*, it handed down a significant decision concerning executive agreements. *United States v. Belmont* was based on the following facts: In 1918, the government of the Soviet Union dissolved, terminated, and liquidated the Petrograd Metal Works and appropriated all of its assets "wherever situated" including the Belmont bank in New York.[19] Later, under the Litvinov Assignment signed on November 16, 1933, the United States, in the person of President Franklin Roosevelt, recognized the Soviet Union and, in turn, the Soviet government agreed to take no steps to enforce claims against American nationals. All such claims were released and were assigned to the United States; however, the Belmont bank refused to comply with the government's demand for the assets. The controversy centered on the fact that the Litvinov arrangement was an executive agreement between the President and the Foreign Minister that had *not* been approved by the Senate. Speaking for six members of the Court, Justice Sutherland defended the President's action:[20]

The recognition, establishment of diplomatic relations the assignment, and agreements with respect thereto, were all parts of one transaction resulting in an international compact between the two governments. That the negotiations...were within the competence of the President may not be doubted. Governmental power over internal affairs is distributed between the national government and the several states. Governmental power over external affairs is *not* distributed, but is vested *exclusively* in the national government.

At this point, the Associate Justice went out of his way to, in effect, to reaffirm his dicta in *Curtiss-Wright*:

And in respect of what was done here, the Executive had
authority to speak as the *sole organ* of that government. The
assignment and the agreement...did *not*, as in the case of
treaties, as that term is used in the treaty making clause of the
Constitution (Art.II, section 2), require the advice and consent
of the Senate [emphasis added].[21]

In distinguishing between a treaty and an executive agreement,
Sutherland cited *Altman R. Co. v. United States*, 224 US 583 (1912)
which was based on section 3 of the Tariff Act of 1897; it allowed the
President to make commercial agreements with other nations in certain
cases. Although this may not be a treaty requiring ratification by the
Senate, it *was* a compact negotiated and proclaimed under the authority
of the President, and as such it was a "treaty" within the meaning of the
Circuit Court of Appeals Act"[22] The principle established by *Belmont*
was to be an important factor in American diplomatic relations during
World War II.

President Roosevelt relied heavily on the use of executive agreements with other countries, thus effectively bypassing the Senate. (Since
the end of the Second World War, Presidents have increased the use of
such agreements on an unparalleled scale; in 1988 alone, for example,
well over 400 executive agreements were signed by President Reagan.)[23]

In the first of six significant cases affecting foreign policy during
World War II, the Court, with Sutherland having departed in 1938,
reaffirmed *Belmont* in *United States v. Pink* (1942).[24] The facts of the
case were essentially the same as its predecessor except that the company
involved was the New York branch of the First Russian Insurance Co.
The majority opinion was given by the youngest and least experienced
Court member, Associate Justice William O. Douglas, who without any
apparent hesitation, embraced the "sole organ" concept of Sutherland.[25]
On the sweeping authority of the President to recognize foreign
governments, Douglas pointed out that,

The powers of the President in the conduct of foreign relations
included the power, without the consent of the Senate, to
determine the public policy of the United States with respect to
the Russian nationalization decrees.... That authority is not

limited to a determination of the government to be recognized. It includes the power to determine the policy, which is to govern the question of recognition. Objections to the underlying policy as well as objections to recognition, are to be addressed to the political departments and not to the courts.... Power to remove such obstacles to full recognition as settlement of claims of our nationals certainly is a modest implied power of the President who is the "sole organ of the federal government in the field of international relations."[26]

In *Pink*, what was once George Sutherland's considered opinion had now become established legal precedent. Its influence was to have an *overwhelming* effect on the members of the Supreme Court for years to come. Citing *Hines v. Davidowitz*, 312 U.S. 52 (1941), Justice Douglas dismissed any state claims with respect to confiscation:[27]

Here, we are dealing with an exclusive federal function. If state laws and policies did not yield before the exercise of the external powers of the United States then our foreign policy might be thwarted. These are delicate matters. If state action could defeat or alter our foreign policy serious consequences might ensue. The motion as a whole would be held to answer if a state created difficulties with a foreign power.[28]

As the Court was concerned, the states had no choice but to accept and enforce federal (now presidential) sovereignty as exercised in either a treaty *or* an *executive agreement*; it made no legal difference to the Court *which* of the devices was employed by the President.

In a number of the remaining cases decided by the Court during the war, questions concerning the President's almost unlimited powers in conducting wartime policy were brought to the forefront. On June 17, 1942, four German-trained saboteurs came ashore at night in Ponte Vedra Beach, Florida, carrying with them numerous fuses and explosives, as well as incendiary and timing devices. They proceeded to various points in the United States with the intention of destroying war industries and facilities. Four other German saboteurs had landed on Amagansett Beach in Long Island, New York, four days earlier. Within days, all of the saboteurs were arrested in New York and Chicago by

FBI agents. On July 2, President Roosevelt, as Commander in Chief of the Army and Navy, appointed a military commission to try them for offenses against the law of war and the Articles of War. He also issued a proclamation which declared:

> All persons who are subjects, citizens or residents of any nation at war with the United States...and who during time of war enter or attempt to enter the United States... through coastal or boundary defenses and are charged with committing or attempting or preparing to commit sabotage, espionage, hostile or warlike acts, or violations of the law of war and [are subject] to the jurisdiction of military tribunals.[29]

Both the order and the proclamation were challenged by the German agents on the grounds that the civil courts were open and functioning, and that the President had no statutory or constitutional authority to require trial by military tribunal. Called into a special term by Chief Justice Stone, the members of the Supreme Court convened on Wednesday, July 29, to consider the defendants' applications in *United States ex rel. Quirin et al. v. Cox, Provost Marshal*.[30] Noting that Congress had enacted the Articles, the Chief Justice stated:

> The Constitution thus invests the President, as Commander in Chief, with the power to wage war which Congress has declared, and to carry into effect all law passed by Congress for the conduct of the war...and all laws defining and punishing offenses against the law of nations....[31]

The Chief Justice was careful to point out that the President's conduct was authorized by Congress:

> By his order creating the present Commission, he has undertaken to exercise the authority conferred upon him by Congress, and also such authority as the Constitution itself gives the Commander in Chief, to direct the performance of those functions which may constitutionally be performed by the military arm of the nation in time of war.[32]

Against the claim by the agents, including one who possessed United States citizenship, that their Fifth and Sixth Amendment rights were being violated by a military trial, Harlen F. Stone retorted:

By universal agreement and practice, the law of war draws a distinction between the armed forces and the peaceful populations of belligerent nations and also between those who are lawful and unlawful combatants...an enemy combatant who without uniform comes secretly through the lines for the purpose of waging war by destruction of life or property, are familiar examples of belligerents who are generally deemed not to be entitled to the status of prisoners of war, but to be offenders against the law of war subject to trial and punishment by military tribunals.[33]

On the matter of citizenship, the Chief Justice concluded:

Citizenship in the United States of an enemy belligerent does not relieve him from the consequences of a belligerency which is unlawful because in violation of the law of war. Citizens who associate themselves with the military arm of the enemy government, and with its aid, guidance and direction enter this country bent on hostile acts, are enemy belligerents within the meaning of the Hague Convention and the law of war.[34]

The next four decisions were directly related to acts of Congress and executive orders issued by the President which imposed curfew, relocation and other military restrictions upon Japanese residents on the West Coast and Hawaii during the period between 1942 and 1946. Significantly, the Court in each of these decisions resorted to the traditional concept of *mutual cooperation* between the President and Congress as it had done on previous occasions of declared war. On February 19, 1942, President Franklin Roosevelt issued Executive Order 9066 which authorized the Secretary of War and the military commander under his command to promulgate regulations prescribing military areas on the West Coast of the United States off limits to persons of Japanese ancestry—citizen and non citizen. In all, military commanders were to take "every possible protection" against espionage and sabotage to national-defense material, premises and utilities, as so ordered by the Commander in Chief of the Army and Navy.[35] Given the fear of imminent Japanese invasion of the West Coast, Congress passed the War Act of March 21, which clearly authorized and ratified the action taken by the President in his executive order. Three days later, Lt. General J.L. DeWitt, Military Commander of the Western Defense Command, comprising the Pacific Coast States among others, issued a regulation imposing a curfew on "all alien Germans, all alien Italians and all persons of Japanese ancestry."[36]

Gordon K. Hirabayashi, an American citizen and resident of the State of Washington, refused to comply with the curfew order on the grounds that the military commander's order was an exercise of an unconstitutional delegation by Congress of its legislative power and that it discriminated against citizens of Japanese ancestry, and those of other ancestries, in violation of the Fifth Amendment. In a case certified to the Supreme Court, Chief Justice Stone rejected the plaintiffs contentions.[37] Speaking for the majority, Stone's words rang of an earlier period in judicial history:

> We have no occasion to consider whether the President, acting alone, could lawfully have made the curfew order in question or have authorized others to make it, for the President's action has the support of an Act of Congress, and we are immediately concerned with the question whether it is within the constitutional power of the national government, through *joint action* of Congress and the Executive to impose this restriction as an emergency war measure [emphasis added][38]

The Chief Justice noted that the Constitution grants to the political branches the power to wage war in all of its "vicissitudes and conditions," and therefore:

> ...it has necessarily given them wide scope for the exercise of judgment and discretion in determining the nature and extent of the threatened injury or danger and in the selection of the means for resisting it...it is not for any court to sit in review of the wisdom of their action or substitute its judgment for theirs.[39]

Concerning Hirabayashi's claim of racial discrimination, Stone pointed out that since the attack on Pearl Harbor the attachment of Japanese residents to their ancestral homeland was "a matter of grave concern" because the Japanese, he continued, "...have in large measure *prevented* their assimilation as an integral part of the white population." At this point, Chief Justice Stone referred to footnote #4 which, in fact, contained nothing less than a recitation of legal "discriminations" against Japanese residents of the United States. These included federal legislation denying to the Japanese, American citizenship by (8 USCA section 703), state laws denying to Japanese aliens the privilege of owning land, and the intermarriage of persons of the aforementioned race with Caucasians.[40] Given these circumstances, he concluded:

> We cannot say that the war-making branches of the Government did not have grounds believing that in a critical hour such persons could not readily isolated and separately dealt with, and constituted a menace to the national defense and safety, which demanded that prompt and adequate measures be taken to guard against it.[41]

Associate Justices William O. Douglas and Wiley Rutledge concurred. Frank Murphy also concurred, but warned:

> ...[Japanese-Americans'] status as citizens, though subject to requirements of national security and military necessity, should at all times be accorded the fullest consideration and respect. When the danger is past, the restrictions imposed on them should be promptly removed and their freedom of action fully restored.[42]

The most infamous and well-documented case to reach the Court during the Second World War was *Korematsu v. United States*, 323 US 214 (1944). Fred T. Korematsu, an American citizen residing in San Leandro, California, charged that the exclusion orders were beyond the war powers of Congress, the President and the military authorities. While upholding the *Hirabayashi* decision, Justice Hugo Black, who delivered the opinion, separated his reasoning from that of Chief Justice Stone represented in footnote #4:

It should be noted, to begin with, that all legal restrictions which curtail the civil rights of a single racial group are immediately suspect...courts must subject them to the most rigid scrutiny. Pressing public necessity may sometimes justify the existence of such restrictions; racial antagonism never can.[43]

Only the "gravest imminent danger to the public safety," argued the Associate Justice, could justify exclusion from the threatened area. Additionally, it was "impossible" for the military authorities to immediately segregate "the disloyal from the loyal."[44] Justice Black proceeded:

Citizenship has its responsibilities as well as its privileges, and in time of war the burden is always heavier. Compulsory exclusion of large groups of citizens from their homes...is inconsistent with our basic governmental institutions. But when, under conditions of modern warfare, our shores are threatened by hostile forces, the power to protect must be commensurate with the threatened danger.[45]

Upholding the exclusion order at "the time it was made and when the petitions violated it," Black angrily responded to those Justices who dissented on the grounds of racial discrimination:

To cast this case into outlines of racial prejudice, without reference to the real military dangers which were presented, merely confuses the issue. Korematsu was not excluded... because of hostility to him or his race. He was excluded because we are at war with the Japanese Empire, because the properly constituted military authorities feared an invasion of our West Coast and felt constrained to take proper security... because Congress reposing its confidence in this time of war in our military leaders—as inevitably it must—determined that they should have the power to do just this....We cannot—by availing ourselves of the calm perspective of hindsight—now say that at that time these actions were unjustified.[46]

It is not insignificant that Hugo Black, always suspicious of excessive presidential discretion as seen in the above quotation, acknowledged the primacy of Congress under the war powers *without* also referring to the President. As to the other participants, Justice Felix Frankfurter concurred adhering to the view that "within their sphere, military authorities are no more outside the bounds of obedience to the Constitution than are judges within theirs."[47]

In dissent, Associate Justice Owen Roberts objected to Korematsu's conviction because he "according to the uncontradicted evidence, is a loyal citizen of the nation."[48] (The question of individual loyalty would come back to haunt the Court's majority in the next case). Finally, in a more vigorous dissent most often cited by liberal constitutional commentators, Associate Justice Frank Murphy argued:

> Such exclusion goes over "the very brink of constitutional power" and falls into the ugly abyss of *racism*.... Being an obvious racial discrimination, the order deprives all those within its scope of the equal protection of the laws as guaranteed by the Fifth Amendment... [and] also deprives them of all their constitutional rights to procedural due process.[49]

Many contemporary civil libertarians rank *Korematsu* second only to *Dred Scott* (1857) and *Plessy* (1896) as the worst cases adjudicated in the history of the Supreme Court of the United States.[50] (The author would certainly include *Curtiss-Wright* in such a list.) In 1988, Congress motivated by sentiments of past guilt enacted a law, signed by President Ronald Reagan, that provided a $20,000,000 compensation to the nearly 60,000 surviving Japanese internees.

To supplement Executive Order 9066, President Roosevelt promulgated Order 9012 on March 18, 1942, which created the War Relocation Authority, a principal function of which was to segregate the loyal from the disloyal evacuees.[51] On May 7, General DeWitt issued Civilian Exclusion Order No. 52 which ordered that "all persons of Japanese ancestry, both alien and non-alien" be excluded from Sacramento, California. One resident so affected was Mitsuyi Endo, an American citizen who was in the Tule Lake Relocation Center on June 19. She was later transferred from California to the Central Utah Center at Topaz, Utah. Months later, Miss Endo filed a petition for a writ of habeas corpus in the United States District Court alleging that she is "a loyal and law-abiding citizen...that no charge has been made against her... [and] that she is being unlawfully detained...under arms and held there against her will."[52] The Court for the Northern District of California denied the writ and the U.S. Circuit Court of Appeals (Ninth Circuit) certified the case to the Supreme Court. Citing the *Curtiss-Wright* decision, *inter alia*, Associate Justice Douglas, who read the opinion, agreed that:

> *Broad* powers frequently granted to the President or other executive offices by Congress so that they may deal with the *exigencies* of wartime have been sustained. And the Constitution when it committed to the Executive and to Congress the exercise of the *war power* necessarily gave them wide scope for the exercise of judgement and discretion so that war might be waged effectively and successfully. [emphases added].[53]

Justice Douglas' reliance on *Curtiss-Wright* to justify the kind of sweeping power granted to President Franklin Roosevelt by the congressional enactments in this case, clearly *betrays* the degree of potential *danger* to personal liberty *inherent* in the 1936 decision. In no way did the circumstances nor the environment, politically or militarily, at the time of *Curtiss-Wright* resemble either *Korematsu* or *Endo*; the United States was *not* at war *nor* did government officials fear an imminent invasion by a foreign enemy. Justice Sutherland, unfortunately, could not have made such a claim. However, Douglas did call attention to the fact that the Constitution "is as specific in its enumeration of many of the civil rights of the individual as it is in the enumeration of the powers of his government," by citing the Fifth and Sixth Amendments.[54] Therefore, in approaching an executive order or congressional statute during wartime, the Court:

> ...has quite consistently given a narrower scope for the operation of the presumption of constitutionality when legislation appeared on its face to violate a specific prohibition of the Constitution. We have likewise favored that interpretation of legislation which gives it the greater chance of surviving the test of constitutionality... [and] that the law makers intended to

place no greater restraint on the citizen than was clearly an
unmistakenly indicated by the language they used.[55]

Holding that Miss Endo was entitled to an unconditional release by
the War Relocation Authority, thus creating an exception to the rule of
Korematsu, the Associate Justice declared:

> A citizen who is concededly loyal presents no problem of
> espionage or sabotage. Loyalty is a matter of the heart and
> mind, not of race, creed, or color. He who is loyal is by
> definition not a spy or a saboteur. When the power to detain is
> derived from the power to protect the war effort against
> espionage and sabotage, detention which has no relationship to
> that objective is unauthorized.[56]

Exactly how does a detained *citizen* prove his/her loyalty? What
documentation will *satisfy* the government? Are personal references from
neighbors, employers or the clergy sufficient? To these questions,
Douglas provided *no* answers! Justices Murphy and Roberts wrote
separate concurring opinions in a case that was to have an almost
negligible impact on the detention of most Japanese Americans until the
conclusion of the war.

Unlike the World War I period (1917-1919), the Second World War
resulted in a plethora of litigation stemming from the exercise of the war
powers.[57] While not having a weight of significant importance to the
thesis of this study, several decisions should, at least, be cited. The
Court upheld the Selective Service (draft) Law against the claim that it
violated the Thirteenth Amendment prohibiting slavery or "involuntary
servitude"; in *Fallo v. United States* (1944),[58] it viewed the draft as a
"necessary and proper" means to raise and support the military forces,
and in *Silesian-American Corp. v. Clark* (1947) the Court embraced the
authority of the President or Congress to seize the property of the
enemy, or of enemy aliens, in the United States during wartime.[59]
Without question, to wage war effectively the government must sequester
unfriendly property.[60] In another decision, the Court upheld the application of the Alien Enemy Act (1798) which empowers the President, in
the case of declared war, to order the removal or expulsion of enemy
aliens *if* they are dangerous to "the public safety."[61] Finally, in 1950,

the Court sustained the power of Congress "to provide for the trial and punishment of military and naval offenses," which is not hindered by Article III of the Constitution defining the judicial power. Such cases are subject to judicial review only in cases of "*gross* abuse."[62]

In retrospect, up to the advent of the Korean War (1950-1953), it could be said that the presidency enjoyed a supremacy over foreign policy that the Supreme Court supported, if not enhanced, with but few exceptions. Certainly, this was true of Franklin Delano Roosevelt's vigorous prosecution of the War. In six of the nine major decisions analyzed since *Curtiss-Wright*, the Court *legitimized* extraordinary power-plays for the wartime President that years earlier, it had been reluctant to do for even Abraham Lincoln. Moreover, even in *Hiraboyashi* and *Korematsu*, in which the Court had recognized the important role of accompanying legislation, Congress did not do so until more than a month *after* the President had issued Executive Order No. 9066 and the military authorities on the West Coast had *already* acted. Even setbacks like *Endo* and *Duncan* were virtually meaningless afterthoughts of the Court's majority; merely legal "scraps" for those few Americans who, at the time, displayed a legitimate concern for individual liberties.[63] This legacy of judicial enhancement of presidential powers would, only occasionally, be tempered by the Constitution as we proceed to a *different* Court, a *different* President, and a *different* war—the "Cold War"!

UNITED STATES v. CURTISS-WRIGHT
299 U.S. 304; 57 S. Ct. 216; 81 L. Ed. (1936)

On May 23, 1934, President Franklin D. Roosevelt issued a proclamation forbidding any American company to sell armaments to the warring Countries of Bolivia and Paraguay (the Chaco). The President's announcement was supported by a joint resolution of Congress which permitted him to take such action if, in his judgment, it might help to restore the peace in that area of the hemisphere. The Curtiss-Wright Export Corporation was charged with conspiracy to violate the proclamation; it argued that Congress had no authority to delegate its legislative power to the p resident. The Federal District Court in New York sustained the Corporation's claim, and they appealed directly to the Supreme Court. (From such "mustard seeds," mighty "oaks" do grow.) Since this innocent-looking case, American foreign policy-making has never been the same.

[excerpts]

MR. JUSTICE SUTHERLAND delivered the opinion of the Court:

On January 27, 1936, an indictment was returned in the court below, the first count of which charges that appellees, beginning with the 29th day of May, 1934,...in violation of the Joint Resolution of Congress approved May 28, 1934, and the provisions of a proclamation issued on the same day by the President of the United States pursuant to authority conferred by section 1 of the resolution....

The President's proclamation...after reciting the terms of the Joint Resolution, declares: "Now, therefore, I, Franklin D. Roosevelt, President of the United States of America, acting under and by virtue of the authority conferred in me by the said joint resolution of Congress, do hereby declare and proclaim that I have found that the prohibition of the sale of arms and munitions of war in the United States to those countries now engaged in armed conflict in the Chaco may contribute to the reestablishment of peace between those countries....

"And I do hereby delegate to the Secretary of State the power of prescribing exceptions and limitations to the application of the said joint resolution of May 28, 1934, as made effective by this my proclamation issued thereunder."

On November 14, 1935, this proclamation was revoked....

First. It is contended that by the Joint Resolution, the going into effect and continued operation of the resolution was conditioned (a) upon the President's judgment as to its beneficial effect upon the reestablishment of peace between the countries engaged in armed conflict in the Chaco; (b) upon the making of a proclamation, which was left to his unfettered discretion, thus constituting an attempted substitution of the President's will for that of Congress; (c) upon the making of a proclamation putting an end to the operation of the resolution, which again was left to the President's unfettered discretion; and (d) further, that the extent of its operation in particular cases was subject to limitation and exception by the President, controlled by no standard. In each of these particulars, appellees urge that Congress abdicated its essential functions and delegated them to the Executive. *Whether, if the Joint Resolution had related solely to internal affairs it would be open to the challenge that it constituted an unlawful delegation of legislative power to the Executive, we find it unnecessary to determine. The whole aim of the resolution is to affect a situation entirely external to the United States, and falling within the category of foreign affairs.* The determination which we are called to make, therefore, is whether the Joint Resolution, as applied to that situation, is vulnerable to attack under the rule that forbids a delegation of the law-making power. In other words, assuming (but not deciding) that the challenged delegation, if it were confined to internal affairs, would be invalid, may it nevertheless be sustained on the ground that its exclusive aim is to afford a remedy for a hurtful condition within foreign territory? It will contribute to the elucidation of the question if we first consider the differences between the powers of the federal government in respect of foreign or external affairs and those in respect of domestic or internal affairs. That there are differences between them, and that these differences are fundamental, may not be doubted. *The two classes of powers are different, both in respect of their origin and their nature.* The broad statement that the federal government can exercise no powers except those specifically enumerated in the Constitution, and such implied powers as are necessary and proper to carry into effect the enumerated powers, is categorically true only in respect of our internal affairs. In that field, the primary purpose of the Constitution was to carve from the general mass of legislative powers then possessed by the states such portions as it was thought desirable to vest in the federal government, leaving those not included in the enumeration still in the states.... That this doctrine applies only to powers which the states had, is self evident. And since the states severally never possessed international powers, such powers could not have been carved from the mass of state powers but obviously were transmitted to the United States from some other source. During the colonial period, those powers were possessed exclusively by and were entirely under the control of the Crown. By the Declaration of Independence, "the Representatives of the United States of America" declared the United colonies to be free and independent states, and as such to have "full Power to levy War, conclude Peace, contract Alliances, establish Commerce and to do all other Acts and Things which Independent States may of right do." *As a result of the separation from Great Britain by the colonies acting as a unit, the powers of external sovereignty passed from the Crown not to the colonies severally, but to the colonies in their collective and corporate capacity as the United States of America.* Even before the Declaration, the colonies were a unit in foreign affairs, acting through a common agency—namely the Continental Congress, composed of delegates from the thirteen colonies. That agency exercised the powers of war and peace, raised an army, created a navy, and finally adopted the Declaration of Independence. Rulers come and go; governments end and forms of government change; but sovereignty survives. *A political society cannot endure without a supreme will somewhere. Sovereignty is never held in suspense. When, therefore, the external sovereignty of Great Britain in respect of the colonies ceased, it immediately passed to the Union....* That fact was given practical application almost at once. The treaty of peace, made on September 23, 1783, was concluded between his Britannic Majesty and the "United States of America."....

The Union existed before the Constitution, which was ordained and established among other things to form "a more perfect Union." Prior to that event, it is clear that the Union, declared by the Articles of Confederation to be "perpetual," was the sole possessor of external sovereignty and in the Union it remained without change save in so far as the Constitution in express terms qualified its exercise. The Framers' Convention was called and exerted its powers upon the irrefutable postulate that though the states were several their people in respect of foreign affairs were one....

It results that the investment of the federal government with the powers of external sovereignty did *not* depend upon the affirmative grants of the Constitution. *The powers to declare and wage war, to conclude peace, to make treaties, to maintain diplomatic relations with other sovereignties, if they had never been mentioned in the Constitution, would have vested in the federal government as necessary concomitants of nationality.* Neither the Constitution nor the laws passed in pursuance of it have any force in foreign territory unless in respect of our own citizens...and operations of the nation in such territory must be governed by treaties, international understandings and compacts, and the principles of international law. As a member of the family of nations, the right and power of the United States in that field are equal to the right and power of the other members of the international family. Otherwise, the United States is not completely sovereign....

Not only, as we have shown, is the federal power over external affairs in origin and essential character different from that over internal affairs, but participation in the exercise of the power is significantly limited. *In this vast external realm, with its important, complicated, delicate and manifold problems, the President alone has the power to speak or listen as a representative of the nation.* He makes treaties with the advice and consent of the Senate; but he alone negotiates. Into the field of negotiation the Senate cannot intrude; and Congress itself is powerless to invade it. As Marshall said in his great argument of March 7, 1800, in the House of Representatives, "*The President is the sole organ of the nation in its external relations, and its sole representative with foreign nations.*"...

It is important to bear in mind that we are here dealing not alone with an authority vested in the President by an exertion of legislative power, but *with such an authority plus the very delicate, plenary and exclusive power of the President as the sole organ of the federal government in the field of international relations—a power which does not require as a basis for its exercise an Act of Congress, but which, of course, like every other governmental power, must be exercised in subordination to the applicable provisions of the Constitution....*

The marked difference between foreign affairs and domestic affairs in this respect is recognized by both houses of Congress in the very form of their requisitions for information from the executive departments. In the case of every department except the Department of State, the resolution directs the official to furnish the information. In the case of the State Department, dealing with foreign affairs, the President is requested to furnish the information "if not incompatible with the public interest." A statement that to furnish the information is not compatible with the public interest rarely, if ever, is questioned. When the President is to be authorized by legislation to act in respect of a matter intended to affect a situation in foreign territory, the legislator properly bears in mind the important consideration that the form of the President's action—or, indeed, whether he shall act at all—may well depend, among other things, upon the nature of the confidential information which he has or may thereafter receive, or upon the effect which his action may have upon our foreign relations. This consideration, in connection with what we have already said on the subject, discloses the *unwisdom* of requiring Congress in this field of governmental power to lay down narrowly definite standards by which the President is to be governed....

In the light of the foregoing observations, it is evident that this court should not be in haste to apply a general rule which will have the effect of condemning legislation like that under review as constituting an unlawful delegation of legislative power. The principles which justify such legislation find overwhelming support in the unbroken legislative practice inception of the national government to the present day....

Practically every volume of the United States Statutes contains one or more acts or joint resolutions of Congress authorizing action by the President in respect of subjects affecting foreign relations, which either leave the exercise of the power to his unrestricted judgment, or provide a standard far more general than that which has always been considered requisite with regard to domestic affairs....

The result of holding that the joint resolution here under attack is void and unenforceable as constituting an unlawful delegation of legislative power would be to stamp this multitude of comparable acts and resolutions as likewise invalid. And while this court may not, and should not, hesitate to declare acts of Congress, however many times repeated, to be unconstitutional if beyond all rational doubt it finds them to be so, an impressive array of legislation such as we have just set forth, enacted by nearly every Congress from the beginning of our national existence to the present day, must be given unusual weight in the process of reaching a correct determination of the problem. A legislative practice such as we have here, evidenced not by only occasional instances, but marked by the movement of a steady stream for a century and a half of time, goes a long way in the direction of proving the presence of unassailable ground for the constitutionality of the practice, to be found in the origin and history of the power involved, or in its nature, or in both combined....

It was not within the power of the President to repeal the Joint Resolution; and his second proclamation did not purport to do so. It "revoked" the first proclamation; and the question is, did the revocation of the proclamation have the effect of abrogating the resolution or of precluding its enforcement in so far as that involved the prosecution and punishment of offenses committed during the life of the first proclamation? We are of opinion that it did not. Prior to the first proclamation, the Joint Resolution was an existing law, but dormant, awaiting the creation of a particular situation to render it active. No action or lack of action on the part of the President could destroy its potentiality. Congress alone could do that. The happening of the designated events—namely, the finding of certain conditions and the proclamation by the President—did not call the law into being. It created the occasion for it to function. The second proclamation did not put an end to the law or affect what had been done in violation of the law. The effect of the proclamation was simply to remove for the future, a condition of affairs which admitted of its exercise....

The first proclamation of the President was in force from the 28th day of May, 1934, to the 14th day of November, 1935. If the Joint Resolution had in no way depended upon Presidential action, but had provided explicitly that, at any time between May 28, 1934, and November 14, 1935, it should be unlawful to sell arms or munitions of war to the countries engaged in armed conflict in the Chaco, it certainly could not be successfully contended that the law would expire with the passing of the time fixed in respect of offenses committed during the period.

The judgment of the court below must be reversed and the cause remanded for further proceedings in accordance with the foregoing opinion.

                                                                                    Reversed.

UNITED STATES v. BELMONT
301 U.S. 324; 57 S. Ct. 758; 81L Ed. 1134 (1937)

After seizing power in the Soviet Union in 1917, the Bolsheviks initiated a policy of nationalizing private companies and confiscating their property assets. One such company, the Petrograd Metal Works, had a portion of its assets on deposit at a New York bank owned by Belmont. In 1933, President Franklin D. Roosevelt extended diplomatic recognition to the government of the Soviet Union and, as part of the final agreement between the two countries, it was concluded that the United States would lay claim to all monies owed by American nationals to the U.S.S.R. The settlement, known as the Litvinov Assignments, was an executive agreement that had not been submitted to the Senate for a two-thirds vote of approval. On objection by Belmont, the district court did not grant title to the government on the grounds that the agreement was not a treaty and thus not "the supreme law of the land." The case then proceeded to the Supreme Court for resolution.

[excerpts]

MR. JUSTICE SUTHERLAND delivered the opinion of the Court, saying in part:

First. We do not pause to inquire whether in fact there was any policy of the State of New York to be infringed, since we are of opinion that no state policy can prevail against the international compact here involved.

This court has held, *Underhill v. Hernandez*, [1897], that every sovereign state must recognize the independence of every other sovereign state; and that the courts of one will not sit in judgment upon the acts of the government of another, done within its own territory.

...This court held that the conduct of foreign relations was committed by the Constitution to the political departments of the government, and the propriety of what may be done in the exercise of this political power was not subject to judicial inquiry or decision; that who is the sovereign of a territory is not a judicial question, but one the determination of which by the political departments conclusively binds the courts; and that recognition by these departments is retroactive and validates all actions and conduct of the government so recognized from the commencement of its existence....

We take judicial notice of the fact that coincident with the assignment set forth in the complaint, the President recognized the Soviet Government, and normal diplomatic relations were established between that government and the Government of the United States, followed by an exchange of ambassadors. The effect of this was to validate, so far as this country is concerned, all acts of the Soviet Government here involved from the commencement of its existence. The recognition, establishment of diplomatic relations, the assignment, and agreements with respect thereto, were all parts of one transaction, resulting in an international compact between the two governments. That the negotiations, acceptance of the assignment and agreements and understandings in respect thereof were within the competence of the President may not be doubted. Governmental power over internal affairs is distributed between the national government and the several states. Governmental power over external affairs is not distributed, but is vested exclusively in the national government. And in respect of what was done here, the executive had authority to speak as the sole organ of that government. The assignment and the agreements in connection therewith did not, as in the case of treaties, as that term is used in the treaty making clause of the Constitution (Art. II, § 2), require the advice and consent of the Senate.

A treaty signifies "a compact made between two or more independent nations with a view to the public welfare." *Altman & Co. v. United States*, 224 U.S. 583, 600. But an international compact, as this was, is not always a treaty which requires the participation of the Senate. There are many such compacts, of which a protocol, a modus vivendi, a postal convention, and agreements like that now under consideration are illustrations. See 5 Moore, Int. Law Digest, 210-221. The distinction was pointed out by this court in the *Altman* case, supra, which arose under section 3 of the Tariff Act of 1897, authorizing the President to conclude commercial agreements with foreign countries in certain specified matters. We held that although this might not be a treaty requiring ratification by the Senate, it was a compact negotiated and proclaimed under the authority of the President, and as such was a "treaty" within the meaning of the Circuit Court of Appeals Act, the construction of which might be reviewed upon direct appeal to this court.

Plainly, the external powers of the United States are to be exercised without regard to state laws or policies. The supremacy of a treaty in this respect has been recognized from the beginning. Mr. Madison, in the

Virginia Convention, said that if a treaty does not supersede existing state laws, as far as they contravene its operation, the treaty would be ineffective. "To counteract it by the supremacy of the state laws, would bring on the Union the just charge of national perfidy, and involve us in war." 3 Elliot's Debates 515. And see *Ware v. Hylton*, 3 Dall. 199, 236-237. And while this rule in respect of treaties is established by the express language of cl. 2, Art. VI, of the Constitution, the same rule would result in the case of all international compacts and agreements from the very fact that complete power over international affairs is in the national government and is not and cannot be subject to any curtailment or interference on the part of the several states. Compare *United States v. Curtiss-Wright Export Corp.*, 299 U.S. 304, 316, et seq. In respect of all international negotiations and compacts, and in respect of our foreign relations generally, state lines disappear. As to such purposes the State of New York does not exist. Within the field of its powers, whatever the United States rightfully undertakes, it necessarily has warrant to consummate. And when judicial authority is invoked in aid of such consummation, state constitutions, state laws, and state policies are irrelevant to the inquiry and decision. It is inconceivable that any of them can be interposed as an obstacle to the effective operation of a federal constitutional power....

Second. The public policy of the United States relied upon as a bar to the action is that declared by the Constitution, namely, that private property shall not be taken without just compensation. But the answer is that our Constitution, laws and policies have no extraterritorial operation, unless in respect of our own citizens. Compare *United States v. Curtiss-Wright Export Corp.*, supra, at p. 318. What another country has done in the way of taking over property of its nationals, and especially of its corporations, is not a matter for judicial consideration here. Such nationals must look to their own government for any redress to which they may be entitled. So far as the record shows, only the rights of the Russian corporation have been affected by what has been done; and it will be time enough to consider the rights of our nationals when, if ever, by proper judicial proceeding, it shall be made to appear that affected as to entitle them to judicial relief. The substantive right to the moneys, as now disclosed, became vested in the Soviet Government as the successor to the corporation; and this right that government has passed to the United States. It does not appear that respondents have any interest in the matter beyond that of a custodian. Thus far no question under the Fifth Amendment is involved....

Judgment reversed.

JUSTICES STONE, BRANDEIS and CARDOZO concurred.

UNITED STATES v. PINK
315 U.S. 203; (1942)

*The **Curtiss-Wright** decision in **Pink** was a corollary to **Belmont** v. **U.S.** 301 U.S. 324, that stated courts lack the power to deny the effect of a Soviet nationalization decree upon grounds of a state policy against confiscation, and, more importantly, that a executive argument is the constitutional equivalent of a treaty even though the Senate is not involved.*

The First Russian Insurance Co., organized under the laws of the former Empire of Russia, established a new branch in 1907, and continued to do business until 1925, at which time the state of New York took possession of its assets to pay claims and creditors. After these payments there was $1 million left. The State of New York was ordered to pay foreign creditors and give the remaining money to the Board of Directors.

The United States wanted the fund and was granted a stay on the grounds that in 1933 the United States accepted an assignment of certain claims known as the Litvinov Assignment in the form of an executive agreement.

[excerpts]

MR. JUSTICE DOUGLAS delivered the opinion of the Court:

This action was brought by the United States to recover the assets of the New York branch of the First Russian Insurance Co. which remained in the hands of respondent after the payment of all domestic creditors.... The New York branch of the First Russian Insurance Co. continued to do business in New York until 1925. At that time, respondent, pursuant to an order of the Supreme Court of New York, took possession of its assets for a determination and report upon the claims of the policyholders and creditors in the United States. Thereafter, all claims of domestic creditors, i.e., all claims arising out of the business of the New York branch, were paid by respondent, leaving a balance in his hands of more than $1,000,000....

Thereafter, the present suit was instituted in the Supreme Court of New York. The defendants, other than respondent, were certain designated policyholders and other creditors who had presented in the liquidation proceedings claims against the corporation. The complaint prayed, inter alia, that the United States be adjudged to be the sole and exclusive owner entitled to immediate possession of the entire surplus fund in the hands of the respondent....

It is one thing to hold, as was done in *Guaranty Trust Co. v. United States*,...that under the Litvinov Assignment the United States did not acquire "a right free of a preexisting infirmity," such as the running of the statute of limitations against the Russian Government, its assignor. Unlike the problem presented here and in the Moscow case, that holding in no way sanctions the asserted power of New York to deny enforcement of a claim under the Litvinov Assignment because of an overriding policy of the State which denies validity in New York of the Russian decrees on which the assigned claims rest. That power was denied New York in *United States v. Belmont*,... With one qualification, to be noted, the *Belmont* case is determinative of the present controversy.

That case involved the right of the United States under the Litvinov Assignment to recover, from a custodian or stakeholder in New York, funds which had been nationalized and appropriated by the Russian decrees.

This Court, speaking through Mr. Justice Sutherland, held that *the conduct of foreign relations is committed by the Constitution to the political departments of the Federal Government;* that the propriety of the exercise of that power is not open to judicial inquiry; and that recognition of a foreign sovereign conclusively binds the courts and "is retroactive and validates all actions and conduct of the government so recognized from the commencement of its existence."...

...For, as we shall see, the existence of unpaid claims against Russia and its nationals, which were held in this country, and which the Litvinov Assignment was intended to secure, had long been one impediment to resumption of friendly relations between these two great powers.

The holding in the Belmont case is therefore determinative of the present controversy, unless the stake of the foreign creditors in this liquidation proceeding and the provision which New York has provided for their protection call for a different result....

...There is no constitutional reason why this Government need act as the collection agent for nationals of other countries when it takes steps to protect itself or its own nationals on external debts. There is no reason why it may not, through such devices as the Litvinov Assignment, make itself and its nationals whole from assets here before it permits such assets to go abroad in satisfaction of claims of aliens made elsewhere and not incurred in connection with business conducted in this country. The fact that New York has marshaled the claims of the foreign creditors here involved and authorized their payment does not give them immunity from that general rule....

...*The powers of the President in the conduct of foreign relations included the power, without consent of the Senate, to determine the public policy of the United States with respect to the Russian nationalization decrees....* That authority is not limited to a determination of the government to be recognized. It includes the power to determine the policy which is to govern the question of recognition. Objections to the underlying policy as well as objections to recognition are to be addressed to the political department and not to the courts.... Recognition is not always absolute; it is sometimes conditional.... Power to remove such obstacles to full recognition as settlement of claims of our nationals...certainly is a *modest* implied *power* of the *President* who is the "*sole organ of the federal government in the field of international relations.*" United States v. Curtiss-Wright Corp., supra, p. 320. *Effectiveness* in handling the delicate problems of foreign relations requires *no* less. Unless such a power exists, the power of recognition might be thwarted or seriously diluted. No such obstacle can be placed in the way of rehabilitation of relations between this country and another nation, unless the *historic conception* of the powers and responsibilities of the *President* in the *conduct* of *foreign affairs* (see Moore, Treaties and Executive Agreements, 20 Pol. Sc. Q. 385, 403-417) is to be *drastically* revised. It was the judgment of the political department that full recognition of the Soviet Government required the settlement of all outstanding problems including the claims of our nationals. Recognition and the Litvinov Assignment were interdependent. We would *usurp* the *executive* function if we held that that decision was not final and conclusive in the courts...,

We recently stated in *Hines v. Davidowitz*, 312 U.S. 52, 68, that the field which affects international relations is "the one aspect of our government that from the first has been most generally conceded imperatively to demand broad national authority"; and that any state power which may exist "is restricted to the narrowest of limits." There, we were dealing with the question as to whether a state statute regulating aliens survived a similar federal statute. We held that it did not. Here, we are dealing with an exclusive federal function. If state laws and policies did not yield before the exercise of the external powers of the United States, then our foreign policy might be thwarted. These are delicate matters. If state action could defeat or alter our foreign policy, serious consequences might ensue. The nation as a whole would be held to answer if a State created difficulties with a foreign power....

Such considerations underlie the principle of *Oetjen v. Central Leather Co.*, 246 U.S. 297, 302-303, that when a revolutionary government is recognized as a de jure government, "such recognition is retroactive in effect and validates all the actions and conduct of the government so recognized from the commencement of its existence."...

The action of New York in this case amounts in substance to a rejection of a part of the policy underlying recognition by this nation of Soviet Russia. Such power is not accorded a State in our constitutional system. To permit it would be to sanction a dangerous invasion of Federal authority....

We repeat that there are limitations on the sovereignty of the States. No State can rewrite our foreign policy to conform to its own domestic policies. Power over external affairs is not shared by the States; it is vested in the national government exclusively. It need not be so exercised as to conform to state laws or state policies, whether they be expressed in constitutions, statutes, or judicial decrees. And the policies of the States become wholly irrelevant to judicial inquiry when the United States, acting within its constitutional sphere, seeks enforcement of its foreign policy in the courts....

We hold that the right to the funds or property in question became vested in the Soviet Government as the successor to the First Russian Insurance Co.; that this right has passed to the United States under the Litvinov Assignment; and that the United States is entitled to the property as against the corporation and the foreign creditors.

The judgment is reversed and the cause is remanded to the Supreme Court of New York for proceedings not inconsistent with this opinion.

                                                                   Reversed.

MR. JUSTICE REED and MR. JUSTICE JACKSON did not participate in the consideration or decision of this case.

The nature of the controversy makes it appropriate to add a few observations to my Brother Douglas's opinion. Legal ideas, like other organisms, cannot survive severance from their congenial environment. Concepts like "situs" and "jurisdiction" and "comity" summarize views evolved by the judicial process, in the absence of controlling legislation, for the settlement of domestic issues. To utilize such concepts for the solution of controversies international in nature, even though they are presented to the courts in the form of a private litigation, is to invoke a narrow and inadmissible frame of reference....

It is not consonant with the sturdy conduct of our foreign relations that the effect of Russian decrees upon Russian funds in this country should depend on such gossamer distinctions as those by which courts have determined that Russian branches survive the death of their Russian origin. *When courts deal with such essentially political phenomena as the taking over of Russian businesses by the Russian government by resorting to the forms and phrases of conventional corporation law, they inevitably fall into a dialectic quagmire....* It does violence to the course of negotiations between the United States and Russia, and to the scope of the final adjustment, to assume that a settlement thus made on behalf of the United States—to settle both money claims and to soothe feelings—was to be qualified by the variant notions of the courts of the forty-eight states regarding "situs" or "jurisdiction" over intangibles or the survival of extinct Russian corporations. In our dealings with the outside world, the United States speaks with one voice and acts as one, unembarrassed by the complications as to domestic issues which are inherent in the distribution of political power between the national government and the individual states.

CHIEF JUSTICE STONE, dissented:

...I assume for present purposes that these sweeping alterations of the rights of states and of persons could be achieved by treaty or even executive agreement, although we are referred to no authority which would sustain such an exercise of power as is said to have been exerted here by mere assignment unratified by the Senate. It is true that, in according recognition and in establishing friendly relations with a foreign country, this Government speaks for all the forty-eight states. But it was never true that recognition alters the substantive law of any state or prescribes uniform state law for the nationals of the recognized country. On the contrary, it does not even secure for them equality of treatment in the several states, or equal treatment with citizens in any state, save as the Constitution demands it....

Recognition, like treaty making, is a political act, and both may be upon terms and conditions. But that fact no more forecloses this Court, where it is called upon to adjudicate private rights, from inquiry as to what those terms and conditions are than it precludes, in like circumstances, a court's ascertaining the true scope and meaning of a treaty. Of course, the national power may by appropriate constitutional means override the power of states and the rights of individuals. But, without collision between them, there is no such loss of power or impairment of rights, and it cannot be known whether state law and private rights collide with political acts expressed in treaties or executive agreements until their respective boundaries are defined.

It would seem, therefore, that in deciding this case some inquiry should have been made to ascertain what public policy or binding rule of conduct with respect to state power and individual rights has been proclaimed by the recognition of the Soviet Government and the assignment of its claims to the United States. The mere act of recognition and the bare transfer of the claims of the Soviet Government to the United States can, of themselves, hardly be taken to have any such effect, and they can be regarded as intended to do so only if that purpose is made evident by their terms, read in the light of diplomatic exchanges between the two countries and of the surrounding circumstances. Even when courts deal with the language of diplomacy, some foundation must be laid for inferring an obligation where previously there was none, and some expression must be found in the conduct of foreign relations which fairly indicates an intention to assume it. Otherwise, courts, *rather than the executive, may shape and define foreign policy which the executive has not adopted.*

We are not pointed to anything on the face of the documents or in the diplomatic correspondence which even suggests that the United States was to be placed in a better position, with respect to the claim which it now asserts, than was the Soviet Government and nationals. Nor is there any intimation in them that recognition was to give to prior public acts of the Soviet Government any greater extraterritorial effect than attaches to such acts occurring after recognition—acts which, by the common understanding of English and American courts, are ordinarily deemed to be without extraterritorial force, and which, in any event, have never before been considered to restrict the power of the states to apply their own rules of law to foreign-owned property within their territory....

Under our dual system of government, there are many circumstances in which the legislative and executive branches of the national government may, by affirmative action expressing its policy, enlarge the exercise of federal authority and thus diminish the power which otherwise might be exercised by the states. It is indispensable to the orderly administration of the system that such alteration of powers and the consequent impairment of state and private rights should not turn on conceptions of policy which, if ever entertained by the only branch of the government authorized to adopt it, has been left unexpressed. It is not for this Court to adopt policy, the making of which has been by the Constitution committed to other branches of the government. It is not its function to supply a policy where none has been declared or defined and none can be inferred.

MR. JUSTICE ROBERTS joined in this opinion.

EX PARTE QUIRIN
317 U.S. 1 (1942)

Quirin arouse out of the apprehension of eight Nazi agents who disembarked from a German submarine and secretly entered the United States for the purpose of sabotage. Upon landing, the Germans discarded their military clothing and disguised themselves as civilians. Approximately two days later, they were apprehended by federal agents. Items found on them included lists of American power plants, railroads, bridges, military bases and factories—along with $175,000 in American currency purportedly to be used for living expenses and bribes.

A military commission was established by President Roosevelt to try the eight agents for violating the laws of war. Writs of habeas corpus were applied for by the Nazi prisoners who contended that they were not subject to military jurisdiction nor should they be tried by the military commission, due to the fact that they had not been apprehended in a "zone of active military operation." The writs were denied.

The Supreme Court met in a special summer session on Wednesday, July 29, 1942 pursuant to a call by the Chief Justice (the Court has done so only on eight occasions since 1790). The Supreme Court convicted the eight agents. Later, six of them were executed and the other two were imprisoned.

MR. CHIEF JUSTICE STONE delivered the opinion of the Court:

...The question for decision is whether the detention of petitioners by respondent for trial by Military Commission, appointed by Order of the President of July 2, 1942, on charges preferred against them purporting to set out their violations of the law of war and of the Articles of War, is in conformity to the laws and Constitution of the United States....

After the declaration of war between the United States and the German Reich, petitioners received training at a sabotage school near Berlin, Germany, where they were instructed in the use of explosives and in methods of secret writing. Thereafter petitioners, with a German citizen, Dasch, proceeded from Germany to a seaport in Occupied France, where petitioners Burger, Heinck and Quirin, together with Dasch, boarded a German submarine which proceeded across the Atlantic to Amagansett Beach on Long Island, New York. The four were there landed from the submarine in the hours of darkness, on or about June 13, 1942, carrying with them a supply of explosives, fuses, and incendiary and timing devices. While landing they wore German Marine Infantry uniforms or parts of uniforms. Immediately after landing they buried their uniforms and the other articles mentioned, and proceeded in civilian dress to New York City.

The remaining four petitioners at the same French port boarded another German submarine, which carried them across the Atlantic to Ponte Vedra Beach, Florida. On or about June 17, 1942, they came ashore during the hours of darkness, wearing caps of the German Marine Infantry and carrying with them a supply of explosives, fuses, and incendiary and timing devices. They immediately buried their caps and the other articles mentioned, and proceeded in civilian dress to Jacksonville, Florida, and thence to various points in the United States. All were taken into custody in New York or Chicago by agents of the Federal Bureau of Investigation. All had received instructions in Germany from an officer of the German High Command to destroy war industries and war facilities in the United States, for which they or their relatives in Germany were to receive salary payments from the German Government. They also had been paid by the German Government during their course of training at the sabotage school and had received substantial sums in United States currency, which were in their possession when arrested. The currency had been handed to them by an officer of the German High Command, who had instructed them to wear their German uniforms while landing in the United States.

The President, as President and Commander in Chief of the Army and Navy, by Order of July 2, 1942, appointed a Military Commission and directed it to try petitioners for offenses against the law of war and the Articles of War, and prescribed regulations for the procedure on the trial and for review of the record of the trial and of any judgment or sentence of the Commission. On the same day, by Proclamation, the President declared that "all persons who are subjects, citizens or residents of any nation at war with the United States or who give obedience to or act under the direction of any such nation, and who during time of war enter or attempt to enter the United States...through coastal or boundary defenses, and are charged with committing or attempting or preparing to commit sabotage, espionage, hostile or warlike acts, or violations of the law of war, shall be subject to the law of war and to the jurisdiction of military tribunals."

The Proclamation also stated in terms that all such persons were denied access to the courts....

Petitioners' main contention is that the President is without any statutory or constitutional authority to order the petitioners to be tried by military tribunal for offenses with which they are charged; that in consequence they are entitled to be tried in the civil courts with the safeguards, including trial by jury, which the Fifth and Sixth Amendments guarantee to all persons charged in such courts with criminal offenses. In any case it is urged that the President's Order, in prescribing the procedure of the Commission and the method for review of its findings and sentence, and the proceedings of the Commission under the Order, conflict with Articles of War adopted by Congress...and are illegal and void....

We are not here concerned with any question of the guilt or innocence of petitioners. Constitutional safeguards for the protection of all who are charged with offenses are not to be disregarded in order to inflict merited punishment on some who are guilty. *Ex parte Milligan....* But the detention and trial of petitioners—ordered by the President in the declared exercise of his powers as Commander in Chief of the Army in time of war and of grave public danger—are not to be set aside by the courts without the clear conviction that they are in conflict with the Constitution or laws of Congress constitutionally enacted. *Congress and the President, like the courts, possess no power not derived from the Constitution.* But one of the objects of the Constitution, as declared by its preamble, is to "provide for the common defence."...

The Constitution thus invests the President, as Commander in Chief, with the power to wage war which Congress has declared, and to carry into effect all laws passed by Congress for the conduct of war and for the government and regulation of the Armed Forces, and all laws defining and punishing offenses against the law of nations, including those which pertain to the conduct of war.... Congress, in addition to making rules for the government of our Armed Forces, has thus exercised its authority to define and punish offenses against the law of nations by sanctioning, within constitutional limitations, the jurisdiction of military commissions to try persons for offenses which, according to the rules and precepts of the law of nations, and more particularly the law of war, are cognizable by such tribunals. And the President, as Commander in Chief, by his Proclamation in time of war has invoked that law. By his Order creating the present Commission he has undertaken to exercise the authority conferred upon him by Congress, and also such authority as the Constitution itself gives the Commander in Chief, to direct the performance of those functions which may constitutionally be performed by the military arm of the nation in time of war.

An important incident to the conduct of war is the adoption of measures by the military command not only to repel and defeat the enemy, but to seize and subject to disciplinary measures those enemies who in their attempt to thwart or impede our military effort have violated the law of war. It is unnecessary for present purposes to determine to what extent the President as Commander in Chief has constitutional power to create military commissions without the support of Congressional legislation. For here Congress has authorized trial of offenses against the law of war before such commissions. We are concerned only with the question whether it is within the constitutional power of the National Government to place petitioners upon trial before a military commission for the offenses with which they are charged. We must therefore first inquire whether any of the acts charged is an offense against the law of war cognizable before a military tribunal, and if so whether the Constitution prohibits the trial. We may assume that there are acts regarded in other countries, or by some writers on international law, as offenses against the law of war which would not be triable by military tribunal here, either because they are not recognized by our courts as violations of the law of war or because they are of that class of offenses constitutionally triable only by a jury. It was upon such grounds that the Court denied the right to proceed by military tribunal in *ex parte Milligan*, supra. But as we shall show, these petitioners were charged with an offense against the law of war which the Constitution does not require to be tried by jury....

...Modern warfare is directed at the destruction of enemy war supplies and the implements of their production and transportation, quite as much as at the armed forces. Every consideration which makes the unlawful belligerent punishable is equally applicable whether his objective is the one or the other. The law of war cannot rightly treat those agents of enemy armies who enter our territory, armed with explosives intended for the destruction of war industries and supplies, as any the less belligerent enemies than are agents similarly entering for the purpose of destroying fortified places or our Armed Forces. By passing our boundaries for such purposes without uniform or other emblem signifying their belligerent status, or by discarding that means of identification after entry, such enemies become unlawful belligerents subject to trial and punishment.

Citizenship in the United States of an enemy belligerent does not relieve him from the consequences of a belligerency which is unlawful because in violation of the law of war. Citizens who associate themselves with the military arm of the enemy government, and with its aid, guidance and direction enter this country bent on hostile acts, are enemy belligerents within the meaning of the Hague Convention and the law of war.... It is as an enemy belligerent that petitioner Haupt is charged with entering the United States, and unlawful belligerency is the gravamen of the offense of which he is accused...

We may assume, without deciding, that a trial prosecuted before a military commission created by military authority is not one "arising in the land...forces," when the accused is not a member of or associated with those forces. But even so, the exception cannot be taken to affect those trials before military commissions which are neither within the exception nor within the provisions of Article III, section 2, whose guaranty the Amendments did not enlarge. No exception is necessary to exclude from the operation of these provisions cases never deemed to be within their terms. An express exception from Article III, section 2, and from the Fifth and Sixth Amendments, of trials of petty offenses and of criminal contempts has not been found necessary in order to preserve the traditional practice of trying those offenses without a jury. It is no more so in order to continue the practice of trying, before military tribunals without a jury, offenses committed by enemy belligerents against the law of war....

We cannot say that Congress in preparing the Fifth and Sixth Amendments intended to extend trial by jury to the cases of alien or citizen offenders against the law of war otherwise triable by military commission, while withholding it from members of our own armed forces charged with infractions of the Articles of War punishable by death. It is equally inadmissible to construe the Amendments—whose primary purpose was to continue unimpaired presentment by grand jury and trial by petit jury in all those cases in which they had been customary—as either abolishing all trials by military tribunals, save those of the personnel of our own armed forces, or, what in effect comes to the same thing, as imposing on all such tribunals the necessity of proceeding against unlawful enemy belligerents only on presentment and trial by jury. We conclude that the Fifth and Sixth Amendments did not restrict whatever authority was conferred by the Constitution to try offenses against the law of war by military commission, and that petitioners, charged with such an offense not required to be tried by jury at common law, were lawfully placed on trial by the Commission without a jury....

We need not inquire whether Congress may restrict the power of the Commander in Chief to deal with enemy belligerents. For the Court is unanimous in its conclusion that the Articles in question could not at any stage of the proceedings afford any basis for issuing the writ. But a majority of the full Court are not agreed on the appropriate grounds for decision. Some members of the Court are of opinion that Congress did not intend the Articles of War to govern a Presidential military commission convened for the determination of questions relating to admitted enemy invaders, and that the context of the Articles makes clear that they should not be construed to apply in that class of cases. Others are of the view that—even though this trial is subject to whatever provisions of the Articles of War Congress has in terms made applicable to "commissions"—the particular Articles in question, rightly construed, do not foreclose the procedure prescribed by the President or that shown to have been employed by the Commission, in a trial of offenses against the law of war and the 81st and 82nd Articles of War, by a military commission appointed by the President.

Accordingly, we conclude that Charge I, on which petitioners were detained for trial by the Military Commission, alleged an offense which the President is authorized to order tried by military commission; that his Order convening the Commission was a lawful order and that the Commission was lawfully constituted; that the petitioners were held in lawful custody and did not show cause for their discharge. It follows that the orders of the District Court should be affirmed, and that leave to file petitions for habeas corpus in this Court should be denied.

MR. JUSTICE MURPHY took no part in the consideration or decision of these cases.

HIRABAYASHI v. UNITED STATES
320 U.S. 81 (1943)

Pursuant to Executive Order No. 9066, promulgated by the President on February 19, 1942 while the United States was at war with Japan, the military commander of the Western Defense Command promulgated an order requiring, inter alia, that all persons of Japanese ancestry within a designated military area "be within their place of residence between the hours of 8:00 p.m. and 6:00 a.m." Mr. Gordon Hirabayashi, a United States citizen of Japanese ancestry, violated this order by not reporting to the Civil Control Station in Seattle, Washington (a preliminary step to Japanese-Americans being excluded from that area).

Mr. Hirabayasi was convicted in a federal district court of violating the Act of Congress of March 21, 1942 which makes it a misdemeanor to knowingly disregard restrictions made applicable by a military commander in such a situation. He challenged the Act as being racially discriminatory in violation of the Fifth Amendment. The U.S. Court of Appeals for the Ninth Circuit certified the case to the Supreme Court.

[excerpts]

MR. CHIEF JUSTICE STONE delivered the opinion of the Court:

[A]n American citizen of Japanese ancestry, was convicted in the district court of violating the Act of Congress of March 21, 1942, 56 Stat. 173, which makes it a misdemeanor knowingly to disregard restrictions made applicable by a military commander to persons in a military area prescribed by him as such, all as authorized by an Executive Order of the President.

The questions for our decision are whether the particular restriction violated, namely that all persons of Japanese ancestry residing in such an area be within their place of residence daily between the hours of 8:00 p. m. and 6:00 a. m., was adopted by the military commander in the exercise of an unconstitutional delegation by Congress of its legislative power, and whether the restriction unconstitutionally discriminated between citizens of Japanese ancestry and those of other ancestries in violation of the Fifth Amendment....

The curfew order which appellant violated, and to which the sanction prescribed by the Act of Congress has been deemed to attach, purported to be issued pursuant to an Executive Order of the President.

In passing upon the authority of the military commander to make and execute the order, it becomes necessary to consider in some detail the official action which preceded or accompanied the order and from which it derives its purported authority.

On December 8, 1941, one day after the bombing of Pearl Harbor by a Japanese air force, Congress declared war against Japan...On *February 19, 1942*, the President promulgated Executive *Order No. 9066*.... The Order recited that... [b]y virtue of the authority vested in him as President and as Commander in Chief of the Army and Navy, the President purported to "authorize and direct the Secretary of War, and the Military Commanders whom he may from time to time designate, whenever he or any designated Commander deems such action necessary or desirable, to prescribe military areas in such places and of such extent as he or the appropriate Military Commander may determine, from which any or all persons may be excluded, and with respect to which, the right of any person to enter, remain in, or leave shall be subject to whatever restrictions the Secretary of War or the appropriate Military Commander may impose in his discretion."...

An Executive Order of the President, No. 9102, of March 18, 1942, established the War Relocation Authority, in the Office for Emergency Management of the Executive Office of the President; it authorized the Director of War Relocation Authority to formulate and effectuate a program for the removal, relocation, maintenance and supervision of persons designated under Executive Order No. 9066,...

Congress, by the Act of March 21, 1942, provided: "That whoever shall enter, remain in, leave, or commit any act in any military area or military zone prescribed, under the authority of an Executive order of the President,...shall, if it appears that he knew or should have known of the existence and extent of the restrictions or order and that his act was in violation thereof, be guilty of a misdemeanor and upon conviction shall be liable" to fine or imprisonment, or both....

Appellant does not deny that he knowingly failed to obey the curfew order as charged in the second count of the indictment, or that the order was authorized by the terms of Executive Order No. 9066, or that the challenged Act of Congress purports to punish with criminal penalties disobedience of such an order. His contentions are only that Congress unconstitutionally delegated its legislative power to the military commander by authorizing him to impose the challenged regulation, and that, even if the regulation were in other respects lawfully authorized, the Fifth Amendment prohibits the discrimination made between citizens of Japanese descent and those of other ancestry....

The conclusion is inescapable that Congress, by the Act of March 21, 1942, ratified and confirmed Executive Order No. 9066.... *We must consider also whether, acting together, Congress and the Executive could leave it to the designated military commander to appraise the relevant conditions and on the basis of that appraisal to say whether, under the circumstances, the time and place were appropriate for the promulgation of the curfew order* and whether the order itself was an appropriate means of carrying out the Executive Order for the "protection against espionage and against sabotage" to national defense materials, premises and utilities. For reasons presently to be stated, we conclude that it was within the constitutional power of Congress and the executive arm of the Government to prescribe this curfew order for the period under consideration and that its promulgation by the military commander involved no unlawful delegation of legislative power....

...We have no occasion to consider whether the President, acting alone, could lawfully have made the curfew order in question, or have authorized others to make it. For the President's action has the support of the Act of Congress, and we are immediately concerned with the question whether it is within the constitutional power of the national government, through the joint action of Congress and the Executive, to impose this restriction as an emergency war measure. The exercise of that power here involves no question of martial law or trial by military tribunal....

The war power of the national government is "the power to wage war successfully."... It extends to every matter and activity so related to war as substantially to affect its conduct and progress. The power is not restricted to the winning of victories in the field and the repulse of enemy forces. It embraces every phase of the national defense, including the protection of war materials and the members of the armed forces from injury and from the dangers which attend the rise, prosecution and progress of war.... Since the Constitution commits to the Executive and to Congress the exercise of the war power in all the vicissitudes and conditions of warfare, it has necessarily given them wide scope for the exercise of judgment and discretion in determining the nature and extent of the threatened injury or danger and in the selection of the means for resisting it. *Ex parte Quirin*, supra, 28-29; cf. Prize Cases, supra, 670; *Martin v. Mott*, 12 Wheat. 19, 29. Where, as they did here, the conditions call for the exercise of judgment and discretion and for the choice of means by those branches of the Government on which the Constitution has placed the responsibility of war-making, it is not for any court to sit in review of the wisdom of their action or substitute its judgment for theirs....

Viewing these data in all their aspects, Congress and the Executive could reasonably have concluded that these conditions have encouraged the continued attachment of members of this group to Japan and Japanese institutions. These are only some of the many considerations which those charged with the responsibility for the national defense could take into account in determining the nature and extent of the danger of espionage and sabotage, in the event of invasion or air raid attack. *The extent of that danger could be definitely known only after the event and after it was too late to meet it.* Whatever views we may entertain regarding the loyalty to this country of the citizens of Japanese ancestry, we cannot reject as unfounded the judgment of the military authorities and of Congress that there were disloyal members of that population, whose number and strength could not be precisely and quickly ascertained, We cannot say that the war-making branches of the Government did not have ground for believing that in a critical hour such persons could not readily be isolated and separately dealt with, and constituted a menace to the national defense and safety, which demanded that prompt and adequate measures be taken to guard against it....

If it was an appropriate exercise of the war power its validity is not impaired because it has restricted the citizen's liberty. Like every military control of the population of a dangerous zone in war time, it necessarily involves some infringement of individual liberty, just as does the police establishment of fire lines during a fire, or the confinement of people to their houses during an air raid alarm—neither of which could be thought to be an infringement of constitutional right. Like them, the validity of the restraints of the curfew order depends on all the conditions which obtain at the time the curfew is imposed and which support the order imposing it.

But appellant insists that the exercise of the power is inappropriate and unconstitutional because it discriminates against citizens of Japanese ancestry, in violation of the Fifth Amendment. The Fifth Amendment contains no equal protection clause and it restrains only such discriminatory legislation by Congress as amounts to a denial of due process.... Distinctions between citizens solely because of their ancestry are by their very nature odious to a free people whose institutions are founded upon the doctrine of equality. For that reason, legislative classification or discrimination based on race alone has often been held to be a denial of equal protection.... We may assume that these considerations would be controlling here were it not for the fact that the danger of espionage and sabotage, in time of war and of threatened invasion, calls upon the military authorities to scrutinize every relevant fact bearing on the loyalty of populations in the danger areas. Because racial discriminations are in most circumstances irrelevant and therefore prohibited, it by no means follows that, in dealing with the perils of war, Congress and the Executive are wholly precluded from taking into account those facts and circumstances which are relevant to measures for our national defense and for the successful prosecution of the war, and which may in fact place citizens of one ancestry in a different category from others. "We must never forget, that it is a constitution we are expounding," "a constitution intended to endure for ages to come, and, consequently, to be adapted to the various crises of human affairs." *McCulloch v. Maryland*.... The adoption by Government, in the crisis of war and of threatened invasion, of measures for the public safety, based upon the recognition of facts and circumstances which indicate that a group of one national extraction may menace that safety more than others, is not wholly beyond the limits of the Constitution and is not to be condemned merely because in other and in most circumstances racial distinctions are irrelevant....

Here the aim of Congress and the Executive was the protection against sabotage of war materials and utilities in areas thought to be in danger of Japanese invasion and air attack. We have stated in detail facts and circumstances with respect to the American citizens of Japanese ancestry residing on the Pacific Coast which support the judgment of the war-waging branches of the Government that some restrictive measure was urgent. We cannot say that these facts and circumstances, considered in the particular war setting, could afford no ground for differentiating citizens of Japanese ancestry from other groups in the United States. The fact alone that attack on our shores was threatened by Japan rather than another enemy power set these citizens apart from others who have no particular associations with Japan....

   ...*We cannot close our eyes to the fact, demonstrated by experience, that in time of war residents having ethnic affiliations with an invading enemy may be a greater source of danger than those of a different ancestry.* Nor can we deny that Congress, and the military authorities acting with its authorization, have constitutional power to appraise the danger in the light of facts of public notoriety. *We need not now attempt to define the ultimate boundaries of the war power....*

   The purpose of Executive Order No. 9066, and the standard which the President approved for the orders authorized to be promulgated by the military commander—as disclosed by the preamble of the Executive Order—was the protection of our war resources against espionage and sabotage....

   The military commander's appraisal of facts in the light of the authorized standard, and the inferences which he drew from those facts, involved the exercise of his informed judgment. But as we have seen, those facts, and the inferences which could be rationally drawn from them, support the judgment of the military commander, that the danger of espionage and sabotage to our military resources was imminent, and that the curfew order was an appropriate measure to meet it....

   The Constitution as a continuously operating charter of government does not demand the impossible or the impractical. The essentials of the legislative function are preserved when Congress authorizes a statutory command to become operative, upon ascertainment of a basic conclusion of fact by a designated representative of the Government.

                                                                              Affirmed.

MR. JUSTICE DOUGLAS, concurred:

   ...It is true that we might now say that there was ample time to handle the problem on the individual rather than the group basis. But military decisions must be made without the benefit of hindsight. The orders must be judged as of the date when the decision to issue them was made. To say that the military in such cases should take the time to weed out the loyal from the others would be to assume that the nation could afford to have them take the time to do it. But as the opinion of the

Court makes clear, speed and dispatch may be of the essence. Certainly we cannot say that those charged with the defense of the nation should have procrastinated until investigations and hearings were completed. At that time further delay might indeed have seemed to be wholly incompatible with military responsibilities. Since we cannot override the military judgment which lay behind these orders, it seems to me necessary to concede that the army had the power to deal temporarily with these people on a group basis. Petitioner therefore was not justified in disobeying the orders.

But I think it important to emphasize that we are dealing here with a problem of loyalty not assimilation. *Loyalty is a matter of mind and of heart not of race. That indeed is the history of America. Moreover, guilt is personal under our constitutional system. Detention for reasonable cause is one thing. Detention on account of ancestry is another....*

...Whether in that event the administrative remedy would be the only one available or would have to be first exhausted is also reserved. The scope of any relief which might be afforded—whether the liberties of an applicant could be restored only outside the areas in question—is likewise a distinct issue. But if it were plain that no machinery was available whereby the individual could demonstrate his loyalty as a citizen in order to be reclassified, questions of a more serious character would be presented. The United States, however, takes no such position. We need go no further here than to deny the individual the right to defy the law. It is sufficient to say that he cannot test in that way the validity of the orders as applied to him.

MR. JUSTICE MURPHY, concurred:

...Today is the first time, so far as I am aware, that we have sustained a substantial restriction of the personal liberty of citizens of the United States based upon the accident of race or ancestry. Under the curfew order here challenged no less than 70,000 American citizens have been placed under a special ban and deprived of their liberty because of their particular racial inheritance. In this sense it bears a melancholy resemblance to the treatment accorded to members of the Jewish race in Germany and in other parts of Europe. The result is the creation in this country of two classes of citizens for the purposes of a critical and perilous hour—to sanction discrimination between groups of United

States citizens on the basis of ancestry. In my opinion this goes to the very brink of constitutional power.

Except under conditions of great emergency a regulation of this kind applicable solely to citizens of a particular racial extraction would not be regarded as in accord with the requirement of due process of law contained in the Fifth Amendment. We have consistently held that attempts to apply regulatory action to particular groups solely on the basis of racial distinction or classification is not in accordance with due process of law as prescribed by the Fifth and Fourteenth Amendments....

...Modern war does not always wait for the observance of procedural requirements that are considered essential and appropriate under normal conditions. Accordingly I think that the military arm, confronted with the peril of imminent enemy attack and acting under the authority conferred by the Congress, made an allowable judgment at the time the curfew restriction was imposed....

In voting for affirmance of the judgment I do not wish to be understood as intimating that the military authorities in time of war are subject to no restraints whatsoever, or that they are free to impose any restrictions they may choose on the rights and liberties of individual citizens or groups of citizens in those places which may be designated as "military areas." While this Court sits, it has the inescapable duty of seeing that the mandates of the Constitution are obeyed....

Nor do I mean to intimate that citizens of a particular racial group whose freedom may be curtailed within an area threatened with attack should be generally prevented from leaving the area and going at large in other areas that are not in danger of attack and where special precautions are not needed. Their status as citizens, though subject to requirements of national security and military necessity, should at all times be accorded the fullest consideration and respect. When the danger is past, the restrictions imposed on them should be promptly removed and their freedom of action fully restored.

MR. JUSTICE RUTLEDGE, concurred:

I concur in the Court's opinion, except for the suggestion, if that is intended (as to which I make no assertion), that the courts have no power to review any action a military officer may "in his discretion" find it necessary to take with respect to civilian citizens in military areas or zones, once it is found that an emergency has created the conditions requiring or justifying the creation of the area or zone and the institution of some degree of military control short of suspending habeas corpus. Given the generating conditions for exercise of military authority and recognizing the wide latitude for particular applications that ordinarily creates, I do not think it is necessary in this case to decide that there is no action a person in the position of General DeWitt here may take, and which he may regard as necessary to the region's or the country's safety, which will call judicial power into play. The officer of course must have wide discretion and room for its operation. But it does not follow there may not be bounds beyond which he cannot go and, if he oversteps them, that the courts may not have power to protect the civilian citizen. But in this case that question need not be faced and I merely add my reservation without indication of opinion concerning it.

KOREMATSU v. UNITED STATES
323 U.S. 214 (1944)

American participation in World War II was initiated on December 7, 1941, with the attack by the Japanese on the Pearl Harbor Naval Base in Oahu, Hawaii. On February 20, 1942, President Roosevelt issued Executive Order #9066 giving the military the discretion and authority to designate certain areas of the United States as "military areas" from which certain individuals were not allowed to "enter, leave or remain."

On March 21, 1942, Congress passed a law making it a criminal offense for anyone to "enter, leave or remain" in any military area in order to commit any acts of espionage of sabotage. Following this, General DeWitt, Commander of the Western Defense Command, declared the western coast of the United States to be in peril of attack and began imposing restrictions on all peoples of Italian, German or Japanese ancestry who resided on the West Coast.

Fred Korematsu, an American citizen of Japanese ancestry, refused to leave his home in California. He was arrested and later convicted in federal district court of violating the executive orders. Mr. Korematsu appealed and the circuit court affirmed the decision of the lower court. Mr. Korematsu challenged the constitutionality of General DeWitt's order and appealed to the Supreme Court.

[excerpts]

MR. JUSTICE BLACK delivered the opinion of the Court:

...[A]n American citizen of Japanese descent, was convicted in a federal district court for remaining in San Leandro, California, a "Military Area," contrary to Civilian Exclusion Order No. 34 of the Commanding General of the Western Command, U.S. Army, which directed that after May 9, 1942, all persons of Japanese ancestry should be excluded from that area...

It should be noted, to begin with, that all legal restrictions which curtail the civil rights of a single racial group are immediately *suspect*. That is not to say that all such restrictions are unconstitutional. It is to say that courts must subject them to the most *rigid scrutiny*. Pressing public necessity may sometimes justify the existence of such restrictions; racial antagonism never can....

In the light of the principles we announced in the *Hirabayashi* case, we are unable to conclude that it was beyond the war power of Congress and the Executive to exclude those of Japanese ancestry from relationship to the prevention of espionage and sabotage. The military authorities, charged with the primary responsibility of defending our shores, concluded that curfew provided inadequate protection and ordered exclusion. They did so, as pointed out in our Hirabayashi opinion, in accordance with Congressional authority to the military to say who should, and who should not, remain in the threatened areas....

Like curfew, exclusion of those of Japanese origin was deemed necessary because of the presence of an unascertained number of disloyal members of the group, most of exclusion of large groups of citizens from their homes, except under circumstances of direst emergency and peril, is inconsistent with our basic governmental institutions. But when under conditions of modern warfare our shores are threatened by hostile forces, the power to protect must be commensurate with the threatened danger....

We are thus being asked to pass at this time upon the whole subsequent detention program in both assembly and relocation centers, although the only issues framed at the imprisonment of a loyal citizen in a concentration camp because of racial prejudice.... To cast this case into outlines of racial prejudice, without reference to the real military dangers which were presented, merely confuses the issue. *Korematsu was not excluded from the Military Area because of hostility to him or his race. He was excluded because we are at war with the Japanese Empire,* because the properly constituted military authorities feared an invasion of our West Coast and felt constrained to take proper security measures, because they decided that the military urgency of the situation demanded that all citizens of Japanese ancestry be segregated from the West Coast temporarily, and finally, because Congress, reposing its confidence in this time of war in our military leaders as inevitably it must determined that they should have the power to do just this.... *We cannot by availing ourselves of the calm perspective of hindsight now say that at that time these actions were unjustified.*

Affirmed.

MR. JUSTICE FRANKFURTER, concurred:

...The provisions of the Constitution which confer on the Congress and the President powers to enable this country to wage war are as much part of the Constitution as provisions looking to a nation at peace. And we have had recent occasion to quote approvingly the statement of former Chief Justice Hughes that the war power of the Government is "the power to wage war successfully." *Hirabayashi v. United....* Therefore, the validity of action under the war power must be judged wholly in the context of war. That action is not to be stigmatized as lawless because like action in times of peace would be lawless. To talk about a military order that expresses an allowable judgment of war needs by those entrusted with the duty of conducting war as "an unconstitutional order" is to suffuse a part of the Constitution with an atmosphere of unconstitutionality. The respective spheres of action of military authorities and of judges are of course very different. But within their sphere, military authorities are no more outside the bounds of obedience to the Constitution than are judges within theirs.... *To recognize that military orders are "reasonably expedient military precautions" in time of war and yet to deny them constitutional legitimacy makes of the Constitution an instrument for dialectic subtleties not reasonably to be attributed to the hard-headed Framers, of whom a majority had had actual participation in war.* If a military order such as that under review does not transcend the means appropriate for conducting war, such action by the military is as constitutional as would be any authorized action by the Interstate Commerce Commission within the limits of the constitutional power to regulate commerce. And being an exercise of the war power explicitly granted by the Constitution for safeguarding the national life by prosecuting war effectively, *I find nothing in the Constitution which denies to Congress the power to enforce such a valid military order by making its violation an offense triable in the civil courts....*

MR. JUSTICE ROBERTS dissented:

I *dissent, because I think the indisputable facts exhibit a clear violation of constitutional rights....* [I]t is the case of convicting a citizen as a punishment for not submitting to imprisonment in a concentration camp, based on his ancestry, and solely because of his ancestry, without evidence or inquiry concerning his loyalty and good disposition towards the United States. If this be a correct statement of the facts disclosed by this record, and facts of which we take judicial notice, I need hardly labor the conclusion that constitutional rights have been violated. The Government's argument, and the opinion of the court, in my judgment, erroneously divide that which is single and indivisible and thus make the case appear as if the petitioner violated a Military Order, sanctioned by Act of Congress, which excluded him from his home, by refusing voluntarily to leave and, so, knowingly and intentionally, defying the order and the Act of Congress....

The predicament in which the petitioner thus found himself was this: He was forbidden, by Military Order, to leave the zone in which he lived; he was forbidden, by Military Order, after a date fixed, to be found within that zone unless he were in an Assembly Center located in that zone. General DeWitt's report to the Secretary of War concerning the programme of evacuation and relocation of Japanese makes it entirely clear, if it were necessary to refer to that document, and, in the light of the above recitation, I think it is not, that an Assembly Center was a euphemism for a prison. No person within such a center was permitted to leave except by Military Order.

In the dilemma that he dare not remain in his home, or voluntarily leave the area, without incurring criminal penalties, and that the only way he could avoid punishment was to go to an Assembly Center and submit himself to military imprisonment, the petitioner did nothing....

The Government has argued this case as if the only order outstanding at the time the petitioner was arrested and informed against was Exclusion Order No. 34 ordering him to leave the area in which he resided, which was the basis of the information against him. That argument has evidently been effective....

Moreover, it is beside the point to rest decision in part on the fact that the petitioner, for his own reasons, wished to remain in his home. If, as is the fact, he was constrained so to do, it is indeed a narrow application of constitutional rights to ignore the order which constrained him, in order to sustain his conviction for violation of another contradictory order.

I would reverse the judgment of conviction.

MR. JUSTICE MURPHY, dissented:

This exclusion of "all persons of Japanese ancestry, both alien and non-alien," from the Pacific Coast area on a plea of military necessity in the absence of martial law ought not to be approved. Such exclusion goes over "the very brink of constitutional power" and falls into the ugly abyss of racism.

...Being an obvious racial discrimination, the order deprives all those within its scope of the equal protection of the laws as guaranteed by the Fifth Amendment. It further deprives these individuals of their constitutional rights to live and work where they will, to establish a home where they choose and to move about freely. In excommunicating them without benefit of hearings, this order also deprives them of all their constitutional rights to procedural due process....

Justification for the exclusion is sought, instead, mainly upon questionable racial and sociological grounds not ordinarily within the realm of expert military judgment, supplemented by certain semi-military conclusions drawn from an unwarranted use of circumstantial evidence....

...But to infer that examples of individual disloyalty prove group disloyalty and justify discriminatory action against the entire group is to deny that under our system of law individual guilt is the sole basis for deprivation of rights. Moreover, this inference, which is at the very heart of the evacuation orders, has been used in support of the abhorrent and despicable treatment of minority groups by the dictatorial tyrannies which this nation is now pledged to destroy....

No adequate reason is given for the failure to treat these Japanese Americans on an individual basis by holding investigations and hearings....

...I dissent, therefore, from this legalization of racism. Racial discrimination in any form and in any degree has no justifiable part whatever in our democratic way of life. It is unattractive in any setting but it is utterly revolting among a free people who have embraced the principles set forth in the Constitution of the United States. All residents of this nation are kin in some way by blood or culture to a foreign land. Yet they are primarily and necessarily a part of the new and distinct civilization of the United States. They must accordingly be treated at all

times as the heirs of the American experiment and as entitled to all the rights and freedoms guaranteed by the Constitution.

MR. JUSTICE JACKSON, dissented:

...Now, if any fundamental assumption underlies our system, it is that guilt is personal and not inheritable. Even if all of one's antecedents had been convicted of treason, the Constitution forbids its penalties to be visited upon him, for it provides that "no attainder of treason shall work corruption of blood, or forfeiture except during the life of the person attainted."...

It would be impracticable and dangerous idealism to expect or insist that each specific military command in an area of probable operations will conform to conventional tests of constitutionality. When an area is so beset that it must be put under military control at all, the paramount consideration is that its measures be successful, rather than legal. The armed services must protect a society, not merely its Constitution. The very essence of the military job is to marshal physical force, to remove every obstacle to its effectiveness, to give it every strategic advantage. Defense measures will not, and often should not, be held within the limits that bind civil authority in peace. No court can require such a commander in such circumstances to act as a reasonable man; he may be unreasonably cautious and exacting. Perhaps he should be. But a commander in temporarily focusing the life of a community on defense is carrying out a military program; he is not making law in the sense the courts know the term. He issues orders, and they may have a certain authority as military commands, although they may be very bad as constitutional law. *But if we cannot confine military expedients by the Constitution, neither would I distort the Constitution to approve all that the military may deem expedient....*

...The chief restraint upon those who command the physical forces of the country, in the future as in the past, must be their responsibility to the political judgments of their contemporaries and to the moral judgments of history....

...I do not suggest that the courts should have attempted to interfere with the Army in carrying out its task. But I do not think they may be asked to execute a military expedient that has no place in law under the Constitution. I would reverse the judgment and discharge the prisoner....

EX PARTE ENDO
323 U.S. 283 (1944)

*Endo was argued on the same day as **Korematsu** and related to the Japanese relocation program and the continued detention of Japanese citizens to relocation centers. Endo, an American citizen of Japanese ancestry, was evacuated from her home in Sacramento, California, and relocated to a detention center—first in California and later in Utah.*

After a writ of habeas corpus filed in July, 1942, in district court was denied, Ms. Endo then appealed to the circuit court that certified the case to the United States Supreme Court. The chief question for the Court was whether or not the detention of citizens of Japanese ancestry authorized by the Act of March 21, 1942, and President's executive orders violated the Bill of Rights to the U.S. Constitution.

[excerpts]

MR. JUSTICE DOUGLAS delivered the opinion of the Court:

...Mitsuye Endo, hereinafter designated as the appellant, is an American citizen of Japanese ancestry. She was evacuated from Sacramento, California, in 1942, pursuant to certain military orders which we will presently discuss, and was removed to the Tule Lake War Relocation Center located at Newell, Modoc County, California. In July, 1942, she filed a petition for a writ of habeas corpus in the District Court of the United States for the Northern District of California, asking that she be discharged and restored to liberty. That petition was denied by the District Court in July, 1943, and an appeal was perfected to the Circuit Court of Appeals in August, 1943. Shortly thereafter appellant was transferred from the Tule Lake Relocation Center to the Central Utah Relocation Center located at Topaz, Utah, where she is presently detained.... (2) the segregation of loyal from disloyal evacuees;...

...An investigation of the applicant is made for the purpose of ascertaining "the probable effect upon the war program and upon the public peace and security of issuing indefinite leave" to the applicant The grant of leave clearance does not authorize departure from the Relocation Center. Application for indefinite leave must also be made. Indefinite leave may be granted under 14 specified conditions. For example, it may be granted (1) where the applicant proposes to accept an employment offer or an offer of support that has been investigated and approved by the Authority; or (2) where the applicant does not intend to work but has "adequate financial resources to take care of himself" and a Relocation Officer has investigated and approved "public sentiment at his proposed destination,"...

...Her petition for a writ of habeas corpus alleges that she is a loyal and law-abiding citizen of the United States, that no charge has been made against her, that she is being unlawfully detained, and that she is confined in the Relocation Center under armed guard and held there against her will.

It is conceded by the Department of Justice and by the War Relocation Authority that appellant is a loyal and law-abiding citizen. They make no claim that she is detained on any charge or that she is even suspected of disloyalty. Moreover, they do not contend that she may be held any longer in the Relocation Center....

Essentially, military necessity required only that the Japanese population be removed from the coastal area and dispersed in the interior, where the danger of action in concert during any attempted enemy raids along the coast, or in advance thereof as preparation for a full scale attack, would be eliminated. That the evacuation program necessarily and ultimately developed into one of complete Federal supervision, was due primarily to the fact that the interior states would not accept an uncontrolled Japanese migration....

...We are of the view that Mitsuye Endo should be given her liberty. In reaching that conclusion we do not come to the underlying constitutional issues which have been argued. For we conclude that, whatever power the War Relocation Authority may have to detain other classes of citizens, it has no authority to subject citizens who are concededly loyal to its leave procedure....

...Broad powers frequently granted to the President or other executive officers by Congress so that they may deal with the exigencies of wartime problems have been sustained. And the Constitution when it committed to the Executive and to Congress the exercise of the war power necessarily gave them wide scope for the exercise of judgment and discretion so that war might be waged effectively and successfully. *Hirabayashi v. United States.... At the same time, however, the Constitution is as specific in its enumeration of many of the civil rights of the individual as it is in its enumeration of the powers of his government....*

We mention these constitutional provisions not to stir the constitutional issues which have been argued at the bar but to indicate the approach which we think should be made to an Act of Congress or an order of the Chief Executive that touches the sensitive area of rights specifically guaranteed by the Constitution. This Court has quite consistently given a narrower scope for the operation of the presumption of constitutionality when legislation appeared on its face to violate a specific prohibition of the Constitution. We have likewise favored that interpretation of legislation which gives it the greater chance of surviving the test of constitutionality....

A citizen who is concededly loyal presents no problem of espionage or sabotage. Loyalty is a matter of the heart and mind, not of race, creed, or color. He who is loyal is by definition not a spy or a saboteur. When the power to detain is derived from the power to protect the war effort against espionage and sabotage, detention which has no relationship to that objective is unauthorized....

Reversed.

MR. JUSTICE MURPHY, concurred:

...Moreover, the Court holds that Mitsuye Endo is entitled to an unconditional release by the War Relocation Authority.... If, as I believe, the military orders excluding her from California were invalid at the time they were issued, they are increasingly objectionable at this late date, when the threat of invasion of the Pacific Coast and the fears of sabotage and espionage have greatly diminished. *For the Government to suggest under these circumstances that the presence of Japanese blood in a loyal American citizen might be enough to warrant her exclusion from a place where she would otherwise have a right to go is a position I cannot sanction.*

MR. JUSTICE ROBERTS concurred:

...I conclude, therefore, that the court is squarely faced with a serious constitutional question,—whether the relator's detention violated the guarantees of the Bill of Rights of the federal Constitution and especially the guarantee of due process of law. There can be but one answer to that question. An admittedly loyal citizen has been deprived of her liberty for a period of years. Under the Constitution she should be free to come and go as she pleases. Instead, her liberty of motion and other innocent activities have been prohibited and conditioned. She should be discharged.

Notes

1. David Gray Adler, "Foreign Policy and the Separation of Powers: The Influence of the Judiciary," Chapter 6 in Michael W. McCann & Gerald Houseman, *Judging the Constitution: Critical Essays on Judicial Lawmaking* (Glenview, Ill: Scott, Forsman and Company, 1989), p. 159.
2. See Randall W. Bland, "The President, the Court and Foreign Policy Leadership," in Thomas Patterson, *The American Democracy* (New York: McGraw-Hill, 1990).
3. *United States v. Curtiss-Wright Export Corp. et al.,* 299 US 304 (1936).
4. See *Schechter Poulty Corporation v. United States,* 295 US 495 (1935). The decision represents the *third* instance in which the Court struck down a presidential order.
5. *United States v. Curtiss-Wright,* p. 315.
6. Ibid, pp. 315-316.
7. Ibid, pp. 319-320. The origin of the "sole organ" argument can probably be traced to John Jay's Paper #64, which justified it on the grounds of "secrecy" and "dispatch." Rossiter, *The Federalist Papers,* p. 390.
8. An acknowledged constitutional expert, Alfred H. Kelly, called Sutherland's opinion "remarkable" because of its "entangled logic." "The Constitution and Foreign Policy," in *The Encyclopedia of American Foreign Policy,* Alexander De Conde, Editor (New York: Charles Scribner's Sons, 1978), p. 178. Also see, Jose F. Paschal. *Mr. Justice Sutherland* (Chicago: University of Chicago Press, 1956) and for Sutherland's own thoughts, see George Sutherland, *Constitutional Power and World Affairs* (New York: Columbia University Press, 1919).
9. "Foreign Policy and the Separation of Powers: The Influence of the Judiciary," Chapter 6 in McCann & Houseman, *Judging the Constitution,* p. 160.

10. 299 US at 316. Later, the author of the opinion, in a rather mystical fashion, wrote: "A political society cannot endure without a *supreme will* somewhere. Sovereignty is never held in suspense."
11. 3 Dall. 54, 80-81.
12. See Adler's extensive treatment of Sutherland's opinion in "The Constitution and Presidential War Making: The Enduring Debate," *Political Science Quarterly*, volume 103, (Spring 1988) pp. 30-34.
13. "The President's Unilateral Termination of the Taiwan Treaty," *Northwestern Law Review*, Volume 75 (November 1980) pp. 591-594. For similar views, see David M. O'Brien, *Constitutional Law and Politics: Struggles for Power and Governmental Accountability* (New York: W.W. Norton R. Company, 1991) p. 197; Charles Lofgen, "United States v. Curtiss Wright Export Corporation: An Historical Reassessment," *Yale Law Journal.* Volume 83 (November 1973); and David M. Levitan, "The Foreign Relations Power: An Analysis of Mr. Justice Sutherland's Theory," *Yale Law Journal.* Volume 55 (April 1946) p. 476.
14. See Louis Henkin, *Foreign Affairs and the Constitution* (Mineola: Foundation Press, 1972) p. 27.
15. "The Constitution and Presidential War-making," *Political Science Quarterly* (1988) p. 31. 26 299 US 318.
16. 299 US 318.
17. *The President* (1984) p. 202.
18. 299 US 324.
19. 301 US 324.
20. Justices Stone, Brandeis and Cardozo concurred in the opinion.
21. 310 US 330.
22. Ibid. 331.
23. O'Brien. *Constitutional Law and Politics*, Volume I, p. 209. In 1972, Congress passed the Case Act which requires the president to notify the legislative branch of "any international agreement."
24. 315 US 203. Legal scholars supported Sutherland's views. For example, see "Executive Agreements: A Study of the Executive in the Control of the Foreign Relations of the United States." 35 *Illinois Law Review* (1940) p. 365.
25. 315 US 223. Justices Reed and Jackson did not participate. Justice Frankfurter concurred and Justice Stone dissented.
26. 315 US 299.

27. In *Hines*, the Court held that congressional statutes regulating aliens superseded similar state laws.
28. 315 US 232.
29. *Federal Register* 5101.
30. *Ex parte Quirin*, 317 US 1 (1942).
31. 317 US 26. See 10 U.S.C. sections 1471-1593.
32. Ibid. 28.
33. Ibid, 30-31.
34. The citizen-agent was Herbert Hans Haupt. Ibid, 37-38.
35. Federal Register 1407. For a detailed discussion of presidential powers in such emergencies, see Louis Hankin, *Constitutionalism, Democracy and Foreign Affairs*, (New York: Columbia University Press, 1989).
36. Public Proclamation No. 3 issued on March 24, 1942 required persons affected to be in their residences each day between 8:00 p.m. and 6:00 a.m. 7 *Federal Register* 2543.
37. 320 US 81 (1942).
38. 48 320 US at 92.
39. Ibid, p. 93.
40. Ibid, p. 97.
41. Ibid, p. 99. Later, Stone argued that since the Fifth Amendment contained no Equal Protection Clause, it could not be used to prohibit racial discrimination. This line of reasoning was overturned twelve years later in *Boiling v. Sharpe*, 347 US 497 (1954).
42. Ibid, p. 113.
43. 323 US at 216. Justice Black's use of terminology is important because he clearly anticipated the "strict scrutiny" test that would be used by the Warren Court in the 1960's in race discrimination cases.
44. Ibid, pp. 218-219. Specifically, *Korematsu* failed to comply with the Civilian Exclusion Order (No. 34) issued by General De Witt.
45. Ibid, pp. 219-220. It should be noted that in the Nineteenth Century, Mr. Justice Story warned us about such extraordinary circumstances. Speaking for a unanimous Supreme Court, he wrote: "It has not been denied [that]...within the constitutional authority of Congress, [it may]...lawfully provide for cases of imminent danger of invasion...for the power to provide for repelling invasions *includes* the power to provide against the attempt and danger of

invasion, as the necessary and proper means to effectuate the object. One of the best means to repel invasions is to provide the requisite force for action *before the* invader himself has reached the soil" [emphasis added]. *Martin v. Mott*, 12 Wheat. 19 at 27 (1827).

46. 323 US at pp.222-223.
47. Ibid, p. 225.
48. Ibid, p. 226.
49. Ibid, pp. 233-234. For a complete assessment of the curfew and exclusion decisions, see Peter Irons. *Justice at War: The Story of the Japanese American Interment Cases* (New York: Oxford University Press, 1983).
50. *Dred Scott v. Sandford*, 60 US 393 (1X57); *Plessy v. Ferguson*, 163 US 537 (1896). "Americans would be prouder of their political record if it did not include [them]," wrote Ronald Dworkin in *Law's Empire* (Cambridge: The Belknap Press of Harvard University, 1986) pp. 374, 376.
51. See *Ex Parte Mitsuye Endo*, 323 US 283 at 287-288.
52. Ibid. p. 294.
53. Ibid, pp. 298-299.
54. Ibid. p. 299.
55. Ibid, pp. 299-300.
56. Ibid, p. 303.
57. The case most cogent to the subject under discussion during World War I was that in which the Court sustained the Selective Draft Law, *Aven v. United States*, 245 US 366 (1918).
58. Also see *Billings v. Touesdale*, 321 US 542 (1944) and *Estep v. United States*, 327 US 114 (1946).
59. 332 US 469. Also, *United States v. Chemical Foundation*, 272 US 1.
60. See *Clark v. Vebersee Funonz-Korporation*, 333 US 480 (1947). The Court also permitted Congress to seize excessive profits realized from federal war contracts, *Lichter v. United States* 334 US 742 (1947).
61. *Ludecker v. Watkins*, 335 US 160 (1948).
62. *Hiatt v. Brown*, 339 US 103 (1950).
63. Also see *Hartzel* v. *United States*, 322 US 680 (1944) and *Cramer v. United States*, 325 US 1.

Chapter Six:
The Apex of Presidential Supremacy:
The Truman Years (1946-1953)

After Roosevelt's death on April 12, 1945, President Harry S. Truman inherited the disillusionment of his vexed predecessor over the possibility of future cooperation with the Soviet Union in maintaining world peace. Despite his earlier optimistic views after both the Yalta and Potsdam Conferences (1945), Truman acted consistently with F.D.R.'s interpretation of those Conferences in assuming a more confrontational approach towards the Communist titan.[1] By March 1946, the President adopted George Kennan's "containment policy" of Soviet expansion in Eastern Europe and the Far East to the extent that Truman pledged: the United States would "maintain Western cohesion, combat Soviet propaganda, educate the public, and improve... [the] health and vigor of our own society."[2] By doing so, the Truman administration found that the Soviets "usually retreated when strong resistance is encountered at any point," since "the U.S.S.R.'s retreat from Iran appeared to validate" Kennan's thesis.[3] This policy, which initiated the participation of the United States in the so-called "Cold War" with first the Soviet Union and later China, was exemplified by the formation of NATO in Western Europe, the Marshall Plan, the Berlin Airlift, the "Truman Doctrine," and by aiding Turkey and Greece between 1946-1950.[4]

After the cessation of hostilities in 1945, the Supreme Court handed down three noteworthy decisions influencing the duration and termination of the wartime powers of the President and Congress. In the first, the Supreme Court, for only the third time in its history, adjudicated a case involving "war crimes." On September 3, 1945, General Tomoyuki Yamashita, Commander of the Fourteenth Army Group of the Imperial Japanese Army, which had occupied the Philippine Islands, surrendered to U. S. Army forces. He was charged with the violation of the law of war in that between October 9, 1944, and September 2, 1945, he failed to control the activities of the members of his command which resulted in brutal atrocities including slaughter, pillaging, rape, and the wanton destruction of religious buildings.[5] Apparently, Japanese soldiers attempted to massacre and exterminate some 25,000 Philippine civilians—unarmed men, women and children—in the Batangas Province. On September 12, 1945, President Harry Truman, as Commander in Chief, directed General Douglas MacArthur, Commander of U. S. Forces in the Pacific, to proceed with the trial before an appropriate military tribunal. Within the next two months, General Yamashita, who pleaded not guilty to the charge, was tried by a commission of five Army officers. On December 7, 1945 the defendant was found guilty and was sentenced to death by hanging. His lawyers filed for a Writ of Habeas Corpus and petitioned for a Writ of Certiorari, first before the Supreme Court of the Philippines and later before the Supreme Court of the United States. The latter Court set the two applications down as one case.[6]

Chief Justice Stone, who delivered the opinion of the Court, began by recognizing the authority of Congress to create military commissions for the trial of enemy combatants for offenses against the law of war under Article I, section 8, clause 10 of the Constitution which states that "[Congress is allowed to] define and punish...offenses against the Law of Nations."[7] Relying on *Quirin,* he further pointed out that the Court was neither concerned with the guilt or innocence of the petitioner, nor were the judgments of such a military tribunal subject to review by it. The Chief Justice then turned to the heart of the Yamashita defense that, as commander, he neither committed nor directed such acts against the civilian population; he was not *personally* responsible for the unauthorized actions of his troops and, as a result, no violation should be charged against him. In what was to serve as a "harbinger" at the Nuremberg Trials of Nazi war criminals in Germany, Stone rejected the General's argument:

It is evident that the conduct of military operations by troops whose excesses are unrestrained by the orders or efforts of their commander would almost certainly result in violations which it is the purpose of the law of war to prevent. Its purpose to protect civilian populations and prisoners of war from brutality would largely be defeated if the commander of an invading army could, with impunity, neglect to take reasonable measures for their protection. Hence, the laws of war presuppose...the control of the operations of war by commanders who are to some extent responsible for their subordinates.[8]

Furthermore, Yamashita was the military governor, as well as, Commander of the Philippines, Stone continued, and therefore had "an affirmative duty" to take measures to protect civilians. Moreover, his military trial did not procedurally violate the Geneva Convention of 1929.[9] Finally, Stone upheld the President's order, and those made in pursuance of it, as being lawful since the trial "did not violate any military, or statutory command."[10]

As for the other members of the Court, Justice Robert Jackson was absent for the whole term since President Harry Truman had appointed him "Chief Prosecutor" for the United States at the Nuremberg Trials in the late 1940's. However, given his arguments at the trials, Jackson would have probably agreed with the Chief Justice's conclusions.[11] Associate Justice Frank Murphy dissented, as he had in *Korematsu*, protesting that the charge was only "an alleged war crime" invented by victorious American leaders and that the Yamashita trial was replete with procedural violations in abridgment of the Due Process Clause of the Fifth Amendment. Convinced that the General was tried for "unrecognized crimes that would serve only to permit his accusers to satisfy their desires for revenge," Justice Murphy then made a *prophetic* statement in light of the American experience in Vietnam years later:

The high feelings of the moment doubtless will be satisfied. But in the sober after glow will come the realization of the boundless and dangerous implications of the procedure sanctioned today. No one in a position of command in an army, from sergeant to general, can escape those implications.... That has been the inevitable effect of every method of punishment disregarding the element of personal culpability.[12]

With the "most deeply felt convictions," Justice Wiley Rutledge wrote a lengthy dissent, joined by his brother Murphy, in which he argued:

> This trial is unprecedented in our history. Never before have we tried and convicted an enemy general for action taken during hostilities or otherwise in the course of military operations or duty. Much less have we condemned one for failing to take action.[13]

In a case involving statutory rather than constitutional interpretation, the Court confronted the issue of whether a loyal citizen could be tried by a military tribunal under martial law declared in the Hawaiian Islands. Immediately after the attack by the Japanese on Pearl Harbor, Joseph B. Poindexter, the Governor of Hawaii, proclaimed the suspension of the Writ of Habeas Corpus and placed the territory under martial law. His authority to do so was based on section 67 of the Hawaiian Organic Act of 1900. The next day, the commanding general declared himself Military Governor, closed existing civil and criminal courts, and established military tribunals to take their place. President Roosevelt approved the Territorial Governor's action on December 9.

More than two years and two months after the Japanese attack, Lloyd C. Duncan, a civilian shipfitter, engaged in a brawl with two armed Marine sentries at the Navy Yard in Honolulu. Later that day, February 24, 1944, he was arrested by the military police and eventually placed in the custody of Duke Papa Kahanamoku, Sheriff of the County of Honolulu. By this time, the administration of martial law had been relaxed by the Military Governor to the extent that civilian courts were once again conducting most criminal trials except those violating military orders.[14] Duncan was tried and convicted by a military tribunal and was sentenced to six months imprisonment. The District Court for Hawaii held the trial void and ordered his release; however the Circuit Court of Appeals, Ninth Circuit, ruled that the trial was valid and reversed the Gerry court's ruling. The Supreme Court granted certiorari and decided the case.[15] In a brief opinion, Associate Justice Hugo Black, speaking for the majority, brought attention to the fact that Congress also added Section 5 to the Organic Act which provided "that the Constitution...shall have the same force and effect within the said Territory as elsewhere in the United States."[16] Justice Black continued by saying:

> It follows that civilians in Hawaii are entitled to the Constitutional guarantee of a fair trial to the same extent as those who live in any other part of our country. We are aware that *conditions peculiar to Hawaii* might imperatively demand extraordinarily speedy and effective measures in the *event of actual or threatened invasion....* Whatever power the Organic Act gave Hawaiian military authorities, such power must therefore be construed *in the same way* as a grant of power to troops stationed in any one of the states. [emphases added].*[17]*

Astonishingly, while two years earlier Hugo Black had granted to the President, Congress and military commanders the extra-constitutional sweep of power to imprison Japanese-Americans on the West Coast under the guise of "imminent invasion," he refused to acknowledge the civil and military authorities of Hawaii after a *real, not* imagined, attack by Japanese forces. The spirit and reasoning of *Korematsu,* if not its ruling, was seriously blunted by the *Duncan* opinion.

Not surprisingly, Associate Justice Murphy concurred saying: "The right to jury trial and the other constitutional rights of an accused individual are too fundamental to be sacrificed merely through a reasonable fear of military assault."[18] Chief Justice Stone concurred in the result, while Justice Jackson remained in Nuremberg. On the other hand, Associate Justice Harold Burton, joined by Felix Frankfurter, vigorously dissented on the grounds of judicial self-restraint:

> For this Court to intrude its judgment into spheres of constitutional discretion that are reserved either to Congress or to the Chief Executive, is to invite disregard of that judgment by the Congress or by executive agencies under a claim of a constitutional right to do so.... That conditions of war and the means of meeting its emergencies were within the contemplation of the Constitution...is shown by the broad authority vested in the President of the United States and as Commander in

Chief...and in the war powers of the Congress and the Chief
Executive to preserve the safety of the nation in time of
war.[19]

The judicial sentiments defending presidential prerogative and the
war powers of Congress as being *supreme* in foreign affairs, expressed
in this dissent, would certainly be embraced by such contemporary
Justices as William Rehnquist, Antonin Scalia, and Clarence Thomas.
The last decision, concerning the duration of the war power after
hostilities had ceased, focused on the continuation of federal rent control
under the Housing and Rent Act of 1947. Congress enacted the law, after
President Truman had issued Proclamation No. 2714 terminating
hostilities on December 31, 1946. Because of the diversion during the
war of labor and materials from domestic house construction, there was
a housing shortage aggravated by millions of returning American troops.
The act which, among other measures, established federal rent regulation
and conferred on the Housing Expediter the authority to remove such
controls, under certain conditions, was based on the war power of
Congress. On July 2, 1947, the Lloyd W. Miller Company demanded of
its apartment tenants increases of 40-60% for rental accommodations in
the Cleveland Defense Rental Area. The Miller Company admitted that
it had violated the act; however, it contended that Congress was without
constitutional power to enact the law since the war had *ended;* also, that
the power delegated to the Expediter is an essential legislative power and
is therefore unconstitutional. In response, the Housing Expediter, Tahoe
E. Woods, filed an application to enjoin the violations in the U. S.
District Court for the Northern District of Ohio. After the District Court
denied relief, Woods appealed to the Supreme Court.[20] Speaking for the
majority, Associate Justice William O. Douglas pointed out that "the war
power does not necessarily end with the cessation of hostilities."[21] He
expounded on the legitimacy of this statement:

> Since the war effort contributed heavily to [the housing
> shortage], Congress has the power, even after the cessation of
> hostilities, to act to control the forces that a short supply of the
> needed article created. If that were not true, the Necessary and
> Proper Clause, Art. 1, [section] 8, Cl. 18, would be drastically
> limited in its application to the several war powers.[22]

Justice Douglas all but *ignored* the "illegal delegation" argument of the defendant and concentrated instead upon the responsibilities of Congress:[23]

> Any power, of course, can be abused. But we cannot assume that Congress is not alert to its constitutional responsibilities. And the question in cases such as this is open to judicial inquiry.... Here, it is plain from the legislative history that Congress was invoking its war power to cope with a current condition of which the war was a direct and immediate cause. Its judgment on that score is entitled to the respect granted like legislation enacted pursuant to the police power.[24]

Associate Justice Frankfurter concurred, and Robert Jackson, having returned from Nuremberg, also filed a concurring opinion with the admonition that "this power is the most dangerous one to free government in the whole catalogue of powers."[25]

On the heels of *Woods* and *Lichter*, the Court rekindled a wartime power of the President in domestic policy. In *Ludecke v. Watkins*, 335 US 160 (1948), the Court approved President Roosevelt's order removing certain aliens, mostly German, who were determined to be dangerous "to the public safety." The Court based its approval on the Alien Enemy Act of 1798, which empowers the President to provide for the removal of such aliens whenever there is a *declared* war. With the last of the wartime cases of the 1940s, the Supreme Court maintained its position of allowing the chief executive the greatest possible latitude in conducting international politics. After all, with the development of the Cold War, the President assumed the mantle of "leader of the free world." The advent of the new decade gave the Court ample opportunity to refine its single-leader philosophy, for unknown to either the justices or the American people, the war just concluded was to be the ninth and *last* war proceeded by a declaration by Congress.[26]

On June 5, 1950, the Supreme Court, still adhering to its notion of presidential supremacy in foreign affairs, rendered a decision that was to be of vital importance only *days* later. In *Johnson v. Eisentrager*, Justice Robert Jackson announced the opinion of the Court—with only three dissenting votes—that it is not "the function of the Judiciary to entertain private litigation—even by a citizen—which challenges the legality, wisdom, or propriety of the Commander in Chief in sending our armed forces abroad or to any particular region."[27] The facts involved were as follows: near the end of the war with Japan, American troops in China captured Eisentrager, a former citizen of the United States, and other nonresident enemy aliens who had worked for Nazi Germany. They were tried and convicted by an American military commission for violations of the laws of war, despite their claims of being denied constitutional rights. The Court rejected these claims and upheld the convictions on the basis that the aliens activities occurred during a time of "declared war."[28] However, the Associate Justice went beyond the necessities of the case by exploring the Court's role in the process of committing American troops abroad. Prior to doing so, Jackson had confined his opinion to the subject of whether the nonresident enemy aliens were entitled to either a civil trial or constitutional rights:

> If the Fifth Amendment confers its rights on all the world except Americans engaged in defending it, the same must be true of the companion civil-rights Amendments, for more of them are limited by its express terms, territorially or as persons.... Such extra-territorial application of organic law would have been so significant an innovation in the practice of governments that, if intended or apprehended, it could scarcely have failed to excite contemporary comment. No one word can be cited. No decision of this Court supports such a view.[29]

Later, to support his notion that a military commission is the lawful tribunal to try such offenses, Justice Jackson cited the *Quirin* and *Yamashita* decisions.[30] Then Jackson laid the foundation for his sweeping dicta to come, by enumerating the totality of constitutional war powers. Given American participation in the major and minor wars of the 1960's to 1990, it seems important to cite the majority's conception of that specified power:

> Among powers granted to Congress by the Constitution is the power to provide for common defense, to declare war, to raise and support armies, to provide and maintain a navy, and to make rules for the government and regulation of the land and naval forces. Article I, section 8. Constitution. It also gives

power [to Congress] to make rules concerning captives on land and water...which this Court has construed as an independent substantive power... Indeed, out of seventeen specific paragraphs of congressional power, *eight* of them are devoted in whole or in part to specification of powers connected with warfare.[31]

The author of the opinion then turned his attention to the other political branch and its list of responsibilities and powers:

The first of the enumerated powers of the President is that he shall be Commander in Chief of the Army and Navy of the United States. Article II, section 2, Constitution. And, of course, a part of the war power includes *all that is necessary and proper for carrying these powers into execution.* [emphasis added].[32]

As to the last sentence, *supra*, Justice Jackson was pointing out that not only does the Doctrine of Implied Powers apply to these enumerated powers, Congress has far *more leeway* in doing so since the war powers are key elements of our nation's *foreign* policy not our internal affairs. Upon this legal foundation, Jackson made a pronouncement, in a manner the late George Sutherland probably would have approved, that the Court is *confined* to public litigation if it is *ever* to determine the *"legality,* the *wisdom* or the *propriety"* of a President using American troops during a *declared* war.[33] Does this mean that only Congress could legitimately initiate litigation before the Supreme Court during a "declared war?" An *undeclared* war? Or, in the latter case, could *private* litigation be adjudicated by the Supreme Court? Aspects of the case, he concluded, involve "a challenge to conduct diplomatic and foreign affairs, for which the President is *exclusively* responsible."[34] *Nothing* was mentioned or implied that the President enjoyed the same status of immunity during an *undeclared* or "presidential war."

Only Justice Hugo Black, joined by his brethren Douglas and Burton, dissented in the case.[35] Even so, the Associate Justice made no reference to Jackson's broad concluding statement; rather, Black displayed his disagreement with the majority's interpretations of *Quirin* and *Yamashita* which "lend no support to" their conclusions.[36] Said Black:

> Our Constitution has led people everywhere to hope and to believe that wherever our laws control, all people, whether our citizens or not, would have equal chance before the bar of criminal of criminal justice.[37]

He then made the following concluding remarks:

> Our constitutional principles are such that their mandate of equal justice under the law should be applied as well as when we occupy lands across the sea as when our flag flew over the thirteen colonies. Our nation proclaims a belief in the dignity of human beings as such, no matter what their nationality or where they happen to live. Habeas corpus, as an instrument to protect against illegal imprisonment, is written into the Constitution. Its use by courts cannot in my judgment be constitutionally abridged by Executive or by Congress.... Courts should not for any reason abdicate this, the loftiest power with which the Constitution has endowed them.[38]

The vital question of whether the Supreme Court of the United States has the authority to intervene, in *any* way or form, into those situations where the President has committed American forces, *short* of a declaration of war, has plagued our legal and political processes particularly since 1950. Thus far, the Court, at best, has given very mixed signals. Only two years earlier, President Truman *asserted* the authority to commit American troops to Palestine—*without* congressional approval—as a part of the United Nations' forces; however, he decided not to do so.[39]

On June 24, 1950, the North Korean army invaded South Korea, on either the covert "advice" or encouragement of the USSR and China, which constituted a "test" of collective security under the Charter of the United Nations. More importantly, with the ascension to power of the Communists in China, the disintegration of the "balance of power" in Asia, and the perceived threat to a defeated and unarmed Japan, the Truman administration considered this Communist invasion of our "protégé" to be a direct threat to our "containment policy."[40] Accordingly, the President ordered American air and sea forces to block the North Korean advance on June 27 and 28; however, Truman finally ordered in American troops, together with certain of our United Nations allies, to stem the tide under the command of General Douglas MacArthur. With the USSR absent (in protest over the U.N.'s ban on admission of Communist China as a voting member), the Security Council voted to intervene on behalf of South Korea. After some initial problems, the U.N. Supreme Commander launched a stunning landing at Inchon, over 150 miles behind the enemy lines, on September 15. Within a month, U.N. forces had crossed the 38th parallel and were headed toward the North Korean border with China. History would demonstrate that Joseph Stalin, whose Russian troops had steadfastly avoided any *direct* confrontation with Western forces, was willing to fight *this war* to the last soldier—the last *Chinese* soldier! In late November, Chinese Communist troops or "volunteers" cut through the Korean border and turned back U.N. forces back below the 38th parallel. Although, the military objective of *unifying* Korea had been sanctioned by a United Nations' resolution on October 7, the U.S. Congress had enacted *no* legislation to support the President's decision to intervene in this dispute.[41]

Incredibly, then, the United States found itself involved not only in a war with North Korea, but in a full-scale military conflict with the most populous nation in the world, under the flimsy legal guise of a United Nations' "police action." For the *first* and, as it would turn out, *only* time in its history, the President had committed our country to a full-scale war *without* a congressional delegation of power *or* declaration of war. In fact, Congress was *not* involved in the formulation, fulfillment, or execution of this American intervention in the Far East. It *was* President Truman's war, because his Secretary of State Dean Atchison, an outstanding constitutional lawyer and former clerk to Justice Louis D. Brandies, had assured the President that as Commander in Chief and a charter member of the United Nations, he had the legal power to act on his *own*.[42] Quite aware that Congress would not have issued a declaration, the President should have *at least* asked for a joint resolution which would have constitutionally involved Congress in the war-making process. Some argue that such "a resolution would have spared troop morale and national unity, not to mention the administration itself from, at least *one* damaging form of attack *after* the war became unpopular."[43]

At first, Congress did not criticize Truman's action on constitutional grounds, with the notable exception of Republican Senate leader, Robert A. Taft of Ohio, who commented that the President had "no legal authority" to act as he had. But *even* Taft admitted that he would support a joint resolution justifying such intervention.[44] However, after one year of fighting, congressional and other opposition began to mushroom. So much so that on January 3, 1951, Representative Frederick R. Coudert, Jr., (R-New York) introduced a resolution, which anticipated by two decades the War Powers Act by stating that "no additional military forces" could be committed by the President abroad *without* "prior authorization of Congress in each instance," except to "extricate" American troops from Korea.[45] Consequently, President Truman, acting upon the seemingly unilateral decisions of the Supreme Court from 1936 to 1950, which supported executive prerogative in foreign policy, had, without intending to do so, *fantastically* increased the power of his successors to involve or take the United States into a major war *without* the participation of Legislative Branch.

Of course, some revisionists, including historians and political scientists, disagree strongly with this assessment. For example, Professor Edward Keynes, whose career encompassed distinctly Western European interests, insists that the Korean War "did not furnish the occasion to test President Truman's authority." If, by this statement, Professor Keynes meant that no justifiable litigation reached the Supreme Court of the United States to test the President's legal discretion against our organic law, he is correct; however, the author goes much further in a completely different, as it turns out, *erroneous* direction. Writes Keynes:

> Inasmuch, as the Second World War did not terminate until April 1952, when the Japanese peace treaty came into effect, Truman had initiated military operation under *operative* wartime statutes. Furthermore, as President Truman observed, his actions were pursuant to a United Nations resolution. In dispatching combat forces to Korea, the President was enforcing the United Nations charter, a treaty that has the *force of domestic law* in the United States. Therefore, the Vietnam War was the *first* modern undeclared war that provided the occasion

to test the President's Constitutional authority as Commander
in Chief. [emphases added][46]

The Professor is entitled to his beliefs and he can, no doubt, attempt
to defend them; however, the historical and legal evidence does not
support his views. If, for example, Korea was of such strategic importance that it was to be covered with the protection of "operative wartime
statutes," why did the Secretary of State, Dean Atchison, state in 1950
that South Korea was *outside* of the "American defense perimeter"? In
my view, Keynes is wrong on the following points: First, to state that
Truman's actions were justified because WW II statutes were operative
until April 1952, is to run the Court's rationale in the *Woods* decision
into the ground! From the signing by the Japanese of the Treaty aboard
the battleship *Missouri* in 1945 until the summer of 1950, the United
States was not involved in any form of open hostilities with the Soviet
Union, Communist China, Japan, and certainly not with *North Korea*[47]
If Keynes' point is correct, then *any* President in the future would be
free to conduct any wars he wishes *if* wartime statutes of some kind have
this sort of *indefinable* "half-life." Second, the author's contention that
the President's enforcement of the "police action" provision of the United
Nations Charter justified Truman's commitment of combat troops to
South Korea because, as a treaty it has the force of domestic law, is
sheer constitutional "heresy." Associate Justice Holmes in *Missouri v.
Holland* (1920) assured the people of this nation that a treaty is "the
Supreme law of the land" if, and *only* if, it "does not contravene any
prohibitory words to be found in the Constitution."[48] Of course the
relevant words in this case are found in Article I, section 8, clause 11,
"The Congress shall have Power...to declare war." If Holmes' reasoning
is, for some rationale, found wanting, I would suggest an examination
of a much later decision, *Reid v. Covert* (1947). Third, and finally, all
of Keynes' arguments were presented in the government's brief in the
Youngstown case to justify Truman's seizure of the nation's steel mills
as "defense plants" and all were *rejected* in Justice Black's opinion on
the grounds that such "takings," or seizure, is *solely* within the discretion
of the national legislature.[49] Would the Court have regarded the
Constitutional power of Congress to declare or initiate a state of war in
any *lesser* light? Later, Presidents Bush (in the case of Iraq) and Clinton
(in the case of Bosnia) were to make equally erroneous and unsuppor-

table claims. The Constitution of the United States and our common law tradition are *clear*: the President may not initiate a war using American combat forces without *either* a declaration of war or a joint resolution by Congress as required by the *Curtiss-Wright* decision, unless the United States, its possessions, its armed forces or its citizens are *first* attacked. As Justice Hugo L. Black said forcefully a year after the armed intervention, "The Constitution does not subject this lawmaking power of Congress to presidential or military suppression or control."

As previously mentioned, as the Korean War continued on with no end in sight, a labor dispute at home permitted President Truman to make another fateful decision having an eventual impact on American foreign affairs. Indeed, it was yet another instance in which the President acted on his own authority *without* the expressed consent of Congress.

Late in 1951, labor problems arose between the United Steelworkers of America, and the nation's steel companies over the terms and conditions to be included in new bargaining agreements. With differences unresolved, the Union stated its intention to strike, and thus shut down steel production, on December 31. The matter was first brought before the Federal Mediation and Conciliation Board and then the Federal Wage Stabilization Board, and *both* failed to reach a settlement. On April 4, 1952, the Steelworkers' Union announced a nationwide strike to begin on April 9. Several hours before this deadline, President Truman issued Executive Order 10340 which "directed the Secretary of Commerce [Sawyer] to take possession of most of the steel mills and keep them running." Congress took *no* action.[50]

It is significant that the following events took place: the Supreme Court, after taking the case from the U.S. Court of Appeals for the District of Columbia Circuit recognized, from the outset, the argument that the President acted to protect the "national defense" by entering the Korean conflict;[51] that the respected lawyer, John W. Davis, and the other counsel for the major steel companies, took notice of this fact;[52] and that President Truman in his executive order clearly stated that "American fighting men...are now engaged in deadly combat with the forces of aggression in Korea and...weapons and other materials are needed by our armed forces...and steel is an indispensable component of all such weapons and materials...."[53] Therefore, the overriding question which haunted the members of the Supreme Court, although they never mentioned it specifically, was whether the Korean War was a *sufficient* danger to the national security and safety of the United States to *justify,* in extraconstitutional terms, the President's independent decision to act *alone* to seize the mills?

Mr. Justice Hugo L. Black, a close friend of the President, delivered the opinion of the Court, while Justices Frankfurter, Douglas, Jackson, Burton, and Clark wrote concurring opinions. Chief Justice Vinson, joined by his brethren Read and Milton, filed a dissenting opinion. Four of the Justices—Burton, Vinson, Clark, and Milton—had been appointed by President Truman and had changed the political coloration of the Supreme Court markedly between 1945-1949.[54] This body was *not* the same "friendly" Court that had, so willingly approved Franklin Roosevelt's exertions of power during World War II, or shortly thereafter.

Justice Black was an "absolutist" who based his interpretation of the Constitution of the United States on the bedrock of its "plain language" and the original intent of the Framers of that document. He often referred to the Constitution as "my legal bible."[55] In front of Black and his colleagues, stood John W. Davis, the lawyer Black most admired and, admittedly, one of the greatest advocates of the twentieth century. On May 12, 1952, Davis arguing for the major steel companies thus proclaimed:

> Is it or is it not an immutable principle that our Government is one of limited powers? Is it or is it not an immutable principle that we have a...tripartite system of legislation, execution and judgment? Is it or is it not an immutable principle that the powers of government are based on a government of laws and are not based on a government of men? You cannot dispose of those immutable principles merely by a seizure of this kind.[56]

It is obvious that Davis and his legal staff had a tremendous impact on a majority of the Justices on the Court, but apparently not as much as their own reading of the Constitution's mandate of separation of powers. On June 2, Black announced the Court's opinion:

> The mill owners argue that the President's order amounts to lawmaking, a legislative function which the Constitution has expressly confided to the Congress and not to the President.

The Government's position is that the order was made on findings of the President, that his action was necessary to avert a national catastrophe which would inevitably result from a stoppage of steel production, and that in meeting this grave emergency the President was acting within the aggregate of his constitutional powers as the Nation's Chief Executive and the Commander in Chief of the Armed Forces of the United States [of America].[57]

The Associate Justice, after reviewing the background of the litigation, announced what was later to be one of the most cited paragraphs in the entire opinion:

The President's power, if any, to issue the order [to exercise this power] must stem *either* from an act of Congress *or* from the Constitution itself. There is no statute that expressly authorizes the President to take possession of property as he did here. Nor is there any act of Congress to which our attention has been directed from which such a power can fairly be implied. Indeed, we do not understand the Government to rely on statutory authorization for this seizure. [emphasis added][58]

Black focused attention on the fact that Congress, in the past, had enacted two laws which "do authorize the President to take both personal and real property under certain conditions": (1) The Selective Service Act of 1948 (62 Stat. 604); and (2) The Defense Production Act of 1950 (64 Stat. 798). The President had also refused to invoke the terms of the Taft-Hartley Act (The Labor Management Restorations Act of 1947) *against* which he had campaigned vigorously in his successful presidential election campaign of 1948.[59] Having rejected legislative justification, the author of the opinion then turned to the Constitution and, specifically, to the executive powers granted by Article II:

It is clear that if the President had authority to issue the order he did, it *must* be found in some provision of the Constitution. And it is not claimed that express constitutional language grants this power to the President. The contention is that presidential power should be *implied* from the aggregate [Hamilton's term] of his powers under the Constitution. [emphasis added][60]

Black noted that President Truman had placed particular reliance upon Article II, section 2 (the Commander in Chief clause), and 3 (the faithfully execute clause). Did the President have the legal discretion to *imply* the authority from clause 2 to seize or nationalize private property? The Associate Justice responded:

> The order *cannot* properly be sustained as an exercise of the President's military power as Commander in Chief of the Armed Forces. The Government attempts to do so by citing a number of cases upholding broad powers in military commanders engaged in day-to-day fighting in a *theater of war.* Such cases need not concern us here. Even though "theater of war" is an expanding concept, we cannot with faithfulness to our constitutional system hold that the Commander in Chief of the Armed Forces has the ultimate power [in this existing conflict] as such to take possession of private property in order to keep labor disputes from stopping production. *This* is a job for the Nation's lawmakers, *not* for its military authorities. [emphases added][61]

In many important ways, this quotation from the Court's opinion, *supra,* is the most important citation from the entire decision. As a matter of fact, it could be fairly argued that the Commander in Chief clause provides the constitutional "linchpin" of the case for the following reasons: *First,* in stating his interpretation of Article II, section 2, Justice Black produced *no* proof, either by citing previous Court decisions, or from governmental practices throughout American history. In fact, there were *several* earlier decisions of the Supreme Court which supported the government's position.[62] *Second,* as Justice Felix Frankfurter provided in the appendix, submitted with his concurring opinion, historical precedent had been established by former Commanders-in-Chief. With the outbreak of the Civil War, President Lincoln seized sections of the nation's railroads and telegraph lines *without* statutory authorization.[63] During World War I, President Wilson's administration made *eight* such seizures; while *before,* and after, the attack on Pearl Harbor, President

Franklin Roosevelt exerted such "emergency" seizures on eleven occasions, four of which took place *prior* to December 7, 1941. The most controversial and publicized example was F.D.R.'s seizure of the Montgomery Ward Company in 1945.[64] In addition, there were eighteen instances where Congress did pass implementing legislation to comply with presidential intentions to seize such property. Finally, only *four* of the concurring Justices *agreed* with Black's basic argument. On the other hand, Justices Frankfurter, Jackson, and, particularly, Tom Clark, as well as three dissenting Justices, agreed that: "the President *does* possess, in the absence of restrictive legislation, a residual of resultant power above, or in consequence of those granted powers, to deal with *emergencies* which he regards as *threatening* the national security."[65] This claim was asserted most clearly, by Justice Clark, when he wrote:

> I conclude that where Congress has laid down specific proce-
> dures to deal with the type of crisis confronting the President,
> he *must* follow those procedures in meeting the crisis; *but* that
> in the *absence* of such action by Congress, the President's
> *independent* power to act [on his own] depends upon the
> *gravity* of the situation confronting the nation. [emphases
> added][66]

As previously demonstrated, Clark's (or more likely, Edward Corwin's) constitutional "tests of validity"—the *type* and *gravity* of the crisis—is supported by historical, legal and administrative precedent *throughout* the evolution of the presidential office since 1790. In application, the type of the crisis determines whether it is a domestic or foreign problem since the Framers' gave much *more* discretion to the national government in its handling of foreign or external affairs. Part two of the test is the *gravity,* or the actual seriousness of the threat to the safety and security of the United States. Had the Supreme Court specifically applied Clark's two-prong test in *Korematsu*, one could argue that it would have decided exactly in the same manner as the Roosevelt Court had done in 1944. This type of crisis was indeed *foreign* and the gravity was *most* extreme; however, Truman's undeclared "police action" *failed* the test. No reasonable scholar could rationally argue that the Korean War posed the *same* degree of danger or threat to the nation's security in the 1950's that World War II had done in the 1940's. As Hans J. Morgenthau, a leading expert in world politics, observed (eight years after the conclusion of the Korean War) after the Second World War, "the United States replaced Japan as a check upon Russian ambitions in Korea. China, by intervening in the Korean War, resumed its *traditional* interest in the control of Korea."[67] The actual sense of the *threat* posed to world peace was verified, Morgenthau pointed out, by the fact that of the sixty members of the United Nations, which was founded on the concept of collective security, *only* fifteen countries sent armed forces of *any* kind to South Korea from 1950-1954, and that *only* the United States, Canada, and Great Britain were sufficiently convinced that the gravity of the situation warranted a *full* military response.[68]

Returning to Justice Black's opinion, it drew attention to the *weaker* presidential basis of power in Article 11, section 3, which provided the Court's *apologia*:

> Nor can the seizure order be sustained because of the several constitutional provisions that grant executive power to the President. In the framework of our Constitution, the President's power to see that the laws are faithfully executed *refutes* the idea that he is a *lawmaker*. The Constitution limits his functions in the lawmaking process to the recommending of laws he thinks wise and vetoing of laws he thinks bad. And the Constitution is neither silent nor equivocal about *who* shall make laws which the President is to execute. [emphasis added][69]

As to the similar actions of *past* Presidents, the Associate Justice concluded by casting aside historical precedent:

> It is said that other Presidents without congressional authority have taken possession of private business enterprises in order to settle labor disputes. *But* even if this be true, Congress has *not* thereby *lost* its exclusive constitutional authority to make laws necessary and proper to carry out the powers vested by the Constitution "in the Government of the United States or any Department or Office thereof" [emphasis added][70]

Accordingly, the decision of the federal district court, which had issued the preliminary injunction to restrain the Secretary from carrying out Truman's order, was affirmed. President Truman's reputation as a "tough" decision-maker suffered because of this decision. His effectiveness as President in his relationship with Congress, never very strong, was further tarnished by verbal assaults from both sides of the aisle: Senator John Bricker (R-Ohio) had commented that the presidential seizure was "smacking of a totalitarian philosophy," while his colleague, and future ("imperial") President of the United States, Senator Lyndon B. Johnson (D-Texas), shouted that the President's action displayed a trend toward "dictatorship."[71] The decision, coupled with the President's dismissal of Douglas MacArthur as commanding general of UN forces in Korea, resulted in a public furor. The American people were disillusioned with the "containment policy," and, in a "storm of disapproval," they denounced Truman for the "firing" of MacArthur.[72] When Harry Truman left the White House in January 1953, he had the lowest popularity rating, according to national pollsters, than any President since the polls had begun to take the nation's pulse. (*Only* Richard M. Nixon, upon his resignation twenty-one years later, would finally sink further than Truman's low marks).

For his part, the President from Missouri would describe *Youngstown* as "that crazy decision that has tied up the Country."[73] As for Tom Clark's participation, Truman would remark, that "damn fool from Texas [was] my biggest mistake.... Well, it wasn't so much that he is a bad man. It's just that he is such a dumb son of a bitch. He's about the dumbest man I think I've ever run across."[74]

What may we conclude, then, about *Youngstown's* long-term consequences on the President's prerogative to exercise his emergency powers to meet the crucial stages of future events? The *only* reasonable response is that *only* in the most grave and critical cases, where the people and the Justices perceive "a clear and present danger," may the President exercise his *own* discretion in the absence of confirming congressional legislation or explicit constitutional sanction.

Succeeding Truman was the former WW II General of the Army, Dwight David Eisenhower, the *first* Republican elected to the Presidency since Herbert Hoover in 1928. He, along with congressional Republicans, engaged in a successful political campaign in the 1952 election in their opposition to "Communism, Corruption and Korea." Not long after

President Eisenhower had taken his oath of office, Joseph Stalin, the brutal enemy of the western world, died of still "undetermined" causes in 1953. His multiple successors pledged "peaceful coexistence with the Western and non-Communist countries," but the members of the Eisenhower administration, especially the Secretary of State John Foster Dulles ignored it. The new administration seemed dead set on *confrontation* with the "Communist World." The international scene was characterized as a *bi-polar* world and the "Containment" policy was to be replaced by world "brinkmanship." Doomed to failure from the outset, Communist expansionism was not curtailed by the idle threat of "massive retaliation" on the part of the United States. Fortunately, as shall be demonstrated in Volume II [forthcoming], President Eisenhower learned quickly once in office and, for the most part, relied on power politics and *not* the policies of his Secretary of State.

IN RE YAMASHITA
327 U.S. 1 (1946)

After the completion of all combat involving the United States and Japan in World War II, Japanese General Yamashita was charged with a violation of the law of war. Yamashita had been in command of several divisions of Japanese army troops in the Philippine Islands and was accused of failure to control the illegal conduct and actions of the troops under his control, thus violating of the laws of war.

A military commission was appointed to try Yamashita. On December 18, 1945, Yamashita was found guilty and sentenced to death by hanging. Counsel for Yamashita then filed a writ of habeas corpus and a writ of prohibition to the United States Supreme Court alleging that the military commission was without lawful authority or jurisdiction to place Yamashita on trial.

[excerpts]

MR. CHIEF JUSTICE STONE delivered the opinion of the Court:

...We also emphasized in *ex parte Quirin*, as we do here, that on application for habeas corpus we are not concerned with the guilt or innocence of the petitioners. We consider here only the lawful power of the commission to try the petitioner for the offense charged. In the present cases it must be recognized throughout that the military tribunals which Congress has sanctioned by the Articles of War are not courts whose rulings and judgments are made subject to review by this Court....

By direction of the President, the Joint Chiefs of Staff of the American Military Forces, on September 12, 1945, instructed General MacArthur, Commander in Chief, United States Army Forces, Pacific, to proceed with the trial, before appropriate military tribunals, of such Japanese war criminals "as have been or may be apprehended."...

The Charge. Neither Congressional action nor the military orders constituting the commission authorized it to place petitioner on trial unless the charge preferred against him is of a violation of the law of war. The charge, so far as now relevant, is that *petitioner*, between October 9, 1944 and September 2, 1945, in the Philippine Islands, *"while commander of armed forces of Japan at war with the United States of America and its allies, unlawfully disregarded and failed to discharge his duty as commander to control the operations of the* *members of his command, permitting them to commit brutal atrocities and other high crimes against people of the United States and of its allies and dependencies*, particularly the Philippines; and he...thereby violated the laws of war."...

The first item specifies the execution of a "a deliberate plan and purpose to massacre and exterminate a large part of the civilian population of Batangas Province, and to devastate and destroy public, private and religious property therein, as a result of which more than 25,000 men, women and children, all unarmed noncombatant civilians, were brutally mistreated and killed, without cause or trial, and entire settlements were devastated and destroyed wantonly and without military necessity." Other items specify acts of violence, cruelty and homicide inflicted upon the civilian population and prisoners of war, acts of wholesale pillage and the wanton destruction of religious monuments....

The question then is whether the law of war imposes on an army commander a duty to take such appropriate measures as are within his power to control the troops under his command for the prevention of the specified acts which are violations of the law of war and which are likely to attend the occupation of hostile territory by an uncontrolled soldiery, and whether he may be charged with personal responsibility for his failure to take such measures when violations result....

These provisions plainly imposed on petitioner, who at the time specified was military governor of the Philippines, as well as commander of the Japanese forces, an affirmative duty to take such measures as were within his power and appropriate in the circumstances to protect prisoners of war and the civilian population. This duty of a commanding officer has heretofore been recognized, and its breach penalized by our own military tribunals. A like principle has been applied so as to impose liability on the United States in international arbitrations. Case of Jenaud, 3 Moore, International Arbitrations, 3000; Case of "The Zafiro," 5 Hackworth, Digest of International Law, 707.

We do not make the laws of war but we respect them so far as they do not conflict with the commands of Congress or the Constitution. There is no contention that the present charge, thus read, is without the support of evidence, or that the commission held petitioner responsible for failing to take measures which were beyond his control or inappropriate for a commanding officer to take in the circumstances....

It thus appears that the order convening the commission was a lawful order, that the commission was lawfully constituted, that petitioner was charged with violation of the law of war, and that the commission had authority to proceed with the trial, and in doing so did not violate any military, statutory or constitutional command. We have considered, but find it unnecessary to discuss other contentions which we find to be without merit....

MR. JUSTICE JACKSON took no part in the consideration or decision of these cases.

MR. JUSTICE MURPHY, dissenting:

...The significance of the issue facing the Court today cannot be overemphasized. An American military commission has been established to try a fallen military commander of a conquered nation for an alleged war crime. The authority for such action grows out of the exercise of the power conferred upon Congress by Article I, § 8, Cl. 10 of the Constitution to "define and punish... Offenses against the Law of Nations...." The grave issue raised by this case is whether a military commission so established and so authorized may disregard the procedural rights of an accused person as guaranteed by the Constitution, especially by the due process clause of the Fifth Amendment.

The answer is plain. The Fifth Amendment guarantee of due process of law applies to "any person" who is accused of a crime by the federal government or any of its agencies. No exception is made as to those who are accused of war crimes or as to those who possess the status of an enemy belligerent. Indeed, such an exception would be contrary to the whole philosophy of human rights which makes the Constitution the great living document that it is. The immutable rights of the individual, including those secured by the due process clause of the Fifth Amendment, belong not alone to the members of those nations that excel on the battlefield or that subscribe to the democratic ideology. They belong to every person in the world, victor or vanquished, whatever may be his race, color or beliefs. They rise above any status of belligerency or outlawry....

He was not charged with personally participating in the acts of atrocity or with ordering or condoning their commission. Not even knowledge of these crimes was attributed to him. It was simply alleged that he unlawfully disregarded and failed to discharge his duty as commander to control the operations of the members of his command, permitting them to commit the acts of atrocity....

In my opinion, *such a procedure is unworthy of the traditions of our people or of the immense sacrifices that they have made to advance the common ideals of mankind. The high feelings of the moment doubtless will be satisfied. But in the sober afterglow will come the realization of the boundless and dangerous implications of the procedure sanctioned today.* No one in a position of command in an army, from sergeant to general, can escape those future. *Indeed, the fate of some future President of the United States and his chiefs of staff and military advisers may well have been sealed by this decision....*

International law makes no attempt to define the duties of a commander of an army under constant and overwhelming assault; nor does it impose liability under such circumstances for failure to meet the ordinary responsibilities of command. The omission is understandable. Duties, as well as ability to control troops, vary according to the nature and intensity of the particular battle. To find an unlawful deviation from duty under battle conditions requires difficult and speculative calculations. Such calculations become highly untrustworthy when they are made by the victor in relation to the actions of a vanquished commander. Objective and realistic norms of conduct are then extremely unlikely to be used in forming a judgment as to deviations from duty. The probability that vengeance will form the major part of the victor's judgment is an unfortunate but inescapable fact. So great is that probability that international law refuses to recognize such a judgment as a basis for a war crime, however fair the judgment may be in a particular instance. It is this consideration that undermines the charge against the petitioner in this case... Life and liberty are made to depend upon the biased will of the victor rather than upon objective standards of conduct....

No one denies that inaction or negligence may give rise to liability, civil or criminal. But it is quite another thing to say that the inability to control troops under highly competitive and disastrous battle conditions renders one guilty of a war crime in the absence of personal culpability. Had there been some element of knowledge or direct connection with the atrocities the problem would be entirely different....

MR. JUSTICE RUTLEDGE, dissented:

Not with ease does one find his views at odds with the Court's in a matter of this character and gravity. Only the most deeply felt convictions could force one to differ. That reason alone leads me to do so now, against strong considerations for withholding dissent.

More is at stake than General Yamashita's fate. There could be no possible sympathy for him if he is guilty of the atrocities for which his death is sought. But there can be and should be justice administered according to law. In this stage of war's aftermath it is too early for Lincoln's great spirit, best lighted in the Second Inaugural, to have wide hold for the treatment of foes. It is not too early, it is never too early, for the nation steadfastly to follow its great constitutional traditions, none older or more universally protective against unbridled power than due process of law in the trial and punishment of men, that is, of all men, whether citizens, aliens, alien enemies or enemy belligerents. It can become too late....

This trial is unprecedented in our history. *Never before have we tried and convicted an enemy general for action taken during hostilities or otherwise in the course of military operations or duty. Much less have we condemned one for failing to take action....*

DUNCAN v. KAHANAMOKU
327 U.S. 304 (1946)

This case focused attention on the question of whether a civilian, Mr. Lloyd Duncan, could be tried under martial law in Hawaii by a military tribunal when the civil courts were able to exercise their normal territorial functions. Late one night, Duncan, a civilian shipfitter employed in the Naval Yard in Honolulu, engaged in a brawl with two armed Marine sentries at the yard. He was arrested and placed in detention under the authority of Sheriff Kahanamoku. Duncan was tried and convicted for having violated the law of war, but the territorial federal district court overturned the conviction. The U. S. Court of Appeals for the Ninth Circuit reversed and Duncan petitioned the Supreme Court of the United States.

[excerpts]

MR. JUSTICE BLACK delivered the opinion of the Court.

On December 7, 1941, immediately following the surprise air attack by the Japanese on Pearl Harbor, the Governor of Hawaii by proclamation undertook to suspend the privilege of the writ of habeas corpus and to place the Territory under 'martial law.'...

The President approved the Governor's action on December 9th. The Governor's proclamation also authorized and requested the Commanding General, "during...the emergency and until danger of invasion is removed, to exercise all the powers normally exercised" by the Governor and by "the judicial officers and employees of the Territory."

Pursuant to this authorization the Commanding General immediately proclaimed himself Military Governor and undertook the defense of the Territory and the maintenance of order. On December 8th, both civil and criminal courts were forbidden to summon jurors and witnesses and to try cases. The Commanding General established military tribunals to take the place of the courts....

Duncan, the petitioner in No. 14, was a civilian shipfitter employed in the Navy Yard at Honolulu. On February 24, 1944, more than two years and two months after the Pearl Harbor attack, he engaged in a brawl with two armed Marine sentries at the yard. He was arrested by the military authorities. By the time of his arrest the military had to some extent eased the stringency of military rule. Schools, bars and motion picture theatres had been reopened. Courts had been authorized to "exercise their normal functions." They were once more summoning jurors and witnesses and conducting criminal trials. There were important exceptions, however. One of these was that only military tribunals were to try "Criminal Prosecutions for violations of military orders." As the record shows, these military orders still covered a wide range of day to day civilian conduct. Duncan was charged with violating one of these orders, paragraph 8.01, Title 8, of General Order No. 2, which prohibited assault on military or naval personnel with intent to resist or hinder them in the discharge of their duty. He was therefore, tried by a military tribunal rather than the Territorial Court, although the general laws of Hawaii made assault a crime. Revised L.H.1935, ch. 166. A conviction followed and Duncan was sentenced to six months imprisonment....

The Circuit Court of Appeals, assuming without deciding that the District Court had jurisdiction to entertain the petitions, held the military trials valid and reversed the ruling of the District Court....

Did the Organic Act during the period of martial law give the armed forces power to supplant all civilian laws and to substitute military for judicial trials under the conditions that existed in Hawaii at the time these petitioners were tried? The relevant conditions, for our purposes, were the same when both petitioners were tried. The answer to the question depends on a correct interpretation of the Act. But we need not construe the Act, insofar as the power of the military might be used to meet other and different conditions and situations. The boundaries of the situation with reference to which we do interpret the scope of the Act can be more sharply defined by stating at this point some different conditions which either would or might conceivably have affected to a greater or lesser extent the scope of the authorized military power. We note first that at the time the alleged offenses were committed the dangers apprehended by the military were not sufficiently imminent to cause them to require civilians to evacuate the area or even to evacuate any of the buildings necessary to carry on the business of the courts. In fact, the buildings had long been open and actually in use for certain kinds of trials. Our question does not involve the well-established power of the military to exercise jurisdiction over members of the armed forces, those directly connected with such forces, or enemy belligerents, prisoners of war, or others charged with violating the laws of war. We are not concerned with the recognized power of the military to try civilians in tribunals established as a part of a temporary military government over occupied enemy territory or territory regained from an enemy where civilian government cannot and does not function. For Hawaii since annexation has been held by and loyal to the United States. Nor need we here consider the power of the military simply to arrest and detain civilians interfering with a necessary military function at a time of turbulence and danger from insurrection or war. And finally, there was no specialized effort of the military, here, to enforce orders which related only to military functions, such as, for illustration, curfew rules or blackouts. For these petitioners were tried before tribunals set up under a military program which took over all government and superseded all civil laws and courts. If the Organic Act, properly interpreted, did not give the armed forces this awesome power, both petitioners are entitled to their freedom.

I.

In interpreting the Act we must first look to its language. Section 67 makes it plain that Congress did intend the Governor of Hawaii, with the approval of the President, to invoke military aid under certain circumstances. But Congress did not specifically state to what extent the army could be used or what power it could exercise. It certainly did not explicitly declare that the Governor in conjunction with the military could for days, months or years close all the courts and supplant them with military tribunals....

II.

Since the Act's language does not provide a satisfactory answer, we look to the legislative history for possible further aid in interpreting the term "martial law" as used in the statute. The government contends that the legislative history shows that Congress intended to give the armed forces extraordinarily broad powers to try civilians before military tribunals....

But when the Organic Act is read as a whole and in the light of its legislative history it becomes clear that Congress did not intend the Constitution to have a limited application to Hawaii. Along with § 67

Congress enacted § 5 of the Organic Act which provides "that the Constitution...shall have the same force and effect within the said Territory as elsewhere in the United States."...

Even when Hawaii was first annexed Congress had provided that the Territory's existing laws should remain in effect unless contrary to the Constitution.... Congress thus expressed a strong desire to apply the Constitution without qualification.

It follows that civilians in Hawaii are entitled to the Constitutional guarantee of a fair trial to the same extent as those who live in any other part of our country. We are aware that conditions peculiar to Hawaii might imperatively demand extraordinarily speedy and effective measures in the event of actual or threatened invasion. But this also holds true for other parts of the United States. Extraordinary measures in Hawaii, however necessary, are not supportable on the mistaken premise that Hawaiian inhabitants are less entitled to Constitutional protection than others....

III.

Since both the language of the Organic Act and its legislative history fail to indicate that the scope of "martial law" in Hawaii includes the supplanting of courts by military tribunals, we must look to other sources in order to interpret that term. We think the answer may be found in the birth, development and growth of our governmental institutions up to the time Congress passed the Organic Act....

People of many ages and countries have feared and unflinchingly opposed the kind of subordination of executive, legislative and judicial authorities to complete military rule which according to the government Congress has authorized here. In this country that fear has become part of our cultural and political institutions. The story of that development is well known and we see no need to retell it all. But we might mention a few pertinent incidents. As early as the 17th Century our British ancestors took political action against aggressive military rule. When James I and Charles I authorized martial law for purposes of speedily punishing all types of crimes committed by civilians the protest led to the historic Petition of Right which in uncompromising terms objected to this arbitrary procedure and prayed that it be stopped and never repeated. When later the American colonies declared their independence one of the grievances listed by Jefferson was that the King had endeavored to render the military superior to the civil power....

Courts and their procedural safeguards are indispensable to our system of government. They were set up by our founders to protect the liberties they valued... Our system of government clearly is the antithesis of total military rule and the founders of this country are not likely to have contemplated complete military dominance within the limits of a Territory made part of this country and not recently taken from an enemy. They were opposed to governments that placed in the hands of one man the power to make, interpret and enforce the laws. Their philosophy has been the people's throughout our history. For that reason we have maintained legislatures chosen by citizens or their representatives and courts and juries to try those who violate legislative enactments. We have always been especially concerned about the potential evils of summary criminal trials and have guarded against them by provisions embodied in the constitution itself....

We believe that when Congress passed the Hawaiian Organic Act and authorized the establishment of "martial law" it had in mind and did not wish to exceed the boundaries between military and civilian power, in which our people have always believed, which responsible military and executive officers had heeded, and which had become part of our political philosophy and institutions prior to the time Congress passed the Organic Act. The phrase "martial law" as employed in that Act, therefore, while intended to authorize the military to act vigorously for the maintenance of an orderly civil government and for the defense of the island against actual or threatened rebellion or invasion, was not intended to authorize the supplanting of courts by military tribunals. Yet the government seeks to justify the punishment of both White and Duncan on the ground of such supposed Congressional authorization. We hold that both petitioners are now entitled to be released from custody.

Reversed.

MR. JUSTICE JACKSON took no part in the consideration or decision of this case.

MR. JUSTICE MURPHY, concurred:

The Court's opinion, in which I join, makes clear that the military trials in these cases were unjustified by the martial law provisions of the Hawaiian Organic Act. Equally obvious, as I see it, is the fact that these trials were forbidden by the Bill of Rights of the Constitution of the United States, which applies in both spirit and letter to Hawaii. Indeed, the unconstitutionality of the usurpation of civil power by the military is so great in this instance as to warrant this Court's complete and out-right repudiation of the action.

Abhorrence of military rule is ingrained in our form of government. Those who founded this nation knew full well that the arbitrary power of conviction and punishment for pretended offenses is the hallmark of despotism....

There is a very necessary part in our national life for the military; it has defended this country well in its darkest hours of trial. But militarism is not our way of life. It is to be used only in the most extreme circumstances. Moreover, we must be on constant guard against an excessive use of any power, military or otherwise, that results in the needless destruction of our rights and liberties. There must be a careful balancing of interests. And we must ever keep in mind that "The Constitution of the United States is a law for rulers and people, equally in war and in peace, and covers with the shield of its protection all classes of men, at all times, and under all circumstances."...

MR. CHIEF JUSTICE STONE, concurred:

...I find nothing in the entire record which would fairly suggest that the civil courts were unable to function with their usual efficiency at the times these petitioners were tried, or that their trial by jury in a civil court would have endangered good order or the public safety. The Governor of Hawaii and the Chief Justice of the Hawaiian Supreme Court testified to the contrary. The military authorities themselves testified and advanced no reason which has any bearing on public safety or good order for closing the civil courts to the trial of these petitioners, or for trying them in military courts. I can only conclude that the trials and the convictions upon which petitioners are now detained, were unauthorized by the statute, and without lawful authority.

We have no occasion to consider whether the arrest and detention of petitioners by the military authorities, pending their delivery to the civil authorities for trial, would have been lawful. The judgment of the Circuit Court of Appeals should be reversed and the petitioners discharged from custody forthwith.

MR. JUSTICE BURTON, with whom MR. JUSTICE FRANKFURTER joined, dissented:

...The conduct of war under the Constitution is largely an executive function. Within the field of military action in time of war, the executive is allowed wide discretion. While, even in the conduct of war, there are many lines of jurisdiction to draw between the proper spheres of legislative, executive and judicial action, it seems clear that at least on an active battle field, the executive discretion to determine policy is there intended by the Constitution to be supreme. The question then arises: What is a battle field and how long does it remain one after the first barrage?

It is well that the outer limits of the jurisdiction of our military authorities is subject to review by our courts even under such extreme circumstances as those of the battle field....

For this Court to intrude its judgment into spheres of constitutional discretion that are reserved either to the Congress or to the Chief Executive, is to invite disregard of that judgment by the Congress or by executive agencies under a claim of constitutional right to do so. On the other hand, this Court can contribute much to the orderly conduct of government, if it will outline reasonable boundaries for the discretion of the respective departments of the Government, with full regard for the limitations and also for the responsibilities imposed upon them by the Constitution.

It is important to approach the present cases with a full appreciation of the responsibility of the executive branch of the Government in Hawaii under the invasion which occurred on December 7, 1941....

Whether or not from the vantage post of the present this Court may disagree with the judgment exercised by the military authorities in their schedule of relaxation of control is not material unless this Court finds that the schedule was so delayed as to exceed the range of discretion which such conditions properly vest in the military authorities.

It is all too easy in this postwar period to assume that the success which our forces attained was inevitable and that military control should have been relaxed on a schedule based upon such actual developments....

In order to recognize the full strength of our Constitution, both in time of peace and in time of war, it is necessary to protect the authority of our legislative and executive officials, as well as that of our courts, in the performance of their respective obligations to help to "establish Justice, insure domestic Tranquility, provide for the common defence, promote the general Welfare and secure the Blessings of Liberty to ourselves and our Posterity."...

The provision of § 67 of the Hawaiian Organic Act conferring power upon the territorial governor to place the Territory under martial law "in case of rebellion or invasion, or imminent danger thereof, when the public safety requires it" may not, in view of the provision of § 5 of the Act that the Federal Constitution shall have the same force and effect in the Territory as elsewhere in the United States....

Civilians in Hawaii are entitled to the Constitutional guaranty of a fair trial to the same extent as those who live in the continental United States....

Power to declare martial law does not include the power to supplant civilian laws by military orders and to supplant courts by military tribunals, where conditions are not such as to prevent the enforcement of the laws by the courts....

Trial of a civilian by a military tribunal for an offense other than against the law of war is not justified by § 67 of the Hawaiian Organic Act....

WOODS v. MILLER
333 U.S. 138 (1948)

After World War II, Mr. Miller and others had demanded rental increases of 40 to 60 percent from their tenants in housing located in the Cleveland Defense Rental Area. This increase clearly violated Title II of the Housing and Rent Act passed by Congress in 1947. Woods, a housing official, sued in an Ohio federal district court to enjoin these violations of the act. The federal court denied the injunction on the ground that the Act was unconstitutional. Woods then appealed directly to the Supreme Court.

[excerpts]

MR. JUSTICE DOUGLAS delivered the opinion of the Court:

...The District Court was of the view that the authority of Congress to regulate rents by virtue of the war power...ended with the Presidential Proclamation terminating hostilities on December 31, 1946, since that proclamation inaugurated "peace-in-fact" though it did mark termination of the war. It also concluded that, even if the war power continues, Congress did not act under it because it did not say so, and only if Congress says so, or enacts provisions so implying, can it be held that Congress intended to exercise such power. That Congress did not so intend, said the District Court, follows from the provision that the Housing Expediter can end controls in any area without regard to the official termination of the war, and from the fact that the preceding federal rent-control laws (which were concededly exercises of the war power) were neither amended nor extended. The District Court expressed the further view that rent control is not within the war power because "the emergency created by housing shortage came into existence long before the war."...

We conclude, in the first place, that the war power sustains this legislation....
[T]he war power includes the power "to remedy the evils which have arisen from its rise and progress" and continues for the duration of that emergency. *Whatever may be the consequences when war is officially terminated, the war power does not necessarily end with the cessation of hostilities....*

The legislative history of the present Act makes abundantly clear that there has not yet been eliminated the deficit in housing which in considerable measure was caused by the heavy demobilization of veterans and by the cessation or reduction in residential construction during the period of hostilities due to the allocation of building materials to military projects. Since the war effort contributed heavily to that deficit, Congress has the power even after the cessation of hostilities to act to control the forces that a short supply of the needed article created. If that were not true, the Necessary and Proper Clause, Art. I, § 8, cl. 18, would be drastically limited in its application to the several war powers. The Court has declined to follow that course in the past.... We decline to take it today. The result would be paralyzing. It would render Congress powerless to remedy conditions the creation of which necessarily followed from the mobilization of men and materials for successful prosecution of the war. So to read the Constitution would be to make it self-defeating.

We recognize the force of the argument that the effects of war under modern conditions may be felt in the economy for years and years, and that if the war power can be used in days of peace to treat all the wounds which war inflicts on our society, it may not only swallow up all other powers of Congress but largely obliterate the Ninth and Tenth Amendments as well. There are no such implications in today's decision. We deal here with the consequences of a housing deficit greatly intensified during the period of hostilities by the war effort. Any power, of course, can be abused. But we cannot assume that Congress is not alert to its constitutional responsibilities. And the question whether the war power had been properly employed in cases such as this is open to judicial inquiry....

The question of the constitutionality of action taken by Congress does not depend on recitals of the power which it undertakes to exercise. *Here it is plain from the legislative history that Congress was invoking its war power to cope with a current condition of which the war was a direct and immediate cause.* Its judgment on that score is entitled to the respect granted like legislation enacted pursuant to the police power....

Reversed.

MR. JUSTICE FRANKFURTER and JUSTICE JACKSON concurred:

I agree with the result in this case, but the *arguments that have been addressed to us lead me to utter more explicit misgivings about war powers than the Court has done. The Government asserts no constitutional basis for this legislation other than this vague, undefined and undefinable "war power. "*

No one will question that this power is the *most dangerous* one to free government in the whole catalogue of powers. It usually is invoked in haste and excitement when calm legislative consideration of constitutional limitation is difficult. It is executed in a time of patriotic fervor that makes moderation unpopular. And, worst of all, it is interpreted by judges under the influence of the same passions and pressures. Always, as in this case, the Government urges hasty decision to forestall some emergency or serve some purpose and pleads that paralysis will result if its claims to power are denied or the confirmation delayed.

Particularly when the war power is invoked to do things to the liberties of people, or to their property or economy that only indirectly affect conduct of the war and do not relate to the management of the war itself, the constitutional basis should be scrutinized with care.

I think we can hardly deny that the war power is as valid a ground for federal rent control now as it has been at any time. We still are technically in a state of war. *I would not be willing to hold that war powers may be indefinitely prolonged merely by keeping legally alive a state of war that had in fact ended. I cannot accept the argument that war powers last as long as the effects and consequences of war, for if so they are permanent—as permanent as the war debts.* But I find no reason to conclude that we could find fairly that the present state of war is merely technical. We have armies abroad exercising our war power and have made no peace terms with our allies, not to mention our principal enemies. I think the conclusion that the war power has been applicable during the lifetime of this legislation is unavoidable.

JOHNSON v. EISENTRAGER
339 U.S. 763 (1950)

Eisentrager (alias Ehrhardt) and twenty other German agents were captured in China by American troops. They were tried and convicted for violations of the laws of war by a military commission. Eisentrager, a former citizen and resident in the United States, claimed that his military trial violated his procedural rights under Articles I, II, and the Fifth Amendment, inter alia, under the Constitution of the United States. The critical element of the decision was the Court's retreat on stressing presidential supremacy and thus the genesis of the judiciary's evolution in law toward the "political question" doctrine in foreign policy matters. The defendants petitioned the federal district court for habeas corpus relief directed at Johnson, the Secretary of Defense and others. The district court refused to grant the writ, while the court of appeals reversed. The government petitioned to the U.S. Supreme Court for a review of the case.

[excerpts]

MR. JUSTICE JACKSON delivered the opinion of the Court:

It is claimed that their trial, conviction and imprisonment violate Articles I and III of the Constitution, and the Fifth Amendment thereto, and other provisions of the Constitution and laws of the United States and provisions of the Geneva Convention governing treatment of prisoners of war....

We are cited to no instance where a court, in this or any other country where the writ is known, has issued it on behalf of an alien enemy who, at no relevant time and in no stage of his captivity, has been within its territorial jurisdiction. Nothing in the text of the Constitution extends such a right, nor does anything in our statutes. Absence of support from legislative or juridical sources is implicit in the statement of the court below that "The answers stem directly from fundamentals. They cannot be found by casual reference to statutes or cases." The breadth of the court's premises and solution requires us to consider questions basic to alien enemy and kindred litigation which for some years have been beating upon our doors.

Modern American law has come a long way since the time when outbreak of war made every enemy national an outlaw, subject to both public and private slaughter, cruelty and plunder. But even by the most magnanimous view, our law does not abolish inherent distinctions recognized throughout the civilized world between citizens and aliens, nor between aliens of friendly and of enemy allegiance, nor between resident enemy aliens who have submitted themselves to our laws and nonresident enemy aliens who at all times have remained with, and adhered to, enemy governments.

With the citizen we are now little concerned, except to set his case apart as untouched by this decision and to take measure of the difference between his status and that of all categories of aliens. Citizenship as a head of jurisdiction and a ground of protection was old when Paul invoked it in his appeal to Caesar. The years have not destroyed nor diminished the importance of citizenship nor have they sapped the vitality of a citizen's claims upon his government for protection. If a person's claim to United States citizenship is denied by any official, Congress has directed our courts to entertain his action to declare him to be a citizen "regardless of whether he is within the United States or abroad." This Court long ago extended habeas corpus to one seeking admission to the country to assure fair hearing of his claims to citizenship, *Chin Yow v. United States*, 208 U.S. 8, and has secured citizenship against forfeiture by involuntary formal acts, *Perkins v. Elg, 307 U.S. 325.* Because the Government's obligation of protection is correlative with the duty of loyal support inherent in the citizen's allegiance, Congress has directed the President to exert the full diplomatic and political power of the United States on behalf of any citizen, but of no other, in jeopardy abroad. When any citizen is deprived of his liberty by any foreign government, it is made the duty of the President to demand the reasons and, if the detention appears wrongful, to use means not amounting to acts of war to effectuate his release. It is neither sentimentality nor chauvinism to repeat that "Citizenship is a high privilege."....

Mere lawful presence in the country creates an implied assurance of safe conduct and gives him certain rights; they become more extensive and secure when he makes preliminary declaration of intention to become a citizen, and they expand to those of full citizenship upon naturalization. During his probationary residence, this Court has steadily enlarged his right against Executive deportation except upon full and fair hearing... And, at least since 1886, we have extended to the person and property of resident aliens important constitutional guaranties—such as the due process of law of the Fourteenth Amendment. *Yick Wo v. Hopkins*, 118 U.S. 356.

But, in extending constitutional protections beyond the citizenry, the Court has been at pains to point out that it was the alien's presence within its territorial jurisdiction that gave the Judiciary power to act....

It is war that exposes the relative vulnerability of the alien's status. The security and protection enjoyed while the nation of his allegiance remains in amity with the United States are greatly impaired when his nation takes up arms against us. While his lot is far more humane and endurable than the experience of our citizens in some enemy lands, it is still not a happy one. But disabilities this country lays upon the alien who becomes also an enemy are imposed temporarily as an incident of war and not as an incident of alienage....

The essential pattern for reasonable Executive constraint of enemy aliens, not on the basis of individual prepossessions for their native land but on the basis of political and legal relations to the enemy government, was laid down in the very earliest days of the Republic and has endured to this day. It was established by the Alien Enemy Act of 1798....

Executive power over enemy aliens, undelayed and unhampered by litigation,has been deemed, throughout our history, essential to war-time security. This is in keeping with the practices of the most enlightened of nations and has resulted in treatment of alien enemies more considerate than that which has prevailed among any of our enemies and some of our allies.

The resident enemy alien is constitutionally subject to summary arrest, internment and deportation whenever a "declared war" exists. Courts will entertain his plea for freedom from Executive custody only to ascertain the existence of a state of war and whether he is an alien enemy and so subject to the Alien Enemy Act. Once these jurisdictional elements have been determined, courts will not inquire into any other issue as to his internment. *Ludecke v. Watkins*....

But the nonresident enemy alien, especially one who has remained in the service of the enemy, does not have been this qualified access to our courts, for he neither has comparable claims upon our institutions nor could his use of them fail to be helpful to the enemy. Our law on this subject first emerged about 1813 when the Supreme Court of the State of New York had occasion, in a series of cases, to examine the foremost authorities of the Continent and of England. It concluded the rule of the common law and the law of nations to be that alien enemies resident in the country of the enemy could not maintain an action in its courts during the period of hostilities....

When we analyze the claim prisoners are asserting and the court below sustained, it amounts to a right not to be tried at all for an offense against our armed forces. If the Fifth Amendment protects them from military trial, the Sixth Amendment as clearly prohibits their trial by civil courts. The latter requires in all criminal prosecutions that "the accused" be tried "by an impartial jury of the State and district wherein the crime shall have been committed, which district shall have been previously ascertained by law." And if the Fifth be held to embrace these prisoners because it uses the inclusive term "no person," the Sixth must, for it applies to all "accused." No suggestion is advanced by the court below or by prisoners of any constitutional method by which any violations of the laws of war endangering the United States forces could be reached or punished, if it were not by a Military Commission in the theater where the offense was committed....

If this Amendment invests enemy aliens in unlawful hostile action against us with immunity from military trial, it puts them in a more protected position than our own soldiers. American citizens conscripted into the military service are thereby stripped of their Fifth Amendment rights and as members of the military establishment are subject to its discipline, including military trials for offenses against aliens or Americans....

If the Fifth Amendment confers its rights on all the world except Americans engaged in defending it, the same must be true of the companion civil-rights Amendments, for none of them is limited by its express terms, territorially or as to persons. Such a construction would mean that during military occupation irreconcilable enemy elements, guerrilla fighters, and "were-wolves" could require the American Judiciary to assure them freedoms of speech, press, and assembly as in the First Amendment, right to bear arms as in the Second, security against "unreasonable" searches and seizures as in the Fourth, as well as rights to jury trial as in the Fifth and Sixth Amendments. Such extraterritorial application of organic law would have been so significant an innovation in the practice of governments that, if intended or apprehended, it could scarcely have failed to excite contemporary comment. Not one word can be cited. No decision of this Court supports such a view....

We hold that the Constitution does not confer a right of personal security or an immunity from military trial and punishment upon an alien enemy engaged in the hostile service of a government at war with the United States....

Among powers granted to Congress by the Constitution is power to provide for the common defense, to declare war, to raise and support armies, to provide and maintain a navy, and to make rules for the government and regulation of the land and naval forces, Art. I, § 8, Const. It also gives power to make rules concerning captures on land and water, ibid., which this Court has construed as an independent substantive power. *Brown v. United States*, 8 Cranch 110, 126. Indeed, out of seventeen specific paragraphs of congressional power, eight of them are devoted in whole or in part to specification of powers connected with warfare. The first of the enumerated powers of the President is that he shall be Commander in Chief of the Army and Navy of the United States. Art. II, § 2, Const. And, of course, grant of war power includes all that is necessary and proper for carrying these powers into execution.

Certainly it is not the function of the Judiciary to entertain private litigation—even by a citizen—which challenges the legality, the wisdom, or the propriety of the Commander in Chief in sending our armed forces abroad or to any particular region....

We are unable to find that the petition alleges any fact showing lack of jurisdiction in the military authorities to accuse, try and condemn these prisoners or that they acted in excess of their lawful powers....

For reasons stated, the judgment of the Court of Appeals is reversed and the judgment of the District Court dismissing the petition is affirmed.

Reversed.

MR. JUSTICE BLACK, with whom MR. JUSTICE DOUGLAS and MR. JUSTICE BURTON joined, dissented:

Not only is United States citizenship a "high privilege," it is a priceless treasure. For that citizenship is enriched beyond price by our goal of equal justice under law—equal justice not for citizens alone, but for all persons coming within the ambit of our power. This ideal gave birth to the constitutional provision for an independent judiciary with authority to check abuses of executive power and to issue writs of habeas corpus liberating persons illegally imprisoned....

In *ex parte Quirin*, we held that status as an enemy alien did not foreclose "consideration by the courts of petitioners' contentions that the Constitution and laws of the United States constitutionally enacted forbid their trial by military commission." This we did in the face of a presidential proclamation denying such prisoners access to our courts. Only after thus upholding jurisdiction of the courts to consider such habeas corpus petitions did we go on to deny those particular petitions upon a finding that the prisoners had been convicted by a military tribunal of competent jurisdiction for conduct that we found constituted an actual violation of the law of war. Similarly, in *re Yamashita*, 327 U.S. 1, we held that courts could inquire whether a military commission, promptly after hostilities had ceased, had lawful authority to try and condemn a Japanese general charged with violating the law of war before hostilities had ceased....

When a foreign enemy surrenders, the situation changes markedly. If our country decides to occupy conquered territory either temporarily or permanently, it assumes the problem of deciding how the subjugated people will be ruled, what laws will govern, who will promulgate them, and what governmental agency of ours will see that they are properly administered. This responsibility immediately raises questions concerning the extent to which our domestic laws, constitutional and statutory, are transplanted abroad. Probably no one would suggest, and certainly I would not, that this nation either must or should attempt to apply every constitutional provision of the Bill of Rights in controlling temporarily occupied countries. But that does not mean that the Constitution is wholly inapplicable in foreign territories that we occupy and govern....

Our Constitution has led people everywhere to hope and believe that wherever our laws control, all people, whether our citizens or not, would have an equal chance before the bar of criminal justice.... Our constitutional principles are such that their mandate of equal justice under law should be applied as well when we occupy lands across the sea as when our flag flew only over thirteen colonies. *Our nation proclaims a belief in the dignity of human beings as such, no matter what their nationality or where they happen to live.* Habeas corpus, as an instrument to protect against illegal imprisonment, is written into the Constitution. Its use by courts cannot in my judgment be constitutionally abridged by Executive or by Congress.... *Courts should not for any reason abdicate this, the loftiest power with which the Constitution has endowed them.*

YOUNGSTOWN SHEET & TUBE CO.
v. SAWYER
343 U.S. 579 (1952)

*Even though the crux of this case centered on President Truman's seizure order to his Secretary of Commerce, Mr. Sawyer, nationalizing the nation's privately-owned steel mills, it had extremely important overtones, more implied than stated, with respect to the war powers shared by the political branches. It is instructive to recall that **Curtiss-Wright** did not grant "carte blanc" to the Commander in Chief in foreign policy. Without being first attacked or having a declaration of war, the President cannot legally initiate conflict in the absence of a joint resolution from Congress; nor can he exercise emergency powers not yielded to him by the Constitution including the "taking of private property." [**Contrast:** the Court's judgment on Truman's order in this case with that of F.D.R.'s executive order in **Korematsu**.]*

[excerpts]

MR. JUSTICE BLACK delivered the opinion of the Court:

The mill owners argue that the President's order amounts to lawmaking, a legislative function which the Constitution has expressly confided to the Congress and not to the President. The Government's position is that the order was made on findings of the President that his action was necessary to avert a national catastrophe which would inevitably result from a stoppage of steel production, and that in meeting this grave emergency the President was acting within the aggregate of his constitutional powers as the Nation's Chief Executive and the Commander in Chief of the Armed Forces of the United States. The issue emerges here from the following series of events:

In the latter part of 1951, a dispute arose between the steel companies and their employees over terms and conditions that should be included in new collective bargaining agreements. Long-continued conferences failed to resolve the dispute. On December 18, 1951, the employees' representative, United Steelworkers of America, C.I.O., gave notice of an intention to strike when the existing bargaining agreements expired on December 31. The Federal Mediation and Conciliation Service then intervened in an effort to get labor and management to agree. This failing, the President on December 22, 1951, referred the dispute to the Federal Wage Stabilization Board to investigate and make recommendations for fair and equitable terms of settlement. This Board's report resulted in no settlement. On April 4, 1952, the Union gave notice of a nation-wide strike called to begin at 12:01 a.m. April 9. The indispensability of steel as a component of substantially all weapons and other war materials led the President to believe that the proposed work stoppage would immediately jeopardize our national defense and that governmental seizure of the steel mills was necessary in order to assure the continued availability of steel. Reciting these considerations for his action, the President, a few hours before the strike was to begin, issued Executive Order 10340, a copy of which is attached as an appendix, *post*, p. 589. The order directed the Secretary of Commerce to take possession of most of the steel mills and keep them running. The Secretary immediately issued his own possessory orders, calling upon the presidents of the various seized companies to serve as operating managers for the United States. They were directed to carry on their activities in accordance with regulations and directions of the Secretary....

Obeying the Secretary's orders under protest, the companies brought proceedings against him in the District Court. Their complaints charged that the seizure was not authorized by an act of Congress or by any constitutional provisions. The District Court was asked to declare the orders of the President and the Secretary invalid and to issue preliminary and permanent injunctions restraining their enforcement. Opposing the motion for preliminary injunction, the United States asserted that a strike disrupting steel production for even a brief period would so endanger the well being and safety of the Nation that the President had "inherent power" to do what he had done—power "supported by the Constitution, by historical precedent, and by court decisions." The Government also contended that in any event no preliminary injunction should be issued because the companies had made no showing that their available legal remedies were inadequate or that their injuries from seizure would be irreparable. Holding against the Government on all points, the District Court on April 30 issued a preliminary injunction restraining the Secretary from 'continuing the seizure and possession of the plants...and from acting under the purported authority of Executive Order No. 10340....'

Two crucial issues have developed: First. Should final determination of the constitutional validity of the President's order be made in this case which has proceeded no further than the preliminary injunction stage? Second. If so, is the seizure order within the constitutional power of the President?

I.

It is urged that there were nonconstitutional grounds upon which the District Court could have denied the preliminary injunction and thus have followed the customary judicial practice of declining to reach and decide constitutional questions until compelled to do so. On this basis it is argued that equity's extraordinary injunctive relief should have been denied because (a) seizure of the companies' properties did not inflict irreparable damages, and (b) there were available legal remedies adequate to afford compensation for any possible damages which they might suffer....

II.

The President's power, if any, to issue the order must stem either from an act of Congress or from the Constitution itself. There is no statute that expressly authorizes the President to take possession of property as he did here. Nor is there any act of Congress to which our attention has been directed from which such a power can fairly be implied. Indeed, we do not understand the Government to rely on statutory authorization for this seizure. There are two statutes which do authorize the President to take both personal and real property under certain conditions. However, the Government admits that these conditions were not met and that the President's order was not rooted in either of the statutes. The Government refers to the seizure provisions of one of these statutes (s 201(b) of the Defense Production Act) as "much too cumbersome, involved, and time-consuming for the crisis which was at hand." Moreover, the use of the seizure technique to solve labor disputes in order to prevent work stoppages was not only unauthorized by any congressional enactment; prior to this controversy, Congress had refused to adopt that method of settling labor disputes....

It is clear that if the President had authority to issue the order he did, it must be found in some provisions of the Constitution. And it is not claimed that express constitutional language grants this power to the President. The contention is that presidential power should be implied from the aggregate of his powers under the Constitution. Particular reliance is placed on provisions in Article II which say that "the executive power shall be vested in a President..." that "he shall take care that the laws be faithfully executed"; and that he "shall be Commander in Chief of the Army and Navy of the United States."

The order cannot properly be sustained as an exercise of the President's military power as Commander in Chief of the Armed Forces. The Government attempts to do so by citing a number of cases upholding broad powers in military commanders engaged in day-to-day fighting in a theater of war. Such cases need not concern us here. Even though "theater of war" be an expanding concept, we cannot with faithfulness to our constitutional system hold that the Commander in Chief of the Armed Forces has the ultimate power as such to take possession of private property in order to keep labor disputes from stopping production. This is a job for the Nation's lawmakers, not for its military authorities.

Nor can the seizure order be sustained because of the several constitutional provisions that grant executive power to the President. *In the framework of our Constitution, the President's power to see that the laws are faithfully executed refutes the idea that he is to be a lawmaker.* The Constitution limits his functions in the lawmaking process to the recommending of laws he thinks wise and the vetoing of laws he thinks bad. And the Constitution is neither silent nor equivocal about who shall make laws which the President is to execute....

The President's order does not direct that a congressional policy be executed in a manner prescribed by Congress—it directs that a presidential policy be executed in a manner prescribed by the President. The preamble of the order itself, like that of many statutes, sets out reasons why the President believes certain policies should be adopted, proclaims these policies as rules of conduct to be followed, and again, like a statute, authorizes a government official to promulgate additional rules and regulations consistent with the policy proclaimed and needed to carry that policy into execution. The power of Congress to adopt such public policies as those proclaimed by the order is beyond question. It can authorize the taking of private property for public use. It can makes laws regulating the relationships between employers and employees, prescribing rules designed to settle labor disputes, and fixing wages and working conditions in certain fields of our economy. The Constitution did not subject this law-making power of Congress to presidential or military supervision or control....

It is said that other Presidents without congressional authority have taken possession of private business enterprises in order to settle labor disputes. But even if this be true, Congress has not thereby lost its exclusive constitutional authority to make laws necessary and proper to carry out the powers vested by the Constitution "in the Government of the United States, or in any Department or Officer thereof."

The Founders of this Nation entrusted the law making power to the Congress alone in both good and bad times. It would do no good to recall the historical events, the fears of power and the hopes for freedom that lay behind their choice. Such a review would but confirm our holding that this seizure order cannot stand.

The judgment of the District Court is Affirmed.

MR. JUSTICE FRANKFURTER concurred:

Although the considerations relevant to the legal enforcement of the principle of separation of powers seem to me more complicated and flexible than any appear from what Mr. Justice Black has written, I join his opinion because I thoroughly agree with the application of the principle to the circumstances of this case. Even though such differences in attitude toward this principle may be merely differences in emphasis and nuance, they can hardly be reflected by a single opinion for the Court. Individual expression of views in reaching a common result is therefore important....

Whereas American fighting men and fighting men of other nations of the United Nations are now engaged in deadly combat with the forces of aggression in Korea, and forces of the United States are stationed elsewhere overseas for the purpose of participating in the defense of the Atlantic Community against aggression; and

Whereas the weapons and other materials needed by our armed forces and by those joined with us in the defense of the free world are produced to a great extent in this country, and steel is an indispensable component of substantially all of such weapons and materials; and....

A constitutional democracy like ours is perhaps the most difficult of man's social arrangements to manage successfully. Our scheme of society is more dependent than any other form of government on knowledge and wisdom and self-discipline for the achievement of its aims. For our democracy implies the reign of reason on the most extensive scale. The Founders of this Nation were not imbued with the modern cynicism that the only thing that history teaches is that it teaches nothing. They acted on the conviction that the experience of man sheds a good deal of light on his nature. It sheds a good deal of light not merely on the need for effective power, if a society is to be at once cohesive and civilized, but also on the need for limitations on the power of governors over the governed.

To that end they rested the structure of our central government on the system of checks and balances. For them the doctrine of separation of powers was not mere theory; it was a felt necessity. Not so long ago it was fashionable to find our system of checks and balances obstructive to effective government. It was easy to ridicule that system as outmoded—too easy. The experience through which the world has passed in our own day has made vivid the realization that the Framers of our Constitution were not inexperienced doctrinaires. These long-haired statesmen had no illusion that our people enjoyed biological or psychological or sociological immunities from the hazards of concentrated power....

Rigorous adherence to the narrow scope of the judicial function is especially demanded in controversies that arouse appeals to the Constitution. The attitude with which this Court must approach its duty when confronted with such issues is precisely the opposite of that normally manifested by the general public. So called constitutional questions seem to exercise a mesmeric influence over the popular mind. This eagerness to settle—preferably forever—a specific problem on the basis of the broadest possible constitutional pronouncements may not unfairly be called one of our minor national traits....

The path of duty for this Court, it bears repetition, lies in the opposite direction. Due regard for the implications of the distribution of powers in our Constitution and for the nature of the judicial process as the ultimate authority in interpreting the Constitution, has not only confined the Court within the narrow domain of appropriate adjudication.

It has also led to "series of rules under which it has avoided passing upon a large part of all the constitutional questions pressed upon it for decision."... A basic rule is the duty of the Court not to pass on a constitutional issue at all; however narrowly it may be confined, if the case may, as a matter of intellectual honesty, be decided without even considering delicate problems of power under the Constitution. It ought to be, but apparently is not, a matter of common understanding that clashes between different branches of the government should be avoided if a legal ground of less explosive potentialities is properly available. Constitutional adjudications are apt by exposing differences to exacerbate them....

The utmost that the Korean conflict may imply is that it may have been desirable to have given the President further authority, a freer hand in these matters. Absence of authority in the President to deal with a crisis does not imply want of power in the Government. Conversely the fact that power exists in the Government does not vest it in the President. The need for new legislation does not enact it. Nor does it repeal or amend existing law....

It is not a pleasant judicial duty to find that the President has exceeded his powers and still less so when his purposes were dictated by concern for the Nation's well-being, in the assured conviction that he acted to avert danger. But it would stultify one's faith in our people to entertain even a momentary fear that the patriotism and the wisdom of the President and the Congress, as well as the long view of the immediate parties in interest, will not find ready accommodation for differences on matters which, however close to their concern and however intrinsically important, are overshadowed by the awesome issues which confront the world. When at a moment of utmost anxiety President Washington turned to this Court for advice, and he had to be denied it as beyond the Court's competence to give...

In reaching the conclusion that conscience compels, I too derive consolation from the reflection that the President and the Congress between them will continue to safeguard the heritage which comes to them straight from George Washington....

MR. JUSTICE DOUGLAS, concurred:

There can be no doubt that the emergency which caused the President to seize these steel plants was one that bore heavily on the country. But the emergency did not create power; it merely marked an occasion when power should be exercised. And the fact that it was necessary that measures be taken to keep steel in production does not mean that the President, rather than the Congress, had the constitutional authority to act. The Congress, as well as the President, is trustee of the national welfare. The President can act more quickly than the Congress. The President with the armed services at his disposal can move with force as well as with speed. All executive power—from the reign of ancient kings to the rule of modern dictators—has the outward appearance of efficiency....

The great office of President is not a weak and powerless one. The President represents the people and is their spokesman in domestic and foreign affairs. The office is respected more than any other in the land. It gives a position of leadership that is unique. The power to formulate policies and mould opinion inheres in the Presidency and conditions our national life. The impact of the man and the philosophy he represents may at times be thwarted by the Congress. Stalemates may occur when emergencies mount and the Nation suffers for lack of harmonious, reciprocal action between the White House and Capitol Hill. That is a risk inherent in our system of separation of powers. The tragedy of such stalemates might be avoided by allowing the President the use of some legislative authority. The Framers with memories of the tyrannies produced by a blending of executive and legislative power rejected that political arrangement. Some future generation may, however, deem it so urgent that the President have legislative authority that the Constitution will be amended. We could not sanction the seizures and condemnations of the steel plants in this case without reading Article II as giving the President not only the power to execute the laws but to make some. Such a step would most assuredly alter the pattern of the Constitution.

We pay a price for our system of checks and balances, for the distribution of power among the three branches of government. It is a price that today may seem exorbitant to many. Today a kindly President uses the seizure power to effect a wage increase and to keep the steel furnaces in production. Yet tomorrow another President might use the same power to prevent a wage increase, to curb trade unionists, to regiment labor as oppressively as industry thinks it has been regimented by this seizure.

Mr. Justice JACKSON, concurred:

A judge, like an executive adviser, may be surprised at the poverty of really useful and unambiguous authority applicable to concrete problems of executive power as they actually present themselves. Just what our forefathers did envision, or would have envisioned had they foreseen modern conditions, must be divined from materials almost as enigmatic as the dreams Joseph was called upon to interpret for Pharaoh. A century and a half of partisan debate and scholarly speculation yields no net result but only supplies more or less apt quotations from respected sources on each side of any question. They largely cancel each other. And court decisions are indecisive because of the judicial practice of dealing with the largest questions in the most narrow way.

The actual art of governing under our Constitution does not and cannot conform to judicial definitions of the power of any of its branches based on isolated clauses or even single articles torn from context. While the Constitution diffuses power the better to secure liberty, it also contemplates that practice will integrate the dispersed powers into a workable government. It enjoins upon its branches separateness but interdependence, autonomy but reciprocity. Presidential powers are not fixed but fluctuate, depending upon their disjunction or conjunction with those of Congress....

When the President acts in absence of either a congressional grant or denial of authority, he can only rely upon his own independent powers, but there is a zone of twilight in which he and Congress may have concurrent authority, or in which its distribution is uncertain. Therefore, congressional inertia, indifference or quiescence may sometimes, at least as a practical matter, enable, if not invite, measures on independent presidential responsibility. In this area, any actual test of power is likely to depend on the imperatives of events and contemporary imponderables rather than on abstract theories of law....

That seems to be the logic of an argument tendered at our bar—that the President having, on his own responsibility, sent American troops abroad derives from that act "affirmative power" to seize the means of producing a supply of steel for them. To quote, "Perhaps the most forceful illustrations of the scope of Presidential power in this connection is the fact that American troops in Korea, whose safety and effectiveness are so directly involved here, were sent to the field by an exercise of the President's constitutional powers." Thus, it is said he has invested himself with "war powers."

I cannot foresee all that it might entail if the Court should indorse this argument. Nothing in our Constitution is plainer than that declaration of a war is entrusted only to Congress. Of course, a state of war may in fact exist without a formal declaration. But no doctrine that the Court could promulgate would seem to me more sinister and alarming than that a President whose conduct of foreign affairs is so largely uncontrolled, and often even is unknown, can vastly enlarge his mastery over the internal affairs of the country by his own commitment of the Nation's armed forces to some foreign venture....

A crisis that challenges the President equally, or perhaps primarily, challenges Congress. If not good law, there was worldly wisdom in the maxim attributed to Napoleon that "The tools belong to the man who can use them." We may say that power to legislate for emergencies belongs in the hands of Congress, but only Congress itself can prevent power from slipping through its fingers.

The essence of our free Government is "leave to live by no man's leave, underneath the law"—to be governed by those impersonal forces which we call law. Our Government is fashioned to fulfill this concept so far as humanly possible. The Executive, except for recommendation and veto, has no legislative power. The executive action we have here originates in the individual will of the President and represents an exercise of authority without law. No one, perhaps not even the President, knows the limits of the power he may seek to exert in this instance and the parties affected cannot learn the limit of their rights. We do not know today what powers over labor or property would be claimed to flow from Government possession if we should legalize it, what rights to compensation would be claimed or recognized, or on what contingency it would end. With all its defects, delays and inconveniences, men have discovered no technique for long preserving free government except that the Executive be under the law, and that the law be made by parliamentary deliberations.

Such institutions may be destined to pass away. But it is the duty of the Court to be last, not first, to give them up.

MR. JUSTICE BURTON, concurred:

Nor is it claimed that the current seizure is in the nature of a military command addressed by the President, as Commander in Chief, to a mobilized nation waging, or imminently threatened with, total war....

MR. JUSTICE CLARK, concurred:

One of this Court's first pronouncements upon the powers of the President under the Constitution was made by Chief Justice John Marshall some one hundred and fifty years ago. In *Little v. Barreme*, he used this characteristically clear language in discussing the power of the President to instruct the seizure of the "Flying-Fish," a vessel bound from a French port.... Accordingly, a unanimous Court held that the President's instructions had been issued without authority and that they could not "legalize an act which without those instructions would have been a plain trespass." I know of no subsequent holding of this Court to the contrary....

I *conclude that where Congress has laid down specific procedures to deal with the type of crisis confronting the President*, he *must follow those procedures* in meeting the crisis; *but* that *in the absence of such action by Congress*, the *President's independent power to act depends upon the gravity of the situation confronting the nation*. I cannot sustain the seizure in question because here, as in *Little v. Barreme, Congress had prescribed methods to be followed by the President in meeting the emergency at hand....*

MR. CHIEF JUSTICE VINSON, with whom MR. JUSTICE REED and MR. JUSTICE MINTON joined, dissented:

The President of the United States directed the Secretary of Commerce to take temporary possession of the Nation's steel mills during the existing emergency because "a work stoppage would immediately jeopardize and imperil our national defense and the defense of those joined with us in resisting aggression, and would add to the continuing danger of our soldiers, sailors and airmen engaged in combat in the field." The District Court ordered the mills returned to their private owners on the ground that the President's action was beyond his powers under the Constitution.

This Court affirms. Some members of the Court are of the view that the President is without power to act in time of crisis in the absence of express statutory authorization. Other members of the Court affirm on the basis of their reading of certain statutes. Because we cannot agree that affirmance is proper on any ground, and because of the transcending importance of the questions presented not only in this critical litigation but also to the powers the President and of future Presidents to act in time of crisis, we are compelled to register this dissent....

Notes

1. See a superb study by Robert James Maddox. *From War to Cold War: The Education of Harry S. Truman.* (Boulder: Westview Press, 1988), pp. 175-178; Also, *Perspective*, Vol. 18, (winter 1989) p. 5.
2. Robert Maddox. *From War to Cold War,* p. 177. There was no reason for Truman to believe that he would not have the full support of the Supreme Court as had his predecessor.
3. Ibid., pp. 5-6 based on *Woods* (1948) and related decisions.
4. See John Spanier. *American Foreign Policy Since World War II* (Washington, D.C.: Congressional Quarterly Press, 1992), pp. 21-86.
5. The Treaty of Versailles following World War I acknowledged the authority of the Allies, including the United States, to try such offenders before military tribunals. The treaty was not approved by the U. S. Senate *despite* Wilson's best efforts and *because* of those of Senator Lodge and his Republican colleagues. See Article 228 of the Treaty of Versailles, June 28, 1919.
6. *In re. Yamashita*, 327 US 1 (1946).
7. Articles of War, 10 USCA sections 1471-1593, 11 FCA title 10, sections 1471-1593.
8. 327 US at 15. See Articles 1 and 43 of the Annex to the Fourth Hague Convention of 1907. 36 Stat. 2295, 2306.
9. 327 US at 19-20.
10. Ibid., p. 25.

11. Professor Abraham argues that while Jackson was "brilliant at Nuremberg," he returned to the Court a *changed* man: "the once libertarian judicial activist...had become profoundly cautious, a markedly narrow interpreter of the Bill of Rights," particularly in cases of national security and criminal procedure. Henry Abraham. *Justices and Presidents: A Political History of Appointments to the Supreme Court*, Third Edition, (New York: Oxford University Press, 1992) pp. 236-237.

12. Murphy also warned that "Indeed, the fate of some future President of the United States and his chiefs of staff and military advisors may well have been sealed by this decision." 327 US at 28.

13. Ibid., p 42.

14. The Military Governor issued a Proclamation dated February 8, 1943, returning some authority to the civil authorities with the proviso that, given certain circumstances, these powers might be returned to his office. The President approved the proclamation and later on October 24, 1944, issued one of his own which restored the original government and terminated martial law in the Territory.

15. *Duncan v. Kahanamoku* was decided along with *White v. Steer*, 327 US 304 on February 25, 1946.

16. Ibid., p. 317. The Court relied, in some measure, on an article by John P. Frank, "*Ex Parte Milligan v. the Five Companies*: Martial Law in Hawaii," 44 *Columbia Law Review* (1944), p. 639.

17. 327 US at 318.

18. Ibid., p. 330.

19. Ibid., pp. 343, 345.

20. *Woods v. Miller*, 333 US 138 (1948); also see *Lichter v. United States*, 334 US 742 (1948), in which the Court upheld the Renegotiation Act of 1942 which enabled Congress to recover excessive profits from companies engaged in war production, as a "necessary and proper" power to "raise and support armies."

21. Ibid., p. 142. For example, see *Fleming v. Mohawk Wrecking & Lumber Co.*, 331 US 111, *Hamilton v. Kentucky Distilleries & Warehouse Co.*, 251 US 146 (1920), *Jacob Ruppert, Inc. v. Caffey*, 251 US 264, and *Stewart v. Kahn*, 11 US 493.

22. 333 US at 143.

23. See *Bowles v. Willingham*. 321 US 503 (1944); *Yakus v. United States*, 321 US 414 (1944); and *Steuart & Bros. v. Bowles*, 322 U.S. 398 (1944).

24. 333 US at 144.

25. Ibid., p. 146.

26. As mentioned earlier, of the *eleven* major conflicts in which the United states was a major participant, only *five* instances were proceeded by Congressional declarations of war. Consequently since 1789, there have been *nine* separate declarations against particular countries within enemy military alliances. See, Louis W. Koenig, *The Chief Executive*. (New York: Harcourt Brace Jovanovich, 1981) p. 216.

27. The complete citation is *Johnson, Secretary of Defense, et al. v. Eisentrager, alias Ernhardt, et al.*' 339 US 763 at 789; the case was argued on April 17, 1950. Earlier, the High Court had ruled that lower federal courts have no authority to review, reaffirm or reverse the decisions of international tribunals, see *Hirota v. United States*, 338 US 197 (1948). *Hawaii v. Mankichi*, 190 U.S. 197 (1903), is also one of the sixteen cases known as the Insular Cases (1903).

28. Ibid., p. 775.

29. Ibid., p. 784.

30. Ibid., p. 786-787.

31. Ibid., p. 788.

32. Ibid.

33. For citations relating to the fact that the quotation, *supra*, applies only to a war that has been declared by Congress, see Ibid., pp. 768-774, 775, 777-778.

34. Ibid., p. 789. See also, *Chicago & Southern Airlines v. Waterman Steamship Corp.*, 333 US 103 (1947).

35. Ibid., pp. 791-798.

36. Ibid., p. 795.

37. Here, the Associate Justice was referring to the fact that the convicted aliens were transported to the American-occupied part of Germany for imprisonment under the custody of the army. Ibid., p. 798.

38. Ibid.

39. Arthur M. Schlesinger, Jr. *The Imperial Presidency*. Revised. (Boston: Houghton Mifflin Company, 1989) p. 131.

40. John Spanier. *American Foreign Policy Since World War II*. Eighth Edition (New York: Holt, Rinehart, and Winston, 1980) pp. 59-60.

41. Ibid., pp. 61-63.

42. Schlesinger. *Imperial Presidency*, p. 132. Although, in Truman's defense, Schlesinger argues that since Congress did enact legislation providing military appropriations and extending selective service, that it had indeed, "confirmed" and even "ratified" American intervention. p. 134.

43. Ibid., pp. 134-135. On June 27, The President met with a small delegation of Congressmen from which he deduced the support of Congress, but even so it was not what the *Curtiss-Wright* decision required.

44. Ibid., p. 132.
45. Congressman Coudert also lamented "how devastating a precedent [that members] have set in remaining silent while the President took over those powers specifically reserved for Congress in the Constitution." Ibid., pp. 135-136.
46. Keynes, *Undeclared War: Twilight Zone of Constitutional Power.* (University Park, PA: Pennsylvania State University Press, 1991) p 111.
47. *Woods v. Miller*, 333 U.S. 138 (1948); op. cit. Even the Supreme Court recognized that W.W.II had ended, in fact, and that a new cold war with Communist Russia and China had begun. In *Harisiades v. Shaughnessy*, 342 U.S. 580 (1952), the Court upheld the application of the Alien Registration Act of 1940—not to Japanese or German aliens—but to deport Communist party members from the United States and to also strip American Communists of their citizenship.
48. 252 U.S. 346, 361.
49. Speaking for the Court, Justice Black reiterated the *Missouri* decision by stating that a treaty can not violate the rights of the United States citizens under the Constitution. In *Federalist Paper* #41, James Madison argued convincingly that war could only be declared by the branch *most* representative of the people, Congress, and as such was a "right" or liberty which, obviously, may not be abridged by a treaty. As a result, Justice Black concluded in *Reid*, "no agreement with a foreign nation [or a United Nations] can confer power on Congress, which is *free* from the restraints of the Constitution. 345 U.S. 1.
50. *Youngstown Sheet & Tube Company, et al. v. Sawyer*, 343 U.S. 579, at 583 (1952); also refer to Appendix, Executive Order # 10340, pp. 589-592.
51. Ibid., pp. 579, 587. As early as 1814, the Court, in John Marshall's words, narrowly interpreted the declaration of war to mean *only* that a state of war exists between the United States and another country. It did *not* include the authority of an executive officer to seize or confiscate enemy property in this country. *Armitz Brown v. United States*, 3 US 504 (1814).
52. Ibid., at 581.
53. "Appendix" in *Ibid*. p. 590.
54. Henry Abraham. *Justices and Presidents*, Second Edition, p. 390.
55. Ibid., pp. 211-216.
56. William H. Harbaugh. *Lawyer's Lawyer: The Life of John W. Davis*, (New York: Oxford University Press, 1973) p. 476. In March, Davis had said: "there is not the slightest doubt that the President's action...is without legal warrant—constitutional or statutory. It is an act of pure usurpation and I hope that Congress as well as the courts would so declare." p. 474.

57. 343 US 582. See,
58. Ibid., p. 585.
59. Only *after* the Court's decision in *Youngstown* was handed down, did *both* Houses of Congress finally approve Senator Harry F. Byrd's (D - Virginia) proposed resolution calling on the President to invoke the Taft-Hartley law. See Harbaugh, *Lawyer's Lawyer*, p. 470.
60. 343 US 587.
61. Ibid.
62. See *Mitchell v. Harmony*, 13 Howard 115 (1852); *United States v. Russell*, 13 Wallace 623 (1871); *Totten v. United States*, 92 US 105 (1876). Also, see Corwin, *The Constitution*, (1978), pp. 160-161.
63. Although Congress did enact authorizing legislation in 1862—a year *after* Lincoln had acted. Corwin, *The Constitution*, p. 199.
64. Ibid., p. 159.
65. Ibid., p. 199. Justice Robert Jackson's lengthy opinion that foreign policy is "a twilight zone of Constitutional power" is obviously a truism endorsed from the beginning by this writer.
66. 343 US 662. Professor Henry J. Abraham accepts the persuasive argument that the venerable Edward S. Corwin gave Justice Clark's law clerks the reasoning that would be used by the Texan in his "controlling" concurring opinion. *Justices and Presidents*, p. 363.
67. Morgenthau served for years as a Professor of Political Science at the University of Chicago. His classic work was *Politics Among Nations: The Struggle for Power and Peace* (1948) 1st Edition.
68. Ibid., p. 420.
69. 343 US 587.
70. 343 US 587, 588. Most liberal-activist writers quote from Justice Robert Jackson's concurring opinion on the "zone of twilight" between the president and Congress in the separation of powers concept which, in their minds, allows the president to use his own discretion when there is "inertia" in Congress. For example, see Louis Fisher, *Constitutional Conflicts*, 1991, p. 20.
71. Morgenthau. *Politics Among Nations*, p. 469.
72. Spanier, *American Foreign Policy*, p. 65.
73. Abraham. *Justices and Presidents*, p. 241.
74. Spanier. *American Foreign Policy*, p. 65.

Chapter Seven: Conclusion

In retrospect, the Truman years represented the *apex* of presidential supremacy in the foreign arena. From his early decision to use atomic bombs on the Japanese to end the Second World War, his threat to use them again in 1947 to prevent a Soviet takeover of northern Iran, his determination to rebuild both the economies and defenses of our former enemies in Western Europe and Asia, to his armed intervention in South Korea, the president was perfectly suited for this leadership role except possibly in physical appearance. Truman was decisive to a fault. He welded a bipartisan congressional majority in support of his post-war policies, and maintained strong popular approval of his leadership both at home and abroad—*until the* long drawn-out stalemate in Korea. This clearly *presidential* war led not only to the downfall of Truman, who refused to stand for re-election, and the Democratic party (at least temporarily), but also of the seventeen year adherence to "presidential supremacy" in foreign policy. Nevertheless, apologists for such executive dominance remained active and have won over numerous contemporary advocates including such diverse personalities as Robert Bork, Laurence Tribe, Associate Justice Antonio Scalia, and Henry Kissinger. How do such leading intellectuals, lawyers, professors and jurists justify "presidential supremacy" in legal or constitutional terms with only *Curtiss-Wright* and its progeny to lean on—out of America's *entire* two-hundred plus seven-year experience since 1789?

The answer is that they *do not*; at least, not *entirely*. Professors Barbara Kellerman and Ryan Banilleaux suggest a response in their joint study entitled, *The President as World Leader* (1991).[1] They cite his constitutional authority under Article II when reinforced by the president's "extraconstitutional powers": (1) *executive power* allows the president to do almost *anything* if it is in the name of "national security"; (2) emerging powers under which "presidents feel that they can argue that the nation's survival requires nothing less than strong, unilateral presidential action"; (3) *executive agreements* permits the president to bypass the "treaty" provision and Senate approval and to make secret pacts with the leader of other nations, until relatively recent times;[2] and (4) *executive privilege*, only somewhat diminished since the *Nixon* decision (1974), implies presidential power to withhold any information that would adversely affect "either the national security or the president's ability to discharge his official duties."[3]

Whatever rationale is devised to push forward the concept of "presidential supremacy" in international affairs, its long term effects will almost certainly result in a direct *threat* to American constitutionalism. The talented gentlemen who authored the Philadelphia document including James Madison, Alexander Hamilton, James Wilson and George Washington, *never* intended that the mantle of "constitutional dictator" be draped on *any* individual—Lincoln, Roosevelt or Truman—no matter *how* capable, decent, moral, responsible or, for that matter, personally popular. Professor Corwin referred to the temptations of the populace, particularly in crisis situations, when he terms the latter category as the "personalized presidency"; of course, he had F.D.R. in mind when he coined the term in 1940.

To reach this conclusion is not to demean the motives, decisions or actions of any president—past or present—who we must all assume tried his best to protect the interests of the United States and to fulfill the aspirations of her people.[4] Nevertheless, the Korean War was a clear and absolute *violation of* not only the Constitution of the United States of America, but every established legal precedent established since the founding of the United States as one nation. No amount of "power politics" or "national-interest" rationalizations will absolve it, nor make it less dangerous as a precedent of its own,[5] and the legacy of this period (1946-1953) was not only Truman's initiation of the only *major* presidential war in our constitutional history, it was an obvious temptation, if not a *sub rosa* invitation, for future presidents confronted with similar circumstances somewhere in our world to take on the role of international police. This will be discussed further in the forthcoming Volume II of this book.

Notes

1. New York: St. Martin's Press, pp. 38-44.
2. Supposedly, the Case Act of 1972 requires the Secretary of State to transmit to the appropriate Congressional Committee the text of executive or other international agreements "other than a treaty."
3. *The President as World Leader* (1991) p. 42.
4. See Robert G. McCloskey's commentary on presidential excesses in his classic work, *The American Supreme Court* (Chicago: The University of Chicago Press, 1960) pp. 188-192. Also, James W. Davis. *The American Presidency: A New Perspective* (New York: Harper and Row, 1987) pp. 179-185, and Arthur Schlesinger, *The Imperial Presidency*, pp. 441-445.
5. For both similar or varying views, see the following texts: Richard E. Neustadt. *Presidential Power* (New York: John Wiley & Sons, Inc., 1980) pp. 182-187; Thomas E. Mann (ed.) *A Question of Balance: The President, the Congress and Foreign Policy* (Washington, D.C.: The Brookings Institution, 1990) pp. 18, 42-44; Louis Henkin, *Constitutionalism, Democracy, and Foreign Affairs* (New York: Columbia University Press, 1990) pp. 26-34; Cecil V. Crabb, Jr. and Pat M. Holt. *Invitation to Struggle: Congress, the President, and Foreign Policy*, Fourth Edition (Washington, D.C.: Congressional Quarterly Press, 1992) pp. 134-139; and James P. Pfiffner, *The Modern Presidency* (New York: St. Martin's Press, 1994) pp. 177-178.

Epilogue

While this volume of *The Black Robe and the Bald Eagle* could aptly be subtitled, "The Rise of Presidential Imperialism," my soon-to-be-written second volume will be called, "The Judicial Evolution to Abstentionism: 1953 to the Present." It will pick up where this volume leaves off, beginning with the dawn of the Eisenhower administration and the conclusion of the Korean War. It will then go on to chronicle the decades of turmoil and change up to the president day.

During this period nine men served in the White House, most of whom were elected for only one term. Three presidents, Eisenhower, Nixon and Reagan—all Republicans—were elected to two terms; however, only two actually served a full eight-year term. During four highly volatile decades, the continuity of presidential policy affecting foreign policy was precarious at best. Moreover, Americans, usually in a state of shock, witnessed political assassinations, a near presidential impeachment, numerous clashes over foreign affairs between Congress and the Chief Executive, one major war in Southeast Asia (which lost 56,000 American lives), and numerous smaller "presidential" wars.

Consequently, the Supreme Court, usually reflective of the public mood, became increasingly more restrained; it began to abstain from crucial foreign polity questions; and it developed the "aloofness" from "political questions" that has been discussed at length by contemporary judicial scholars.

The future Supreme Court involvement in foreign policy is dependent upon a myriad of factors, particularly the uncertainty of congressional reassertion of its authority, the temperament of the sitting president and the consequences of geopolitcal machinations. All of these issues will be discussed in Volume II.

Appendix

The Constitution of the United States of America*

We the people of the United States, in order to form a more perfect union, establish justice, insure domestic tranquility, *provide for the common defense*, promote the general welfare, and secure the blessings of liberty to ourselves and our posterity, *do ordain and establish this Constitution for the United States of America.*

Article I

Section 1. All legislative powers herein granted shall be vested in a Congress of the United States, which shall consist of a Senate and House of Representatives.

Section 2. The House of Representatives shall be composed of members chosen every second year by the people of the several states, and the electors in each state shall have the qualifications requisite for electors of the most numerous branch of the state legislature.

No person shall be a Representative who shall not have attained to the age of twenty five years, and been seven years a citizen of the United States, and who shall not, when elected, be an inhabitant of that state in which he shall be chosen.

Representatives and direct taxes shall be apportioned among the several states which may be included within this union, according to their respective numbers, which shall be determined by adding to the whole number of free persons, including those bound to service for a term of years, and excluding Indians not taxed, three fifths of all other Persons. The actual Enumeration shall be made within three years after the first meeting of the Congress of the United States, and within every subsequent term of ten years, in such manner as they shall by law direct. The number of Representatives shall not exceed one for every thirty thousand, but each state shall have at least one Representative; and until such enumeration shall be made, the state of New Hampshire shall be entitled to chuse three, Massachusetts eight, Rhode Island and Providence Plantations one, Connecticut five, New York six, New Jersey four, Pennsylvania eight, Delaware one, Maryland six, Virginia ten, North Carolina five, South Carolina five, and Georgia three.

When vacancies happen in the Representation from any state, the

---

*
   Emphasis added for clauses affecting American foreign policy

executive authority thereof shall issue writs of election to fill such vacancies.

The House of Representatives shall choose their speaker and other officers; and shall have the sole power of impeachment.

Section 3. The Senate of the United States shall be composed of two Senators from each state, chosen by the legislature thereof, for six years; and each Senator shall have one vote.

Immediately after they shall be assembled in consequence of the first election, they shall be divided as equally as may be into three classes. The seats of the Senators of the first class shall be vacated at the expiration of the second year, of the second class at the expiration of the fourth year, and the third class at the expiration of the sixth year, so that one third may be chosen every second year; and if vacancies happen by resignation, or otherwise, during the recess of the legislature of any state, the executive thereof may make temporary appointments until the next meeting of the legislature, which shall then fill such vacancies.

No person shall be a Senator who shall not have attained to the age of thirty years, and been nine years a citizen of the United States and who shall not, when elected, be an inhabitant of that state for which he shall be chosen.

The Vice President of the United States shall be President of the Senate, but shall have no vote, unless they be equally divided.

The Senate shall choose their other officers, and also a President pro tempore, in the absence of the Vice President, or when he shall exercise the office of President of the United States.

The Senate shall have the sole power to try all impeachments. When sitting for that purpose, they shall be on oath or affirmation. When the President of the United States is tried, the Chief Justice shall preside: And no person shall be convicted without the concurrence of two thirds of the members present.

Judgment in cases of impeachment shall not extend further than to removal from office, and disqualification to hold and enjoy any office of honor, trust or profit under the United States: but the party convicted shall nevertheless be liable and subject to indictment, trial, judgment and punishment, according to law.

Section 4. The times, places and manner of holding elections for Senators and Representatives, shall be prescribed in each state by the legislature thereof; but the Congress may at any time by law make or alter such regulations, except as to the places of choosing Senators.

The Congress shall assemble at least once in every year, and such meeting shall be on the first Monday in December, unless they shall by law appoint a different day.

Section 5. Each House shall be the judge of the elections, returns and qualifications of its own members, and a majority of each shall constitute a quorum to do business; but a smaller number may adjourn from day to day, and may be authorized to compel the attendance of absent members, in such manner, and under such penalties as each House may provide.

Each House may determine the rules of its proceedings, punish its members for disorderly behavior, and, with the concurrence of two thirds, expel a member.

Each House shall keep a journal of its proceedings, and from time to time publish the same, excepting such parts as may in their judgment require secrecy; and the yeas and nays of the members of either House on any question shall, at the desire of one fifth of those present, be entered on the journal.

Neither House, during the session of Congress, shall, without the consent of the other, adjourn for more than three days, nor to any other place than that in which the two Houses shall be sitting.

Section 6. The Senators and Representatives shall receive a compensation for their services, to be ascertained by law, and paid out of the treasury of the United States. They shall in all cases, except treason, felony and breach of the peace, be privileged from arrest during their attendance at the session of their respective Houses, and in going to and returning from the same; and for any speech or debate in either House, they shall not be questioned in any other place.

No Senator or Representative shall, during the time for which he was elected, be appointed to any civil office under the authority of the United States, which shall have been created, or the emoluments whereof shall have been increased during such time: and no person holding any office under the United States, shall be a member of either House during his continuance in office.

Section 7. All bills for raising revenue shall originate in the House of Representatives; but the Senate may propose or concur with amendments as on other Bills.

Every bill which shall have passed the House of Representatives and the Senate, shall, before it become a law, be presented to the President of the United States; if he approve he shall sign it, but if not he shall return it, with his objections to that House in which it shall have originated, who shall enter the objections at large on their journal, and proceed to reconsider it. If after such reconsideration two thirds of that House shall agree to pass the bill, it shall be sent, together with the objections, to the other House, by which it shall likewise be reconsidered, and if approved by two thirds of that House, it shall become a law. But in all such cases the votes of both Houses shall be determined by yeas and nays, and the names of the persons voting for and against the bill shall be entered on the journal of each House respectively. If any bill shall not be returned by the President within ten days (Sundays excepted) after it shall have been presented to him, the same shall be a law, in like manner as if he had signed it, unless the Congress by their adjournment prevent its return, in which case it shall not be a law.

Every order, resolution, or vote to which the concurrence of the Senate and House of Representatives may be necessary (except on a question of adjournment) shall be presented to the President of the United States; and before the same shall take effect, shall be approved by him, or being disapproved by him, shall be repassed by two thirds of the Senate and House of Representatives, according to the rules and limitations prescribed in the case of a bill.

Section 8. *The Congress shall have power*

To lay and collect taxes, *duties, imposts* and excises, to pay the debts and provide for the common defense and general welfare of the United States; *but all duties, imposts* and excises *shall be uniform throughout the United States;*

To borrow money on the credit of the United States;

To regulate commerce with foreign nations, and among the several states, and with the Indian tribes;

To establish a uniform rule of naturalization, and uniform laws on the subject of bankruptcies throughout the United States;

To coin money, *regulate the value* thereof, and of foreign coin, and fix the standard of weights and measures;

To provide for the punishment of counterfeiting the securities and current coin of the United States;

To establish post offices and post roads;

To promote the progress of science and useful arts, by securing for limited times to authors and inventors the exclusive right to their respective writings and discoveries;

To constitute tribunals inferior to the Supreme Court;

To define and punish piracies and felonies committed on the high seas, and offenses against the law of nations;

To declare war, grant letters of marque and reprisal, and make rules concerning captures on land and water;

To raise and support armies, but no appropriation of money to that use shall be for a longer term than two years;

To provide and maintain a navy;

To make rules for the government and regulation of the land and naval forces;

To provide for calling forth the militia to execute the laws of the union, suppress insurrections and *repel invasions;*

To provide for organizing, arming, and disciplining, the militia, and for governing such part of them as may be employed in the service of the United States, reserving to the states respectively, the appointment of the officers, and the authority of training the militia according to the discipline prescribed by Congress;

To exercise exclusive legislation in all cases whatsoever, over such District (not exceeding ten miles square) as may, by cession of particular states, and the acceptance of Congress, become the seat of the government of the United States, and to exercise like authority over all places purchased by the consent *of the legislature of the state in which the same shall be, for the erection of forts, magazines, arsenals, dockyards, and other needful buildings; and*

To make all laws which shall be necessary and proper for carrying into execution the foregoing powers, and all other powers vested by this Constitution in the government of the United States, or in any department or officer thereof.

Section 9. The migration or importation of such persons as any of the states now existing shall think proper to admit, shall not be prohibited by the Congress prior to the year one thousand eight hundred and eight, but a tax or duty may be imposed on such importation, not exceeding ten dollars for each person.

The privilege of the writ of habeas corpus shall not be suspended, unless when in cases of rebellion or invasion the public safety may require it.

No bill of attainder or ex post facto Law shall be passed.

No capitation, or other direct, tax shall be laid, unless in proportion to the census or enumeration herein before directed to be taken.

No tax or duty shall be laid on articles exported from any state.

No preference shall be given by any regulation of commerce or revenue to the ports of one state over those of another: nor shall vessels bound to, or from, one state, be obliged to enter, clear or pay duties in another.

No money shall be drawn from the treasury, but in consequence of appropriations made by law; and a regular statement and account of receipts and expenditures of all public money shall be published from time to time.

No title of nobility shall be granted by the United States: and *no person holding any office of profit or trust under them, shall, without the consent of the Congress, accept of any present, emolument, office, or title, of any kind whatever, from any king, prince, or foreign state.*

Section 10. *No state shall enter into any treaty, alliance, or confederation; grant letters of marque and reprisal;* coin money; emit bills of credit; make anything but gold and silver coin a tender in payment of debts; pass any bill of attainder, ex post facto law, or law impairing the obligation of contracts, or grant any title of nobility.

No state shall, without the consent of the Congress, lay any imposts or duties on imports or exports, except what may be absolutely necessary for executing it's inspection laws: and the net produce of all duties and imposts, laid by any state on imports or exports, shall be for the use of the treasury of the United States; and all such laws shall be subject to the revision and control of the Congress.

No state shall, without the consent of Congress, lay any duty of tonnage, keep troops, or ships of war in time of peace, enter into any agreement or compact with another state, or with a foreign power, or engage in war, unless actually invaded, or in such imminent danger as will not admit of delay.

Article II

Section 1. The executive power shall be vested in a President of the United States of America. He shall hold his office during the term of four years, and, together with the Vice President, chosen for the same term, be elected, as follows:

Each state shall appoint, in such manner as the Legislature thereof may direct, a number of electors, equal to the whole number of Senators and Representatives to which the State may be entitled in the Congress: but no Senator or Representative, or person holding an office of trust or profit under the United States, shall be appointed an elector.

The electors shall meet in their respective states, and vote by ballot for two persons, of whom one at least shall not be an inhabitant of the same state with themselves. And they shall make a list of all the persons voted for, and of the number of votes for each; which list they shall sign and certify, and transmit sealed to the seat of the government of the United States, directed to the President of the Senate. The President of the Senate shall, in the presence of the Senate and House of Representatives, open all the certificates, and the votes shall then be counted. The person having the greatest number of votes shall be the President, if such number be a majority of the whole number of electors appointed; and if there be more than one who have such majority, and have an equal number of votes, then the House of Representatives shall immediately choose by ballot one of them for President; and if no person have a majority, then from the five highest on the list the said House shall in like manner choose the President. But in choosing the President, the votes shall be taken by States, the representation from each state having one vote; A quorum for this purpose shall consist of a member or members from two thirds of the states, and a majority of all the states shall be necessary to a choice. In every case, after the choice of the President, the person having the greatest number of votes of the electors shall be the Vice President. But if there should remain two or more who have equal votes, the Senate shall choose from them by ballot the Vice President.

The Congress may determine the time of choosing the electors, and the day on which they shall give their votes; which day shall be the same throughout the United States.

No person except a natural born citizen, or a citizen of the United States, at the time of the adoption of this Constitution, *shall be eligible to the office of President;* neither shall any person be eligible to that office who shall not have attained to the age of thirty five years, and *been fourteen Years a resident within the United States*.

In case of the removal of the President from office, or of his death, resignation, or inability to discharge the powers and duties of the said office, the same shall devolve on the Vice President, and the Congress may by law provide for the case of removal, death, resignation or inability, both of the President and Vice President, declaring what officer shall then act as President, and such officer shall act accordingly, until the disability be removed, or a President shall be elected.

The President shall, at stated times, receive for his services, a compensation, which shall neither be increased nor diminished during the period for which he shall have been elected, and he shall not receive within that period any other emolument from the United States, or any of them.

Before he enter on the execution of his office, he shall take the following oath or affirmation: — "I do solemnly swear (or affirm) that I will faithfully execute the office of President of the United States, and will to the best of my ability, preserve, protect and defend the Constitution of the United States."

Section 2. *The President shall be commander in chief of the Army and Navy of the United States, and of the militia of the several states, when called into the actual service of the United States;* he may require the

308 Appendix: U.S. Constitution

opinion, in writing, of the principal officer in each of the executive departments, upon any subject relating to the duties of their respective offices, and he shall have power to grant reprieves and pardons for offenses against the United States, except in cases of impeachment.

He shall have power, by and with the advice and consent of the Senate, to make treaties, provided two thirds of the Senators present concur; and he shall nominate, and by and with the advice and consent of the Senate, shall appoint ambassadors, other public ministers and consuls, judges of the Supreme Court, and all other officers of the United States, whose appointments are not herein otherwise provided for, and which shall be established by law: but the Congress may by law vest the appointment of such inferior officers, as they think proper, in the President alone, in the courts of law, or in the heads of departments.

The President shall have power to fill up all vacancies that may happen during the recess of the Senate, by granting commissions which shall expire at the end of their next session.

Section 3. He shall from time to time give to the Congress information of the state of the union, and recommend to their consideration such measures as he shall judge necessary and expedient; he may, on extraordinary occasions, convene both Houses, or either of them, and in case of disagreement between them, with respect to the time of adjournment, he may adjourn them to such time as he shall think proper; *he shall receive ambassadors and other public ministers;* he shall take care that the laws be faithfully executed, *and shall commission all the officers of the United States.*

Section 4. *The President, Vice President and all civil officers of the United States, shall be removed from office on impeachment for, and conviction of, treason, bribery, or other high crimes and misdemeanors.*

Article III

Section 1. The judicial power of the United States, shall be vested in one Supreme Court, and in such inferior courts as the Congress may from time to time ordain and establish. The judges, both of the supreme and inferior courts, shall hold their offices during good behaviour, and shall, at stated times, receive for their services, a compensation, which shall not be diminished during their continuance in office.

Section 2. *The judicial power shall extend to all cases, in law and equity, arising under* this Constitution, the laws of the United States, and *treaties made, or which shall be made, under their authority; — to all cases affecting ambassadors, other public ministers and consuls; — to all cases of admiralty and maritime jurisdiction; — to controversies* to which the United States shall be a party; — to controversies between two or more states; — between a state and citizens of another state; — between citizens of different states; — between citizens of the same state claiming lands under grants of different states, and *between a state, or the citizens thereof, and foreign states, citizens or subjects.*

In all cases affecting ambassadors, other public ministers and consuls, and those in which a state shall be party, the Supreme Court shall have original jurisdiction. In all the other cases before mentioned, the Supreme Court shall have appellate jurisdiction, both as to law and fact, with such exceptions, and under such regulations as the Congress shall make.

The trial of all crimes, except in cases of impeachment, shall be by jury; and such trial shall be held in the state where the said crimes shall have been committed; but when not committed within any state, the trial shall be at such place or places as the Congress may by law have directed.

Section 3. *Treason against the United States, shall consist only in levying war against them, or in adhering to their enemies, giving them aid and comfort. No person shall be convicted of treason unless on the testimony of two witnesses to the same overt act, or on confession in open court.*

The Congress shall have power to declare the punishment of treason, but no attainder of treason shall work corruption of blood, or forfeiture except during the life of the person attainted.

Article IV

Section 1. Full faith and credit shall be given in each state to the public acts, records, and judicial proceedings of every other state. And the Congress may by general laws prescribe the manner in which such acts, records, and proceedings shall be proved, and the effect thereof.

Section 2. The citizens of each state shall be entitled to all privileges and immunities of citizens in the several states.

A person charged in any state with treason, felony, or other crime, who shall flee from justice, and be found in another state, shall on demand of the executive authority of the state from which he fled, be delivered up, to be removed to the state having jurisdiction of the crime.

No person held to service or labor in one state, under the laws thereof, escaping into another, shall, in consequence of any law or regulation therein, be discharged from such service or labor, but shall be delivered up on claim of the party to whom such service or labor may be due.

Section 3. New states may be admitted by the Congress into this union; but no new states shall be formed or erected within the jurisdiction of any other state; nor any state be formed by the junction of two or more states, or parts of states, without the consent of the legislatures of the states concerned as well as of the Congress.

The Congress shall have power to dispose of and make all needful rules and regulations respecting the territory or other property belonging to the United States; and nothing in this Constitution shall be so construed as to prejudice any claims of the United States, or of any particular state.

Section 4. *The United States shall guarantee to every state in this union a republican form of government, and shall protect each of them against invasion;* and on application of the legislature, or of the executive (when the legislature cannot be convened) against domestic violence.

Article V

The Congress, whenever two thirds of both houses shall deem it necessary, shall propose amendments to this Constitution, or, on the application of the legislatures of two thirds of the several states, shall call a convention for proposing amendments, which, in either case, shall be valid to all intents and purposes, as part of this Constitution, when ratified by the legislatures of three fourths of the several states, or by conventions in three fourths thereof, as the one or the other mode of ratification may be proposed by the Congress; provided that no amendment which may be made prior to the year one thousand eight hundred and eight shall in any manner affect the first and fourth clauses in the ninth section of the first article; and that no state, without its consent, shall be deprived of its equal suffrage in the Senate.

Article VI

All debts contracted and engagements entered into, before the adoption of this Constitution, shall be as valid against the United States under this Constitution, as under the Confederation.

This Constitution, and the laws of the United States which shall be made in pursuance thereof; *and all treaties made, or which shall be made, under the authority of the United States, shall be the supreme law of the land; and the judges in every state shall be bound thereby, anything in the Constitution or laws of any State to the contrary notwithstanding.*

The Senators and Representatives before mentioned, and the members of the several state legislatures, and all executive and judicial officers, both of the United States and of the several states, shall be bound by oath or affirmation, to support this Constitution; but no religious test shall ever be required as a qualification to any office or public trust under the United States.

Article VII

The ratification of the conventions of nine states, shall be sufficient for the establishment of this Constitution between the states so ratifying the same. Done in convention by the unanimous consent of the states present the seventeenth day of September in the year of our Lord one thousand seven hundred and eighty seven and of the independence of the United States of America the twelfth. In witness whereof We have hereunto subscribed our Names. [names omitted]

Articles in addition to, and amendment of, the Constitution of the United States of America, proposed by Congress, and ratified by the legislatures of the several States pursuant to the fifth article of the original Constitution.

AMENDMENTS

The first ten amendments [Bill of Rights] was passed by Congress on September 25, 1789, and ratified by three-fourths of the States on December 15, 1791.

Amendment I

Congress shall make no law respecting an establishment of religion, or prohibiting the free exercise thereof; or abridging the freedom of speech, or of the press; or the right of the people peaceably to assemble, and to petition the government for a redress of grievances.

Amendment II

A well regulated militia, being necessary to the security of a free state, the right of the people to keep and bear arms, shall not be infringed.

Amendment III

No soldier shall, in time of peace be quartered in any house, without the consent of the owner, nor in time of war, but in a manner to be prescribed by law.

Amendment IV

The right of the people to be secure in their persons, houses, papers, and effects, against unreasonable searches and seizures, shall not be violated, and no warrants shall issue, but upon probable cause, supported by oath or affirmation, and particularly describing the place to be searched, and the persons or things to be seized.

Amendment V

No person shall be held to answer for a capital, or otherwise infamous crime, unless on a presentment or indictment of a grand jury, except in cases arising in the land or naval forces, or in the militia, when in actual service in time of war or public danger; nor shall any person be subject for the same offense to be twice put in jeopardy of life or limb; nor shall be compelled in any criminal case to be a witness against himself, nor be deprived of life, liberty, or property, without due process of law; nor shall private property be taken for public use, without just compensation.

Amendment VI

In all criminal prosecutions, the accused shall enjoy the right to a speedy and public trial, by an impartial jury of the state and district wherein the crime shall have been committed, which district shall have been previously ascertained by law, and to be informed of the nature and cause of the accusation; to be confronted with the witnesses against him; to have compulsory process for obtaining witnesses in his favor, and to have the assistance of counsel for his defense.

Amendment VII

In suits at common law, where the value in controversy shall exceed twenty dollars, the right of trial by jury shall be preserved, and no fact tried by a jury, shall be otherwise reexamined in any court of the United States, than according to the rules of the common law.

Amendment VIII

Excessive bail shall not be required, nor excessive fines imposed, nor cruel and unusual punishments inflicted.

Amendment IX

The enumeration in the Constitution, of certain rights, shall not be construed to deny or disparage others retained by the people.

Amendment X

The powers not delegated to the United States by the Constitution, nor prohibited by it to the states, are reserved to the states respectively, or to the people.

Amendment XI (1798)

The judicial power of the United States shall not be construed to extend to any suit in law or equity, commenced or prosecuted against one of the United States by citizens of another state, or by citizens or subjects of any foreign state.

Amendment XII (1804)

The electors shall meet in their respective states and vote by ballot for President and Vice-President, one of whom, at least, shall not be an inhabitant of the same state with themselves; they shall name in their ballots the person voted for as President, and in distinct ballots the person voted for as Vice-President, and they shall make distinct lists of all persons voted for as President, and of all persons voted for as Vice-President, and of the number of votes for each, which lists they shall sign and certify, and transmit sealed to the seat of the government of the United States, directed to the President of the Senate; — The President of the Senate shall, in the presence of the Senate and House of Representatives, open all the certificates and the votes shall then be counted; — the person having the greatest number of votes for President, shall be the President, if such number be a majority of the whole number of electors appointed; and if no person have such majority, then from the persons having the highest numbers not exceeding three on the list of those voted for as President, the House of Representatives shall choose immediately, by ballot, the President. But in choosing the President, the votes shall be taken by states, the representation from each state having one vote; a quorum for this purpose shall consist of a member or members from two-thirds of the states, and a majority of all the states shall be necessary to a choice. And if the House of Representatives shall not choose a President whenever the right of choice shall devolve upon them, before the fourth day of March next following, then the Vice-President shall act as President, as in the case of the death or other constitutional disability of the President. The person having the greatest number of votes as Vice-President, shall be the Vice-President, if such number be a majority of the whole number of electors appointed, and if no person have a majority, then from the two highest numbers on the list, the Senate shall choose the Vice-President; a quorum for the purpose shall consist of two-thirds of the whole number of Senators, and a majority of the whole number shall be necessary to a choice. But no person constitutionally ineligible to the office of President shall be eligible to that of Vice-President of the United States.

Amendment XIII (1865)

Section 1. Neither slavery nor involuntary servitude, except as a punishment for crime whereof the party shall have been duly convicted, shall exist within the United States, or any place subject to their jurisdiction.
Section 2. Congress shall have power to enforce this article by appropriate legislation.

Amendment XIV (1868)

Section 1. All persons born or naturalized in the United States, and subject to the jurisdiction thereof, are citizens of the United States and of the state wherein they reside. No state shall make or enforce any law which shall abridge the privileges or immunities of citizens of the United States; nor shall any state deprive any person of life, liberty, or property, without due process of law; nor deny to any person within its jurisdiction the equal protection of the laws.
Section 2. Representatives shall be apportioned among the several states according to their respective numbers, counting the whole number of persons in each state, excluding Indians not taxed. But when the right to

vote at any election for the choice of electors for President and Vice President of the United States, Representatives in Congress, the executive and judicial officers of a state, or the members of the legislature thereof, is denied to any of the male inhabitants of such state, being twenty-one years of age, and citizens of the United States, or in any way abridged, except for participation in rebellion, or other crime, the basis of representation therein shall be reduced in the proportion which the number of such male citizens shall bear to the whole number of male citizens twenty-one years of age in such state.

Section 3. No person shall be a Senator or Representative in Congress, or elector of President and Vice President, or hold any office, civil or military, under the United States, or under any state, who, having previously taken an oath, as a member of Congress, or as an officer of the United States, or as a member of any state legislature, or as an executive or judicial officer of any state, to support the Constitution of the United States, shall have engaged in insurrection or rebellion against the same, or given aid or comfort to the enemies thereof. But Congress may by a vote of two-thirds of each House, remove such disability.

Section 4. The validity of the public debt of the United States, authorized by law, including debts incurred for payment of pensions and bounties for services in suppressing insurrection or rebellion, shall not be questioned. But neither the United States nor any state shall assume or pay any debt or obligation incurred in aid of insurrection or rebellion against the United States, or any claim for the loss or emancipation of any slave; but all such debts, obligations and claims shall be held illegal and void.

Section 5. The Congress shall have power to enforce, by appropriate legislation, the provisions of this article.

Amendment XV (1870)

Section 1. The right of citizens of the United States to vote shall not be denied or abridged by the United States or by any state on account of race, color, or previous condition of servitude.

Section 2. The Congress shall have power to enforce this article by appropriate legislation.

Amendment XVI (1913)

The Congress shall have power to lay and collect taxes on incomes, from whatever source derived, without apportionment among the several states, and without regard to any census of enumeration.

Amendment XVII (1913)

The Senate of the United States shall be composed of two Senators from each state, elected by the people thereof, for six years; and each Senator shall have one vote. The electors in each state shall have the qualifications requisite for electors of the most numerous branch of the state legislatures.

When vacancies happen in the representation of any state in the Senate, the executive authority of such state shall issue writs of election to fill such vacancies: Provided, that the legislature of any state may empower the executive thereof to make temporary appointments until the people fill the vacancies by election as the legislature may direct.

This amendment shall not be so construed as to affect the election or term of any Senator chosen before it becomes valid as part of the Constitution.

Amendment XVIII (1919)

Section 1. After one year from the ratification of this article the manufacture, sale, or transportation of intoxicating liquors within, the importation thereof into, or the exportation thereof from the United States and all territory subject to the jurisdiction thereof for beverage purposes is hereby prohibited.

Section 2. The Congress and the several states shall have concurrent power to enforce this article by appropriate legislation.

Section 3. This article shall be inoperative unless it shall have been ratified as an amendment to the Constitution by the legislatures of the several states, as provided in the Constitution, within seven years from the date of the submission hereof to the states by the Congress.

Amendment XIX (1920)

The right of citizens of the United States to vote shall not be denied or abridged by the United States or by any state on account of sex.

Congress shall have power to enforce this article by appropriate legislation.

Amendment XX (1933)

Section 1. The terms of the President and Vice President shall end at noon on the 20th day of January, and the terms of Senators and Representatives at noon on the 3d day of January, of the years in which such terms would have ended if this article had not been ratified; and the terms of their successors shall then begin.

Section 2. The Congress shall assemble at least once in every year, and such meeting shall begin at noon on the 3d day of January, unless they shall by law appoint a different day.

Section 3. If, at the time fixed for the beginning of the term of the President, the President elect shall have died, the Vice President elect shall become President. If a President shall not have been chosen before the time fixed for the beginning of his term, or if the President elect shall have failed to qualify, then the Vice President elect shall act as President until a President shall have qualified; and the Congress may by law provide for the case wherein neither a President elect nor a Vice President elect shall have qualified, declaring who shall then act as President, or the manner in which one who is to act shall be selected, and such person shall act accordingly until a President or Vice President shall have qualified.

Section 4. The Congress may by law provide for the case of the death of any of the persons from whom the House of Representatives may choose a President whenever the right of choice shall have devolved upon them, and for the case of the death of any of the persons from whom the Senate may choose a Vice President whenever the right of choice shall have devolved upon them.

Section 5. Sections 1 and 2 shall take effect on the 15th day of October following the ratification of this article.

Section 6. This article shall be inoperative unless it shall have been ratified as an amendment to the Constitution by the legislatures of three-fourths of the several states within seven years from the date of its submission.

Amendment XXI (1933)

Section 1. The eighteenth article of amendment to the Constitution of the United States is hereby repealed.

Section 2. The transportation or importation into any state, territory, or possession of the United States for delivery or use therein of intoxicating liquors, in violation of the laws thereof, is hereby prohibited.

Section 3. This article shall be inoperative unless it shall have been ratified as an amendment to the Constitution by conventions in the several states, as provided in the Constitution, within seven years from the date of the submission hereof to the states by the Congress.

Amendment XXII (1951)

Section 1. No person shall be elected to the office of the President more than twice, and no person who has held the office of President, or acted as President, for more than two years of a term to which some other person was elected President shall be elected to the office of the President more than once. But this article shall not apply to any person holding the office of President when this article was proposed by the Congress, and shall not prevent any person who may be holding the office of President, or acting as President, during the term within which this article becomes operative from holding the office of President or acting as President during the remainder of such term.

Section 2. This article shall be inoperative unless it shall have been ratified as an amendment to the Constitution by the legislatures of three-fourths of the several states within seven years from the date of its submission to the states by the Congress.

Amendment XXIII (1961)

Section 1. The District constituting the seat of government of the United States shall appoint in such manner as the Congress may direct: A number of electors of President and Vice President equal to the whole number of Senators and Representatives in Congress to which the District would be entitled if it were a state, but in no event more than the least populous state; they shall be in addition to those appointed by the states, but they shall be considered, for the purposes of the election of President and Vice President, to be electors appointed by a state; and they shall meet in the District and perform such duties as provided by the twelfth article of amendment.

Section 2. The Congress shall have power to enforce this article by appropriate legislation.

Amendment XXIV (1964)

Section 1. The right of citizens of the United States to vote in any primary or other election for President or Vice President, for electors for President or Vice President, or for Senator or Representative in Congress, shall not be denied or abridged by the United States or any state by reason of failure to pay any poll tax or other tax.

Section 2. The Congress shall have power to enforce this article by appropriate legislation.

Amendment XXV (1967)

Section 1. In case of the removal of the President from office or of his death or resignation, the Vice President shall become President.

Section 2. Whenever there is a vacancy in the office of the Vice President, the President shall nominate a Vice President who shall take office upon confirmation by a majority vote of both Houses of Congress.

Section 3. Whenever the President transmits to the President pro tempore of the Senate and the Speaker of the House of Representatives his written declaration that he is unable to discharge the powers and duties of his office, and until he transmits to them a written declaration to the contrary, such powers and duties shall be discharged by the Vice President as Acting President.

Section 4. Whenever the Vice President and a majority of either the principal officers of the executive departments or of such other body as Congress may by law provide, transmit to the President pro tempore of the Senate and the Speaker of the House of Representatives their written declaration that the President is unable to discharge the powers and duties of his office, the Vice President shall immediately assume the powers and duties of the office as Acting President.

Thereafter, when the President transmits to the President pro tempore of the Senate and the Speaker of the House of Representatives his written declaration that no inability exists, he shall resume the powers and duties of his office unless the Vice President and a majority of either the principal officers of the executive department or of such other body as Congress may by law provide, transmit within four days to the President pro tempore of the Senate and the Speaker of the House of Representatives their written declaration that the President is unable to discharge the powers and duties of his office. Thereupon Congress shall decide the issue, assembling within forty-eight hours for that purpose if not in session. If the Congress, within twenty-one days after receipt of the latter written declaration, or, if Congress is not in session, within twenty-one days after Congress is required to assemble, determines by two-thirds vote of both Houses that the

President is unable to discharge the powers and duties of his office, the Vice President shall continue to discharge the same as Acting President; otherwise, the President shall resume the powers and duties of his office.

Amendment XXVI (1971)

Section 1. The right of citizens of the United States, who are 18 years of age or older, to vote, shall not be denied or abridged by the United States or any state on account of age.

Section 2. The Congress shall have the power to enforce this article by appropriate legislation.

Amendment XXVII
(Passed by Congress 1790; Ratified 1992)

No law varying the compensation for the services of the Senators and Representatives shall take effect until an election of Representatives shall have intervened.

Methodology: Research Note and Bibliography

I have used both primary and secondary sources in analyzing the constitutional debates concerning the responsibilities and formulation, as well as execution of American foreign policy, starting at the Philadelphia convention in 1787 and thereafter. The basic sources include: Wilbourne Benton, *1787: Drafting the U. S. Constitution*, 2 volumes (College Station: Texas A & M University Press, 1986); Max Farrand, *The Records of the Federal Convention of 1787*, 4 volumes (New Haven: Yale University Press, 1966); Catherine D. Bowen, *Miracle at Philadelphia: The Story of the Constitutional Convention*, (Boston: Little, Brown, 1966); Breckenridge Long, *The Genesis of the Constitution of the United States of America* (New York, 1926); Adrienne Koch, ed., James Madison's *Notes in the Federal Convention of 1787*, (Athens: Ohio University Press, 1966); Forrest McDonald, *Novus Ordo Seclorum: The Intellectual Origins of the Constitution*, (Lawrence: University Press of Kansas, 1985); Charles Warren, *The Making of the Constitution* , (New York: Barnes & Noble, 1967); Gordon Wood, *The Creation of the American Republic,* 1776-1787 (Chapel Hill: University of North Carolina Press, 1969); and Clinton Rossiter, ed., *The Federalist Papers* by Hamilton, Madison and Jay (New York: Mentor Books, 1961).

In examining the "Traditional" period (1789-1936), I analyzed such studies as George Curtis, *A History of the Origin, Formation, and Adoption of the Constitution of the United States*, (New York: Harper and Bros., 1958); Louis Fisher, *Constitutional Conflicts Between Congress and the President*, 3rd Edition (Lawrence: University Press of Kansas, 1991); Louis Henkin, *Foreign Affairs and the Constitution*, (Mineola, N.Y.: Foundation Press, 1972); Edwin S. Corwin, *The President: Offices and Powers*, 5th Edition (New York University, 1985); Richard Pious, *The American Presidency*, (New York: Basis Books, 1979); Donald Robinson, *"To the Best of My Ability": The President and the Constitution*, (New York: Norton, 1987). In turning to the "Age of Presidential Supremacy: 1936-1950, we will utilize: Michael Glennon, *Constitutional Diplomacy*, (Princeton, N.J.: Princeton University, 1990); Louis Henkin, *Foreign Affairs and the Constitution*, (Mineola, N.Y.: Foundation Press, 1972); Alfred Kelley and Winfred Harbinson, *The American Constitution: Its Origins and Development*, 5th Edition (New York: Norton, 1976); Christopher May, *In the Name of War*, (Cambridge, Mass.: Harvard University Press, 1989); and, Harry

Wellington, *Interpreting the Constitution*, (New Haven: Yale University Press, 1991).

Constructing the important subject of "Judicial Retreat on the War Powers: 1950-1964" I relied heavily on the following works: Stephen Ambrose, *Rise of Globalism: American Foreign Policy Since 1938*, (New York: Penguin Books, 1991); Edward Keyes, *Undeclared War: Twilight Zone of Constitutional Power*, (College Park: Penn State University Press, 1991); Robert Schulzinger, *American Diplomacy in the Twentieth Century*, 2nd Edition (New York: Oxford University Press, 1990); and John Spanier, *American Foreign Policy Since World War II*, (New York: Holt, Rinehart & Winston, 1980).

Finally, on detailing developments during the "Era of Presidential Wars: 1964-1992, I have cited the following sources: Robert Dallek, *The American Style of Foreign Policy: Cultural Politics and Foreign Affairs*, (New York: Oxford University Press, 1990); R. A. Falk, ed., *The Vietnam War and International Law*, (Princeton, N.J.: Princeton University Press, 1969); Charles Lamb and Stephen Halpen, *The Burger Court: Politics and Judicial Profiles*, (Chicago: University of Illinois Press, 1991); Arthur Schlesinger, Jr., *The Imperial Presidency*, Revised Edition (Boston: Houghton Mifflin Company, 1989); and Francis Wormouth and Edwin Firmage, *To Chain the Dog of War: The War Power of Congress in History and Law* (Dallas: Southern Methodist University Press, 1986). Also, the author explored numerous articles in scholarly journals, publications and law reviews relating to all areas covered by the text.

Index of Cases

Major decisions excerpted at *length* in the *text* will appear in *regular type*; those briefly cited will appear (as usual) in *italized* print.)

—W—

—Y—

Index of Subjects

— A —